Canva

Basics

A Beginner's Guide to Designing with Ease

Kiet Huynh

Table of Contents

Introduction

What is Canva?

In today's digital world, creating visually appealing content has become an essential skill for personal, business, and marketing purposes. Whether it's designing social media posts, presentations, flyers, or even resumes, the need for high-quality graphics is ever-increasing. This is where Canva comes into the picture as one of the most popular and user-friendly design tools available. But what exactly is Canva, and why has it become so integral to the way we create and share content online?

Canva is an online graphic design platform that allows users to create a wide range of visual content. It was founded in 2013 by Melanie Perkins, Cliff Obrecht, and Cameron Adams with the goal of making graphic design accessible to everyone, regardless of technical skills or professional background. Canva's mission is to empower the world to design by simplifying the design process and offering a broad library of templates, images, fonts, and tools.

Unlike traditional design software, such as Adobe Photoshop or Illustrator, which require a significant learning curve, Canva is designed for ease of use. It's intuitive enough for beginners but also offers advanced features that appeal to seasoned designers. Canva's drag-and-drop functionality, combined with a vast selection of ready-made templates, allows anyone—from individuals and small business owners to marketers and educators—to create beautiful and professional-looking designs quickly and efficiently.

The Canva Platform: A User-Friendly Design Tool

At its core, Canva is a cloud-based platform. This means you can access your designs from any device with an internet connection. There's no need to install software or worry about device compatibility. Canva runs seamlessly on web browsers, and it also offers apps for both iOS and Android devices, making it possible to design on the go.

The platform's main appeal lies in its simplicity. Canva provides a library of over 250,000 free templates that are pre-designed and categorized based on the type of project you're working on—whether it's a business card, social media graphic, presentation, or poster. Users can either start with one of these templates or create a design from scratch. The drag-and-drop interface allows you to move and edit elements like text, images, and shapes with ease. No prior knowledge of graphic design is needed, and yet the results can be impressive.

In addition to templates, Canva boasts a huge library of free and premium elements, such as stock photos, illustrations, icons, and fonts. These resources are available at your fingertips, enabling you to enhance your designs without having to search for assets outside the platform. Canva also allows users to upload their own images, logos, and other content to customize their designs further.

Types of Designs You Can Create in Canva

One of the most impressive features of Canva is its versatility. Canva isn't limited to one type of design; it supports a vast array of projects, including:

- *Social Media Graphics:* Canva is widely used for creating content tailored to specific social media platforms like Instagram, Facebook, Twitter, and Pinterest. With Canva, you can quickly resize your designs to match the specifications of each platform, ensuring your content looks great wherever it's posted.

- *Presentations:* Canva offers a comprehensive suite of presentation templates, making it easy for users to create stunning slideshows. These templates come with pre-set layouts that can be customized to fit your brand's aesthetic or message.

- *Marketing Materials:* From brochures to flyers, business cards to posters, Canva is a popular choice for creating print-ready marketing collateral. These templates ensure that all aspects of your brand, from color to typography, are consistent and professional.

- *Infographics:* For data visualization and storytelling, Canva offers infographic templates that make presenting complex information more accessible and visually appealing. The use of charts, graphs, and icons allows you to present data in a compelling way.

- *Logos:* Many small businesses and entrepreneurs use Canva to design their own logos. The platform provides access to professional design elements, enabling users to create unique logos without having to hire a designer.

- *Resumes and CVs:* With a variety of resume templates, Canva makes it easy for job seekers to create resumes that stand out. You can design clean, modern, and professional CVs that leave a lasting impression.

These are just a few examples. Canva's flexibility means that whether you're designing for print or digital media, the possibilities are endless. The platform also supports both beginner and advanced designers, so as your skills grow, so too can the complexity of your designs.

The Power of Templates and Customization

One of Canva's standout features is its extensive library of customizable templates. For those new to design, starting with a template provides a helpful foundation. Instead of staring at a blank page, you can begin by choosing a pre-designed layout that fits your needs. Canva's templates cover virtually every type of project imaginable, from simple invitations to detailed marketing campaigns.

However, while templates offer a fantastic starting point, the real power of Canva comes from customization. Every template element can be modified to suit your specific vision. You can adjust colors, fonts, images, and even layout structures. Canva's intuitive tools make it simple to align, resize, and rotate elements, giving users total creative control. The result is a design that feels personalized, even if it began with a template.

For those who prefer to work from scratch, Canva offers a blank canvas option as well. You can start with a completely empty page and add any elements you want from Canva's vast library, or upload your own assets to create a truly unique design.

Collaboration and Sharing

Another advantage of Canva is its collaborative capabilities. In today's remote work environment, being able to collaborate on designs in real time is a huge benefit. Canva allows you to share designs with others and provide them with editing, viewing, or commenting access. This makes it an ideal tool for teams, whether working on a group presentation or developing a marketing campaign.

With Canva Pro, teams can set up a Brand Kit that includes logos, fonts, and colors, ensuring consistency across all designs. This is particularly helpful for businesses looking to maintain a cohesive brand identity across multiple projects.

Once your design is complete, Canva offers various sharing options. You can download your design in several formats (PNG, JPG, PDF, and even MP4 for animated content), print directly through Canva's printing services, or share your designs online via social media, email, or a unique link.

Canva's Free vs. Pro Features

Calculate for your team

How many people?

Save from 16% with yearly

| Custom | People | Monthly | Yearly |

For one person
Canva Free
Design anything and bring your ideas to life. No cost, just creativity.

For one person
Canva Pro
Unlock premium content, more powerful design tools, and AI features.

For your team
Canva Teams
Transform teamwork, grow your brand, and simplify workflows.

While Canva offers a robust free version, users can upgrade to Canva Pro to unlock even more features. The free version provides access to thousands of templates, images, and design elements, which is more than enough for most beginner and casual users. However, Canva Pro comes with added benefits, including:

- *Access to Premium Templates and Images:* Canva Pro users can choose from a larger selection of premium templates and over 100 million stock photos, videos, and audio tracks.

- *Magic Resize:* This feature allows you to instantly resize designs for different social media platforms or formats with just a click, saving hours of manual resizing work.

- *Brand Kit:* Pro users can set up a Brand Kit, which stores brand assets like logos, fonts, and colors for easy access, ensuring consistency across all designs.

- *Custom Fonts and Uploads:* Canva Pro allows you to upload your own fonts and use custom font sets within your designs.

- *Animation Tools:* Pro users can add advanced animations to their designs, making them more dynamic and engaging.

For many small businesses, marketers, and designers, these added features justify the cost of upgrading to Canva Pro. However, for those just starting or with basic design needs, the free version provides more than enough tools to get the job done.

Conclusion

In summary, Canva is a powerful, easy-to-use design platform that has democratized graphic design for millions of people worldwide. With its drag-and-drop interface, customizable templates, and extensive library of design elements, Canva allows anyone to create professional-quality graphics in a matter of minutes. Whether you're a beginner or a seasoned designer, Canva has the tools and resources to bring your creative vision to life.

As you progress through this guide, you'll learn not only how to use Canva's tools but also how to apply design principles to make your creations stand out. Whether you're designing for social media, print, or presentations, Canva provides everything you need to design with ease.

Why Use Canva for Design?

In today's fast-paced digital world, design has become a crucial element in everything from social media marketing to business branding and personal projects. However, not everyone has access to expensive design software or the skillset to use advanced programs like Adobe Photoshop or Illustrator. This is where Canva comes in—a tool that democratizes design for everyone, from beginners to professionals, providing a platform that is both intuitive and powerful. Below are several reasons why Canva stands out as a top choice for design.

1. Ease of Use

Perhaps the most compelling reason to use Canva is its simplicity and ease of use. You don't need a background in graphic design or special training to create stunning visuals. The platform is designed with non-designers in mind, making it accessible to virtually anyone. The interface is clean, intuitive, and user-friendly, enabling users to navigate its features with minimal effort.

Canva eliminates the steep learning curve commonly associated with design tools. Unlike professional software, which often requires tutorials or even formal training, Canva's drag-and-drop functionality allows users to instantly add elements like text, images, and shapes to their designs. From the moment you sign up, you can start creating.

Additionally, Canva provides real-time feedback. As you manipulate your design elements, the program automatically snaps objects into alignment, suggests fonts, and offers color pairings, ensuring that your design is not only functional but visually appealing. This smart assistance allows even beginners to produce professional-looking designs without much trial and error.

2. Wide Range of Templates

One of Canva's most notable features is its vast library of pre-designed templates. Whether you are designing a social media post, business card, presentation, or flyer, Canva has thousands of templates categorized by use case and design style. This means you can find inspiration or a starting point for any project, reducing the time you spend conceptualizing your design from scratch.

Templates make it easy for anyone, including non-designers, to create beautiful, professional-quality designs in minutes. Each template can be fully customized to fit your brand or personal style. You can change colors, fonts, images, and layouts as much as you want while still benefiting from the professionally crafted design framework provided by Canva.

Moreover, templates are regularly updated to reflect current design trends and industry standards. This means that your work will always look modern and relevant, whether you're creating a social media post for Instagram, a professional presentation for work, or a resume to help land your dream job.

3. Cost-Effective Design Solution

Design can be expensive. Traditional design software, like Adobe Creative Suite, often comes with hefty subscription fees, and hiring a professional designer can cost hundreds or even thousands of dollars, depending on the project. Canva offers a highly cost-effective alternative. While there is a premium plan called Canva Pro, which offers additional features and assets, the free version of Canva is more than sufficient for many users.

The free version includes access to thousands of templates, design elements, and photos, making it possible to create high-quality designs without spending a dime. For individuals or small businesses with limited budgets, Canva provides a way to produce professional designs without breaking the bank. Even Canva Pro, the paid subscription, is reasonably priced, especially when compared to other professional design tools, and offers a vast range of premium features such as additional templates, custom fonts, brand kits, and more.

4. Versatility Across Different Media

Another significant advantage of Canva is its versatility. It's not limited to just one type of design. You can use Canva to create a wide variety of media, including:

- Social Media Graphics: Canva makes it easy to create images optimized for platforms like Instagram, Facebook, Twitter, and LinkedIn. The templates are already sized correctly, saving you time and ensuring your posts look perfect.

- Presentations: Canva offers a range of professionally designed slides that are easy to customize. This makes it an excellent tool for students, business professionals, and educators.

- Print Materials: From business cards to brochures, Canva provides a variety of print-friendly templates that can be customized and exported for high-quality printing.

- Web Assets: You can create web banners, ads, and even website graphics using Canva, all optimized for online use.

- Personal Projects: Canva is also great for personal projects such as wedding invitations, event flyers, or even family photo collages.

No matter what type of project you're working on, Canva offers templates and tools to make the design process easier and faster.

5. Collaborative Features

Canva also excels in its collaborative features. For businesses or teams working on projects together, Canva offers real-time collaboration. You can invite team members to your design, allowing them to comment, make edits, or offer feedback. This feature is particularly useful for marketing teams, designers, and business owners who need to work together to maintain brand consistency or streamline workflows.

With Canva Pro, you can also set up brand kits to ensure that everyone on the team uses the same fonts, colors, and logos, preserving your brand identity across all designs. This feature eliminates the guesswork and ensures that everyone is on the same page, literally and figuratively.

Collaboration in Canva is not limited to internal teams. You can share your designs with clients, allowing them to make edits or suggestions without needing to download any software. This ease of collaboration makes Canva a highly efficient tool for both small and large-scale projects.

6. A Broad Selection of Assets

Canva comes equipped with a vast library of assets, including stock photos, illustrations, icons, fonts, and more. This is particularly valuable for users who may not have access to high-quality design assets or who want to avoid the hassle of purchasing and importing stock photos from third-party sources.

Even in the free version, Canva provides access to thousands of free images and graphics, with even more available in Canva Pro. These assets can be easily dragged and dropped into your designs, allowing for endless customization possibilities. Whether you're looking for a specific background image or a unique illustration, chances are you'll find what you need within Canva's library.

This abundance of assets also includes customizable icons, shapes, and other graphic elements, which can be edited in terms of size, color, and position, giving you full control over your design.

7. Mobile Accessibility

In our increasingly mobile world, the ability to work from anywhere is essential. Canva understands this and offers a mobile app that mirrors the desktop experience. Whether you're on a smartphone or a tablet, Canva allows you to design on the go. This is particularly useful for business owners, social media managers, and students who may need to make quick changes or create designs while away from their computers.

The mobile app is equipped with nearly all the same features as the web version, so you're not sacrificing functionality for portability. You can start a design on your desktop and finish it on your phone, or vice versa, making Canva an extremely flexible tool for designers on the move.

8. Constantly Evolving Features

One of Canva's strengths is that it's constantly evolving. The developers frequently update the platform to add new features, templates, and assets. As design trends change and new technologies emerge, Canva stays at the forefront, ensuring that users always have access to the latest tools and resources.

For instance, Canva has recently introduced features such as animated designs, video editing capabilities, and content planning tools, which make it a comprehensive platform for all your design and content creation needs. These constant updates mean that users can continue growing with the platform, gaining access to more advanced tools as they develop their design skills.

9. Branding and Consistency

Maintaining brand consistency across different platforms and media is essential for any business. Canva makes this easy with its brand kit feature, available in the Pro version. A brand kit allows users to save specific fonts, colors, and logos that represent their brand, which can then be applied consistently across all designs.

This feature is incredibly useful for businesses that need to maintain a unified look and feel across marketing materials, social media posts, presentations, and print media. Even if multiple people are working on designs, the brand kit ensures that every piece of content aligns with your brand's identity.

10. Time-Saving Features

Canva is designed to save users time, and it offers several features specifically aimed at increasing efficiency. For example, Canva offers an auto-save feature, so you never have to worry about losing your progress. It also allows for quick resizing of designs with its Magic Resize tool, which can instantly adjust the dimensions of your design for various platforms with just one click.

Additionally, the drag-and-drop interface, pre-made templates, and built-in asset library mean that you can create complex designs in a fraction of the time it would take using other design software. Whether you're working on a last-minute presentation or need to create social media posts on a tight deadline, Canva's time-saving features help you get the job done quickly and efficiently.

In summary, Canva is a versatile, cost-effective, and user-friendly tool that empowers anyone to create professional designs, regardless of their skill level. Its wide range of templates, collaborative features, and constantly evolving toolset make it an invaluable resource for both personal and professional use. Whether you're a small business owner, a student, a social media manager, or simply someone looking to create eye-catching graphics, Canva offers the tools and assets you need to bring your ideas to life.

How to Navigate This Guide

Design can feel overwhelming when you're first starting out, especially when you're diving into a tool as versatile as Canva. With hundreds of templates, design elements, and features available at your fingertips, it's essential to have a clear path forward so you don't get lost in the process. This guide is designed to help you gradually build your skills and understanding of Canva, no matter your starting level, while offering plenty of opportunities for hands-on practice. Whether you're an absolute beginner or have some experience with design tools, this book will help you navigate Canva with ease, from the basics to more advanced features.

In this section, we'll cover how this book is organized, key features that will enhance your learning experience, and tips for getting the most out of each chapter. Let's dive in and set you up for success.

1. Book Organization and Structure

This guide is divided into eight chapters, each focusing on a different aspect of using Canva. Every chapter is structured to guide you through a specific area of design, ensuring a smooth learning curve.

- *Chapter 1: Getting Started with Canva*

   This chapter is designed for absolute beginners who have never used Canva before. It covers the basics, including how to create an account, navigate the dashboard, and understand the different features available on Canva's homepage. By the end of this chapter, you'll know how to log in, set up your profile, and begin exploring Canva's vast library of templates, projects, and design resources.

- *Chapter 2: Canva Interface Overview*

   In Chapter 2, we dive deeper into Canva's design workspace. You'll learn how to navigate the toolbar, understand the role of layers, and how to use grids and guides to create balanced and professional-looking designs. The chapter also includes a guide to using Canva's extensive template library, teaching you how to customize pre-made templates to suit your needs.

- Chapter 3: Designing with Canva Tools

This is where the fun begins! Chapter 3 walks you through Canva's design tools. You'll learn how to add and format text, choose fonts, customize images, create shapes, and work with colors. Each section is packed with tips on how to use these tools efficiently to create polished designs.

- Chapter 4: Advanced Canva Features

Once you've mastered the basics, Chapter 4 introduces more advanced features like photo editing, adding animations, and creating interactive presentations. You'll also learn how to collaborate with team members, share your designs, and streamline your workflow by leveraging Canva's sharing and commenting features.

- Chapter 5: Canva for Social Media

Social media graphics are one of the most popular uses for Canva, and this chapter will show you exactly how to create eye-catching designs for platforms like Instagram, Facebook, and Twitter. You'll learn the optimal dimensions for each platform, how to use Canva's built-in video editing tools, and even how to schedule and post your content directly from Canva.

- Chapter 6: Printing and Exporting Your Designs

Canva isn't just for online designs. In Chapter 6, you'll learn how to prepare your creations for printing, whether it's posters, business cards, or invitations. This chapter also covers how to download your designs in different formats (such as PNG, JPEG, and PDF), ensuring that your creations look their best whether they're printed or shared online.

- Chapter 7: Canva Tips and Tricks for Beginners

In this chapter, you'll find practical tips that will make you more efficient with Canva. Learn about time-saving keyboard shortcuts, how to maintain consistent branding, and troubleshoot common issues that beginners face when designing in Canva.

- Chapter 8: Expanding Your Skills with Canva Pro

If you're ready to take your designs to the next level, this chapter will introduce you to Canva Pro. With access to premium templates, advanced editing tools, and team management features, you'll learn how to enhance your designs and work more efficiently with Canva's paid features.

2. Key Features to Enhance Your Learning

Each chapter includes several key elements designed to reinforce your learning, making it easy to apply what you've read and start designing right away.

2.1 Step-by-Step Instructions

Throughout the book, you'll find detailed step-by-step instructions that walk you through Canva's features. Each instruction is broken down into simple, easy-to-follow steps that ensure you never feel lost or overwhelmed. The goal is to help you gain confidence as you complete each task.

For example, in Chapter 3, when learning how to add text to a design, the instructions will walk you through selecting the text tool, choosing a font, adjusting font size and color, and positioning it on your design. You'll be able to follow along easily, and by the end of each section, you'll have completed a small design task that reinforces your learning.

2.2 Visual Guides and Screenshots

We understand that learning design requires visual support. That's why this guide includes numerous screenshots and illustrations to help you visualize what you're working on. Whether it's the layout of Canva's toolbar, the options in the template library, or the settings for adjusting image filters, the accompanying images will make it easier to follow along.

Every visual guide is placed right alongside the instructions, so you'll always know what your screen should look like and which buttons to click as you progress through the book.

2.3 Hands-On Exercises

Design is all about practice. At the end of each major section, you'll find hands-on exercises that encourage you to apply what you've learned. These exercises range from simple tasks like creating a social media post to more complex projects like designing an interactive presentation.

For example, after learning about Canva's text tools in Chapter 3, you'll be tasked with creating a poster that incorporates different font styles, sizes, and effects. The exercises are designed to be fun and rewarding, giving you tangible results that you can use in real-world projects.

2.4 Tips and Tricks

Each chapter includes tips and tricks that will help you use Canva more efficiently and effectively. These tips come from professional designers and Canva experts, offering insights into how to get the most out of the platform. Whether it's a shortcut for quickly duplicating elements, advice on color harmony, or tips for aligning text and images perfectly, these nuggets of wisdom will save you time and improve the quality of your designs.

2.5 Common Pitfalls to Avoid

Designing with Canva is generally straightforward, but like any tool, it comes with a few potential challenges. Throughout the guide, we've highlighted common pitfalls that beginners often encounter and provided solutions to help you avoid these issues. Whether it's ensuring that your images remain high-resolution when printed or making sure that text aligns properly on different devices, you'll be well-prepared to tackle any problem that arises.

2.6 Chapter Summaries and Checklists

At the end of each chapter, you'll find a summary that recaps the key points covered. These summaries provide a quick refresher and ensure you have a solid grasp of the concepts before moving on to the next section.

In addition to the summaries, each chapter includes a checklist that you can use to track your progress. The checklist serves as a practical tool to make sure you've completed all the key tasks before moving forward. For instance, after completing Chapter 2, your checklist might include items like: "Created a Canva account," "Uploaded an image," and "Used a template to design a social media post."

3. Tips for Using This Guide Effectively

While this guide is designed to be straightforward, there are a few strategies you can use to maximize your learning experience.

3.1 Work Through the Book in Sequence

Although it might be tempting to jump straight to the advanced features or dive into a project without reading the earlier chapters, it's important to follow the book in sequence. Each chapter builds on the concepts introduced in previous ones, ensuring a smooth progression from basic to more advanced techniques. By working through the chapters in order, you'll avoid gaps in your knowledge and feel more confident as you tackle each new design challenge.

3.2 Take Your Time with Hands-On Practice

Don't rush through the hands-on exercises! Design is a skill that improves with practice, and the more time you spend experimenting with Canva, the better your designs will become. After completing an exercise, take a moment to reflect on what you've learned and how you can apply it to future projects. If something doesn't look right or you're not happy with your design, don't hesitate to go back and make adjustments.

3.3 Bookmark Important Sections

As you work through the guide, you'll likely come across sections that you'll want to revisit later. For instance, you might find the chapter on Canva's text tools especially helpful when creating posters, or you might want to refer back to the tips on exporting designs when preparing your creations for print. Bookmark these sections so you can easily find them when needed.

3.4 Use Canva Simultaneously

The best way to learn Canva is to use it while reading this guide. Open Canva in your browser or app as you read through the instructions. This allows you to follow along step-by-step and apply the concepts in real time. Not only will this help reinforce what you're learning, but it will also give you a sense of accomplishment as you see your designs taking shape.

3.5 Ask for Feedback

If you're working on a design project, don't hesitate to ask for feedback from friends, family, or colleagues. Canva makes it easy to share designs with others for review, and receiving constructive criticism can help you identify areas for improvement. Whether it's refining your font choices, adjusting your layout, or experimenting with colors, feedback is invaluable for growing as a designer.

This guide is designed to be your comprehensive companion as you journey into the world of Canva. Whether you're designing a simple social media post or tackling a more complex project like creating a presentation, this book will provide the knowledge, tools, and confidence you need to make the most of Canva's powerful features. With its clear structure, practical tips, and step-by-step instructions, you'll be well on your way to mastering Canva and bringing your creative ideas to life.

Let's get started!

CHAPTER I
Getting Started with Canva

1.1 Creating a Canva Account

1.1.1 Free vs Pro Account

When you first begin using Canva, you'll notice that the platform offers two types of accounts: Free and Pro. Each account type provides users with varying degrees of access to Canva's design tools, templates, and features. Understanding the differences between the Free and Pro accounts will help you determine which option best suits your design needs, especially if you plan to use Canva regularly for personal projects or professional work. Let's break down these two tiers in detail.

The Free Account: A Solid Starting Point

The Free account is an excellent choice for beginners or those looking for a cost-effective way to create professional designs. With this version, Canva provides a generous set of tools and resources, allowing you to create stunning designs without any financial investment.

1. Access to Thousands of Templates and Design Elements

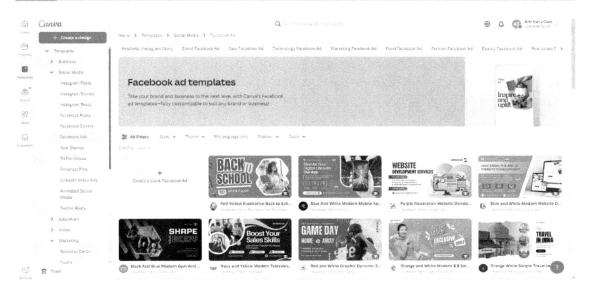

One of the primary advantages of Canva's Free account is access to a large selection of templates and design elements. As a Free user, you can explore over 250,000 free templates across a wide variety of categories—everything from social media posts to business presentations. Canva also offers thousands of free photos, graphics, and fonts that you can easily incorporate into your projects. While the selection is more limited than with the Pro account, it is still robust enough to meet most design needs.

2. Easy-to-Use Drag-and-Drop Interface

Canva's drag-and-drop interface is available to all users, regardless of the account type. This intuitive design process allows Free account users to quickly assemble professional-looking graphics without needing any advanced design knowledge. You can easily move images, shapes, and text around your canvas, experiment with different layouts, and see real-time changes as you work.

3. Basic Photo Editing Tools

For those looking to do light photo editing, the Free account includes several tools to adjust brightness, contrast, and saturation, or to crop and resize images. These features are more than sufficient for users creating simple designs like social media graphics or blog headers. Canva's basic photo editor gives you the ability to fine-tune your images, ensuring that they match your design vision without needing expensive editing software.

4. Limited Cloud Storage

Canva Free users are provided with 5GB of cloud storage, which allows you to store images, designs, and assets within Canva's platform. While this amount of storage is enough for occasional users or those working on smaller projects, those who plan to create multiple large projects or work with high-resolution images may find this limit restrictive. Still, for personal use or small projects, the provided storage should be sufficient.

5. Collaborative Tools

Another valuable feature that comes with Canva Free is the ability to collaborate with others on your design projects. You can share your design with team members, friends, or clients and invite them to view or edit the design in real time. Collaboration features are particularly helpful for group projects, such as when working with a marketing team to create a promotional campaign or with family members on a photo album. While the Free account offers basic collaboration tools, some advanced options—like assigning roles or managing permissions—are reserved for Pro users.

6. Canva's Free Limitations

Although the Free account provides substantial value, it also has certain limitations. Many premium templates, images, videos, and other design elements are locked behind the Pro tier. When browsing through Canva's vast library of resources, Free users will often come across content marked with a crown icon, indicating that it's only available for Pro subscribers. If you're a Free user, you'll need to either substitute those premium elements with free alternatives or purchase individual elements on a pay-per-item basis.

In addition, the Free account does not include access to some of Canva's more advanced features, such as the ability to resize designs for different platforms with a single click, access to more extensive brand management tools, or premium video-editing features. For casual users, this may not be an issue, but for those who require more complex or professional designs, these limitations may become noticeable.

The Pro Account: Power and Flexibility for Serious Designers

If you are looking for a more feature-rich experience, Canva Pro offers significant upgrades over the Free account. Canva Pro is a subscription-based plan, providing users with additional tools, assets, and features that cater to those who need advanced design capabilities, whether for business or personal projects. While the Free account is great for everyday users, Canva Pro is geared towards freelancers, marketers, and teams that need more comprehensive design functionality.

1. Access to Over 100 Million Premium Assets

The most significant advantage of Canva Pro is access to an extensive library of premium resources. Pro users have unlimited access to over 100 million stock photos, illustrations, videos, and audio tracks. These high-quality assets can drastically improve the look and feel of your designs, allowing you to create visually striking content without the need to purchase third-party assets.

The Pro account also unlocks access to over 610,000 premium and free templates, ensuring that you always have a unique starting point for your projects. Additionally, Canva Pro offers a larger variety of fonts and the ability to upload custom fonts, providing even more control over your designs' look and style.

2. Magic Resize

One of the standout features of Canva Pro is the Magic Resize tool. This tool allows users to quickly resize their designs for different platforms with a single click. For instance, you can create a Facebook post and then instantly resize it for Instagram, Twitter, or a blog banner. This feature is particularly useful for social media managers, bloggers, or businesses that need to repurpose content across multiple channels. By eliminating the need to manually resize and reformat designs, Magic Resize saves users valuable time and ensures consistency across platforms.

3. Brand Kit and Advanced Customization

Canva Pro includes advanced tools for businesses and organizations looking to maintain a consistent brand identity. The Brand Kit feature allows Pro users to save their brand's logos, color palettes, and fonts in one central location. This makes it easy to apply your brand's elements across all your designs, ensuring that every piece of content remains on-brand and professional.

For businesses and freelancers, this tool is invaluable. It allows for quick and easy access to pre-approved brand elements and helps maintain consistency across various projects, reducing the risk of design errors or inconsistencies in branding. With Canva Pro, you can also set templates that are aligned with your brand guidelines, making it easier for team members to create on-brand designs.

4. Additional Cloud Storage

Canva Pro subscribers are provided with 1TB (1,000GB) of cloud storage, a substantial upgrade from the Free account's 5GB limit. This additional space is particularly useful for users working on large projects or storing high-resolution images and videos. With 1TB of storage, Canva Pro users can upload and organize an extensive library of assets, keeping everything accessible and neatly stored for future projects.

5. Enhanced Collaboration and Workflow Features

While Canva's Free account offers basic collaboration tools, Canva Pro takes team collaboration to the next level. Pro users can create teams within the platform, assign roles to team members, and control permissions for viewing, editing, or commenting on designs. This makes it easier to manage workflows, especially when working on larger projects with multiple contributors.

For businesses and agencies, this feature allows managers to streamline design processes and improve communication between team members. Furthermore, Canva Pro includes the option to leave feedback and suggestions directly within the design, enhancing the review and approval process.

6. Exporting Options and High-Resolution Downloads

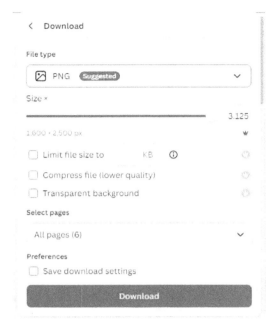

Canva Pro users have more export options than those on the Free plan. Pro subscribers can export their designs with transparent backgrounds, which is essential for logo design or any element that requires integration with other designs or media. Additionally, Pro users can download high-resolution images and PDFs, ensuring that their designs look crisp and professional in both digital and print formats.

7. Advanced Animation and Video Editing

For those creating video content, Canva Pro offers advanced animation tools that enable users to add engaging transitions and animations to their designs. Pro users also have access to additional video editing features, including the ability to adjust frame rates, trim videos, and apply animated text effects. This is ideal for users creating video content for platforms like YouTube, Instagram, or professional presentations.

Which Option is Right for You?

Choosing between Canva's Free and Pro accounts depends largely on how frequently you plan to use the platform and the complexity of the projects you intend to create. The Free account offers more than enough tools and resources for occasional users or those working on simple designs. However, if you need access to a broader range of templates, premium assets, and advanced tools, upgrading to Canva Pro may be a worthwhile investment.

For businesses, marketers, and frequent designers, the Pro account provides exceptional value through its vast library of assets, advanced design tools, and enhanced collaboration features. The ability to save time with tools like Magic Resize, along with the added convenience of features like the Brand Kit, makes Canva Pro a powerful solution for professionals seeking to produce consistent, high-quality designs.

Ultimately, whether you stick with the Free account or upgrade to Pro, Canva offers a user-friendly and versatile platform that can cater to all your design needs.

1.1.2 Signing Up and Logging In

Signing up for Canva is the first step to unleashing your creative potential with this versatile design tool. Whether you're a complete beginner or someone with design experience, Canva offers an intuitive process for setting up an account and logging in. In this section, we'll walk through the steps of creating a new account, logging in to Canva, and understanding the different sign-in options available to users.

Creating a New Account

Getting started with Canva begins with creating an account. Canva makes it easy for users to sign up with multiple methods, allowing for flexibility and convenience. Here are the main methods you can use:

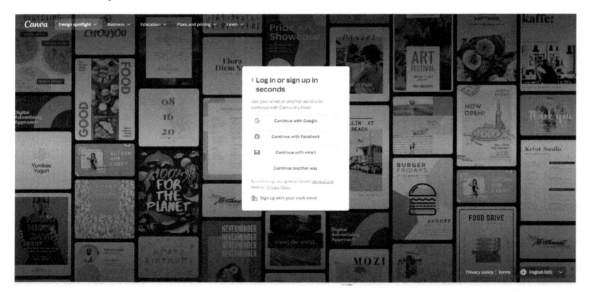

1. Sign up with an email address

2. Sign up with Google

3. Sign up with Facebook

4. Sign up with Apple

Let's dive into each option and how they work:

1. Sign up with an Email Address

The most traditional way of creating a Canva account is by using your email address. This is a straightforward process, especially for those who prefer not to connect their social media or third-party accounts.

1. Go to the Canva Homepage: Start by navigating to www.canva.com using your web browser. On the homepage, you'll see a "Sign up" button at the top right corner.

2. Enter Your Email Address: After clicking "Sign up," you'll be directed to a page where you can enter your email address. Be sure to use an active email address because you will need to verify it.

3. Create a Password: Canva will prompt you to create a password for your account. Choose a strong password that includes a mix of upper- and lower-case letters, numbers, and symbols. Canva recommends using at least eight characters for enhanced security.

4. Submit and Verify Your Email: Once you've entered your details, click "Get started" or a similar button. Canva will send a verification email to the address you provided. Open the email and click the verification link inside. This step confirms your identity and activates your account.

5. Set Up Your Profile: After verifying your email, Canva will ask a few questions to customize your experience. For example, it may ask what types of designs you plan to create (social media posts, presentations, personal projects, etc.). This helps Canva suggest templates and features relevant to your needs.

Congratulations! You've just created your Canva account using your email. You can now start exploring the platform's design tools.

2. Sign up with Google

For users who prefer linking their Canva account to their Google account, Canva offers seamless integration. This method allows you to sign in using your existing Google credentials without the need for additional passwords.

1. Click the "Sign up with Google" Option: From Canva's homepage, click "Sign up" and choose the "Sign up with Google" button.

2. Select Your Google Account: If you're already logged into Google, you'll see a list of accounts associated with your browser. Select the Google account you'd like to use with Canva.

3. Authorize Canva to Access Your Account: You may need to give Canva permission to access certain information from your Google account, such as your name and email address. This is necessary for Canva to create your profile.

4. Finalize the Setup: Once Canva is authorized, your account will be automatically created, and you'll be taken to your Canva dashboard.

Using Google to sign up for Canva can be a timesaver, as you won't need to remember additional passwords. This option is perfect for users who already rely on Google services like Gmail or Google Drive.

3. Sign up with Facebook

Many users find it convenient to sign up for online services using their Facebook accounts, and Canva supports this option as well. Signing up with Facebook can be quick, especially for those who frequently use Facebook for other apps and services.

1. Select the "Sign up with Facebook" Option: From the Canva homepage, click the "Sign up with Facebook" button.

2. Log in to Facebook: If you're not already logged into Facebook on your browser, you'll be prompted to enter your Facebook email or phone number and password. Otherwise, Canva will proceed with the authorization process.

3. Grant Permission: Canva will request permission to access your Facebook profile information, including your name and email address. You'll need to approve this to proceed.

4. Complete the Setup: Once permission is granted, Canva will automatically create your account, linking it to your Facebook profile.

With Facebook, your Canva account is tied to your social media, making it easier to share designs and projects with your network. This is a convenient option for users who regularly use Facebook to log in to various online platforms.

4. Sign up with Apple

Apple users can also sign up for Canva using their Apple ID. This method offers enhanced privacy options, including the ability to hide your email address when signing up.

1. Choose "Sign up with Apple": From Canva's signup options, click "Sign up with Apple."

2. Sign in with Your Apple ID: If you're not already signed into your Apple account, you'll be asked to enter your Apple ID credentials.

3. Decide Whether to Share or Hide Your Email: One of Apple's unique privacy features is the option to hide your email address when signing up for services. You can choose to share your actual email with Canva or use Apple's "Hide My Email" option, which generates a randomized email address.

4. Authorize the Sign-up: Once you've chosen your privacy preferences, authorize Canva to access your Apple account information, such as your name and email.

5. Finalize Account Creation: Canva will complete the account setup, and you'll be directed to the dashboard where you can start creating designs.

Apple's sign-up option is ideal for users concerned about privacy and those who already use Apple's ecosystem extensively.

Logging In to Your Canva Account

Once you've created a Canva account, the next step is logging in. Canva provides a variety of login options, similar to the signup process. Here's how you can log in to your account depending on the method you initially used to sign up.

1. Logging in with Email and Password

If you signed up using your email address and password, follow these steps to log in:

1. Go to the Canva Homepage: Navigate to www.canva.com and click the "Log in" button at the top right of the screen.

2. Enter Your Email and Password: On the login page, enter the email address and password associated with your Canva account. If you forgot your password, click "Forgot password?" to reset it.

3. Access Your Account: After entering your credentials, click "Log in." You'll be taken directly to your Canva dashboard.

2. Logging in with Google

If you signed up using your Google account, the process is even simpler:

1. Click "Log in with Google": On the Canva login page, select the "Log in with Google" option.

2. Choose Your Google Account: If you're already logged into your Google account on your browser, select the appropriate account from the list. If not, you'll be prompted to log into Google first.

3. Access Your Canva Account: Once authenticated, you'll be redirected to your Canva dashboard.

3. Logging in with Facebook

For users who signed up using Facebook, the login process is as follows:

1. Click "Log in with Facebook": On the Canva login page, choose the "Log in with Facebook" button.

2. Authenticate with Facebook: If you're not already logged into Facebook, you'll need to enter your Facebook credentials. Otherwise, Canva will log you in automatically.

3. Start Designing: Once logged in, you'll be taken to your dashboard where you can continue working on existing projects or create new designs.

4. Logging in with Apple

If you signed up using Apple, logging in is equally simple:

1. Select "Log in with Apple": On the Canva login page, choose the "Log in with Apple" option.

2. Authenticate with Your Apple ID: Enter your Apple ID credentials if you're not already logged in through your browser.

3. Access Your Canva Account: After successful authentication, you'll be redirected to your Canva dashboard.

Troubleshooting Login Issues

Sometimes, users may encounter difficulties when trying to log in to Canva. Here are a few common issues and solutions:

Forgotten Password

If you've forgotten your password, don't worry—resetting it is easy:

1. On the login page, click "Forgot password?"

2. Enter the email address associated with your Canva account.

3. Canva will send you a password reset link. Follow the instructions to create a new password.

Can't Access Google, Facebook, or Apple Accounts

If you're having trouble logging in via a third-party account (Google, Facebook, or Apple), ensure that you're logged into the correct account on your browser. Additionally, double-check that Canva has been granted permission to access your account.

Account Verification Issues

If you're unable to log in due to a lack of account verification, try resending the verification email. Ensure the email address you used during signup is correct and check your spam or junk folder for the verification message.

By following these steps, you can successfully create and log into your Canva account, whether you're using an email address, Google, Facebook, or Apple. This is the first step toward exploring the powerful design features Canva has to offer, and once you're in, the creative possibilities are endless!

1.2 Exploring the Dashboard

Once you've signed up for Canva, you'll find yourself in the heart of the platform—the dashboard. The dashboard serves as your control center, where you'll access all your projects, templates, and design tools. Understanding how to navigate it efficiently will save you time and help streamline your design process. Let's dive deeper into the key areas of the Canva dashboard and learn how each section can enhance your overall user experience.

1.2.1 The Homepage Layout

The Canva homepage is your entry point to all things design. As soon as you log in, you're greeted with a well-organized layout that provides quick access to your recent projects, popular templates, and essential tools. Whether you're a beginner or a seasoned designer, knowing where to find the features you need will make your workflow more efficient.

1. The Top Navigation Bar

The top navigation bar of Canva's homepage is a constant presence, regardless of which section you're in. It provides quick access to various tools and features, acting like a universal toolbar to keep you grounded no matter where you are in the platform.

At the top left, you'll notice the Canva Logo, which acts as a shortcut to return to the homepage from anywhere in Canva. This is particularly useful when you're deep into a project but want to start fresh or check out a different design without having to click through multiple screens.

To the right of the Canva logo, you'll find the Templates and Projects tabs. These tabs allow you to jump straight into browsing pre-made templates or managing your ongoing projects. Clicking the Templates tab reveals a categorized menu, where you can explore designs tailored for social media, presentations, documents, and more. It's a great starting point if you're looking for inspiration or need to kickstart a project quickly.

Further along the top navigation bar, you'll encounter the Learn and Pricing tabs. The Learn tab is where Canva houses educational resources like tutorials and design tips. For new users, this section is a goldmine of information. It helps you get up to speed with design techniques and Canva's unique tools, making it easier to master the platform. Meanwhile, the Pricing tab details Canva's subscription options, allowing you to explore the benefits of Canva Pro and other paid features.

Finally, on the far right side of the navigation bar, you'll see your Profile Picture or Account Initials. Clicking on this opens a dropdown menu where you can access your account settings, switch between teams, manage your billing information, or log out. For users working in teams, this dropdown is also where you'll manage team settings and assign roles to collaborators.

2. The Sidebar

To the left of the homepage, you'll find Canva's Sidebar. This vertical menu is where you'll access the majority of Canva's features. The sidebar is divided into several sections:

- Home: This takes you back to the homepage from wherever you are within Canva. It's a quick way to reset your navigation and start a new project or revisit existing ones.

- Templates: Clicking this brings up a comprehensive library of templates. Canva categorizes these templates based on project type, such as social media, business cards, presentations, or flyers. It's designed to help you find the perfect template for your project with minimal effort.

- Projects: This is where all your saved projects live. You can see recent designs, access folders, and even collaborate with team members on shared designs.

- Your Brand: This section is available for Canva Pro users and is designed to help you maintain brand consistency across all your designs. You can upload brand logos, set color palettes, and save fonts, ensuring that every design you create aligns with your brand identity.

- Content Planner: Canva's built-in content planner allows you to schedule posts for your social media channels. You can create posts in advance and set them to publish automatically. This tool is particularly valuable for businesses looking to maintain a consistent online presence.

- Create a Team: Canva's collaboration features shine through this section, where you can invite team members to join your workspace. By creating a team, you can share designs, work together in real-time, and even assign roles to each member.

- Discover Apps: Canva integrates with a variety of third-party apps, such as Google Drive, Dropbox, and Pexels. This section helps you discover useful apps that can enhance your workflow by allowing you to import external assets or export designs to other platforms seamlessly.

Each of these sidebar items opens up additional features and options when clicked, expanding Canva's functionality beyond the initial dashboard.

3. The Main Workspace

The center portion of the homepage is where most of your design journey will take place. This area is dynamic and changes based on what you're currently working on or browsing.

At the top of the main workspace, you'll find a Search Bar. This tool is invaluable for quickly finding templates, design elements, or projects. Whether you're looking for an Instagram post template or a specific graphic element, typing a keyword into the search bar will bring up relevant results in seconds.

Below the search bar, you'll encounter a carousel of Suggested Designs. Canva uses algorithms to recommend templates based on your recent activity or popular trends. This is especially helpful if you're not sure what design to create, as it gives you a variety of options to choose from without having to search manually.

Scrolling further down, you'll see sections such as Your Designs, Shared with You, and Templates for You. These sections offer quick access to your recent work, collaborations, and suggested templates based on your preferences. It's a streamlined way to pick up where you left off or discover new design ideas tailored to your needs.

For users who have been active in Canva, the Your Designs section becomes a hub for revisiting and managing your ongoing projects. This section displays thumbnails of your previous designs, and clicking on one will take you directly into the editor to continue working. The Shared with You section is where designs that others have shared with you will appear, making it easy to collaborate on team projects or provide feedback on others' work.

4. Customization and Personalization

Canva also emphasizes personalization, which is evident in the homepage layout. As you use Canva more, the platform will begin to adapt to your preferences, showing you templates and projects that align with your past design choices. The Templates for You section is a prime example of this, offering suggestions based on the types of projects you've created before, whether that's presentations, social media posts, or business cards.

Moreover, Canva gives users the ability to pin frequently-used templates or projects to the top of their dashboard. This is particularly useful for users who work on recurring design types, such as a social media manager who frequently creates Instagram stories or posts. Pinning these templates ensures they're always accessible with just one click.

5. Notifications and Updates

In the top right corner of the homepage, adjacent to your profile picture, you'll find a bell icon, which serves as your notifications center. Canva uses this area to alert you to important updates, such as new template releases, platform announcements, or notifications from your team members. If someone shares a design with you, requests feedback, or comments on a project you're working on together, these notifications will appear here. It's an excellent way to stay in the loop without needing to check multiple places within Canva.

Additionally, Canva periodically rolls out product updates and new features, and you'll often see announcements about these in the notifications area. For example, if Canva adds a new set of templates or introduces an advanced feature, you'll be notified here so that you can explore and take advantage of the new tools right away.

6. Conclusion

Understanding Canva's homepage layout is the first step in becoming proficient with the platform. By familiarizing yourself with the top navigation bar, sidebar, main workspace, and notification center, you'll be able to navigate Canva's features with ease and start creating your designs more efficiently. In the next section, we'll dive into the intricacies of Navigating Templates, Projects, and Folders, where you'll learn how to manage your design assets and streamline your workflow even further.

1.2.2 Navigating Templates, Projects, and Folders

Canva's dashboard is designed to make your design process as smooth and efficient as possible. At the heart of this efficiency lies the ability to seamlessly navigate through templates, projects, and folders, which are essential components of your creative workflow. Understanding how to make the most of these elements will significantly improve your productivity and organization within Canva.

Templates: A Designer's Best Friend

Canva offers a vast library of pre-designed templates that cater to various needs, from social media posts and presentations to flyers, business cards, and beyond. Navigating these templates is one of the first skills any Canva user should master because they offer a powerful starting point for your designs, saving you time and energy.

1. Finding the Right Template

When you first enter Canva's dashboard, you will see a search bar prominently displayed at the top of the screen. This is where you can search for templates that fit your needs. For example, if you're looking to create an Instagram post, simply type "Instagram post" into the search bar, and Canva will display hundreds, if not thousands, of templates specifically designed for that platform.

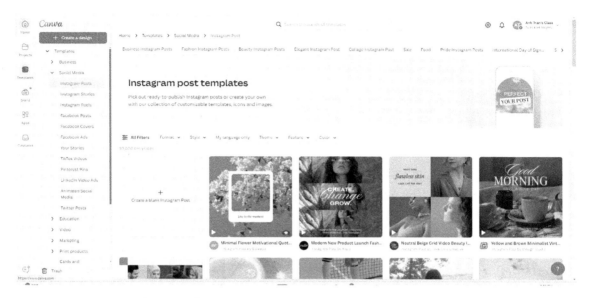

Once you've entered a search query, Canva provides additional filters to help you refine your search. These filters are located on the left-hand side of the screen and allow you to sort templates by style, color, theme, and even size. This is particularly useful when you have a specific visual or branding aesthetic in mind. For instance, if you're creating marketing materials for a luxury brand, you may want to filter by minimalist or elegant styles.

2. Customizing Templates

After selecting a template, Canva takes you to the design workspace, where you can start customizing it to fit your needs. Templates in Canva are fully customizable, allowing you to change fonts, colors, images, and layouts. You can also add or remove elements as needed.

For example, if you are working with a business card template, you can easily replace the placeholder text with your name, title, and contact information. You can also switch out the background image to match your company's branding. This flexibility makes Canva templates versatile, allowing you to create something truly unique without starting from scratch.

3. Saving and Organizing Templates

Once you've customized a template to your liking, you can save it as a project (which we'll cover in more detail shortly) or even save it as a custom template for future use. This feature is especially useful if you frequently need to create similar designs, such as social media posts or presentations for a particular brand or business.

To save a template as your own, simply click on the "..." icon (More Options) next to the design's name in the editor toolbar and select "Save as Template." This will allow you to access your personalized version of the template anytime, speeding up future projects.

Projects: Managing Your Work Efficiently

Every time you work on a design in Canva, it gets saved as a project. Projects in Canva are more than just saved files; they serve as central hubs for all the creative work you've done within the platform. Whether you're working on a single design or multiple iterations of the same concept, understanding how to organize and manage your projects is essential for staying on top of your work.

1. Locating Your Projects

To access your projects, navigate to the "Projects" tab on the left-hand sidebar of your Canva dashboard. Here, you'll find all your saved designs categorized by type. Projects are automatically organized by most recent, so you can quickly pick up where you left off. Canva also provides a thumbnail view of each project, which is particularly useful when you need to visually identify your work.

For instance, if you've recently created a presentation, a business card, and a social media post, you'll see all three designs displayed as thumbnails in your "Projects" area, with the most recent one listed first. Clicking on any project will take you directly to the editing workspace, where you can continue working, make revisions, or download the design.

2. Project Versions and History

One of Canva's most valuable features is its version history. If you've made multiple changes to a project over time and want to revert to an earlier version, Canva makes it easy to do so. By selecting a project and clicking on the "..." icon (More Options), you'll have the option to view version history. From here, you can select a previous version of the design and restore it if necessary.

This feature is especially handy when collaborating with a team or making frequent updates to designs, as it ensures that none of your progress is lost, even if you make major changes.

3. Organizing Projects with Folders

As your body of work grows within Canva, organizing your projects becomes increasingly important. Canva allows you to create folders to categorize and store your projects, making it easier to locate specific designs later on.

To create a folder, go to the "Folders" section in the left-hand sidebar and click the "Create New Folder" button. You can name your folder according to the type of projects it will contain, such as "Social Media," "Client Work," or "Presentations." Once your folder is created, you can drag and drop projects into it, keeping everything organized and easy to find.

This system works particularly well if you're managing multiple clients or brands within Canva. For example, you could create a folder for each client and store all of their related projects inside, ensuring that you can quickly access their designs when needed.

Folders: Your Organizational Toolbox

Folders in Canva aren't just limited to organizing your projects—they can also be used to store assets like images, logos, and fonts that you frequently use in your designs. This is especially useful if you're working on a long-term project or regularly creating designs with consistent branding.

1. Creating and Managing Folders

In addition to organizing projects, Canva's folder system allows you to store and categorize design elements such as uploaded images, brand assets, and even custom templates. This makes it easy to access frequently used items without having to search for them every time you create a new design.

For example, if you are working for a client who has specific brand colors, fonts, and logos, you can create a folder titled "Client Assets" and store all of these elements inside. This ensures that you can quickly add the correct branding elements to any project without hunting through your library.

To create a folder for your assets, click on "Folders" in the left-hand sidebar and select "Create New Folder." Once the folder is created, you can upload files directly into it or move existing uploads into the folder. You can also create subfolders within each folder to further organize your assets. For instance, within your "Client Assets" folder, you might have subfolders for logos, fonts, and color palettes.

2. Collaborating with Shared Folders

If you're working as part of a team, Canva allows you to share folders with your colleagues. This is especially useful for teams working on branding, marketing, or social media campaigns where multiple people need access to the same assets and designs.

To share a folder, simply click on the "..." icon next to the folder name and select "Share." From here, you can invite team members to view, edit, or contribute to the folder. You can also set permissions to ensure that only certain members have editing rights, while others may only view the contents of the folder.

Shared folders keep your team organized and ensure that everyone is working with the same design elements, templates, and brand guidelines. This prevents inconsistencies in design and streamlines the collaborative process.

Conclusion:

Navigating templates, projects, and folders in Canva is an essential skill that will enhance your overall experience with the platform. By mastering these tools, you'll be able to create and manage your designs more efficiently, keep your work organized, and collaborate with others seamlessly.

From selecting the perfect template to organizing your projects and assets, Canva's dashboard is designed with simplicity and functionality in mind. As you become more familiar with these features, you'll find that designing becomes faster, more enjoyable, and more productive. Whether you're working on a personal project, collaborating with a team, or managing multiple clients, understanding how to navigate Canva's templates, projects, and folders will set you up for success in all your creative endeavors.

1.3 Setting Up Your Profile

After creating your Canva account and logging in for the first time, it's essential to set up your profile. A well-organized profile can streamline your workflow, making it easier to manage designs, collaborate with others, and maintain consistency across projects. This section will guide you through the steps of setting up your profile, from customizing your settings to managing team collaboration.

Your Canva profile is more than just a personal identifier – it's a tool that helps you navigate your design journey. Whether you are working solo or part of a team, setting up your profile correctly can save you time, provide easy access to important features, and improve overall efficiency. Additionally, by customizing your profile, you can ensure a consistent professional appearance, which is crucial when sharing designs with others.

1.3.1 Customizing Your Profile Settings

One of the first tasks you should complete after creating your Canva account is customizing your profile settings. Canva provides a range of options that allow you to personalize your experience, whether for individual use, business purposes, or team collaboration. Customizing these settings will make using Canva easier and more efficient as you get into the flow of designing.

Profile Picture

A profile picture is a key part of establishing your identity within Canva. It helps others recognize you, especially when collaborating on projects. Here's how you can add or change your profile picture:

1. Accessing Profile Settings: From the Canva homepage, click on your profile icon in the top right corner of the screen. This will open a drop-down menu where you can find the option labeled "Account Settings." Click on this to navigate to your profile settings.

2. Uploading a Profile Picture: Once inside your profile settings, locate the option to add or update your profile picture. You can upload an image from your computer, ensuring it is clear and professional, especially if you are using Canva for business. Make sure to use a high-resolution image to avoid pixelation.

3. Cropping and Adjusting: Canva allows you to crop and adjust your profile picture directly from the interface, so you don't need additional editing software. Take advantage of this feature to make sure your picture fits well within the display area.

Your profile picture may seem like a minor detail, but it contributes to how others perceive you, especially in team environments. A clear, professional image can create a more polished appearance.

Display Name and Bio

Another essential aspect of customizing your profile is your display name and bio. These elements help convey who you are, your role, and what you bring to a team or project.

1. Setting Your Display Name: Your display name is how others will identify you within Canva. To edit this, navigate to the "Account Settings" section and locate the name field. For personal accounts, use your full name or a preferred alias. For business purposes, it's advisable to use a professional name, especially if you plan on sharing designs with clients or colleagues.

2. Writing a Bio: Canva allows you to add a short bio to your profile. This can be a great way to share information about your background, expertise, and design style. Keep your bio concise but informative. For business or collaborative accounts, mention your role within the company and what type of designs you specialize in. For personal use, feel free to describe your design interests and any relevant skills.

3. Updating Contact Information: While Canva is primarily a design tool, updating your contact information within your profile can help if you plan to use the platform for professional purposes. Some users add their email or website to make it easier for collaborators or clients to reach out.

Language Preferences

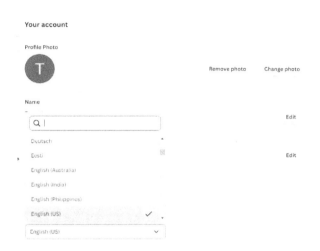

Canva supports multiple languages, allowing you to customize your profile in a language that is most comfortable for you. This is especially helpful for users who work with teams across different regions.

1. Changing Language Settings: To change the language, go to the "Account Settings" and select the "Language" option. From here, you can choose from a variety of languages supported by Canva. Once you've selected your preferred language, the interface will automatically update, making it easier for you to navigate the platform.

2. Designing in Multiple Languages: Canva's flexibility in language settings allows you to create designs in various languages. If you regularly design for audiences that speak different languages, you can switch between languages in your profile settings to match your workflow.

3. Localized Templates: One advantage of setting your language preference is access to localized templates that cater to specific regions and languages. This is particularly useful for users working with international clients or creating content for diverse markets.

Notifications and Alerts

Canva sends notifications for various activities, including project updates, design comments, and team collaboration. Customizing your notification settings allows you to control how and when you receive these alerts.

1. Adjusting Notification Preferences: In your profile settings, find the "Notifications" section. Here, you can choose what types of notifications you'd like to receive, whether via email or directly within Canva. For example, you can opt to receive notifications when someone comments on your design or updates a shared project.

2. Turning Off Unnecessary Alerts: If you find the notifications overwhelming, Canva allows you to disable specific alerts. For instance, if you don't need to know every time a team member logs into Canva, you can turn off that particular notification. Customizing these settings helps reduce distractions while ensuring you stay updated on the most important activities.

3. Email vs. In-App Notifications: Canva lets you choose between receiving notifications via email or within the app. If you prefer fewer emails cluttering your inbox, opt for in-app notifications only. On the other hand, if you rarely log into Canva but want to stay informed, email notifications may be more suitable.

Privacy Settings

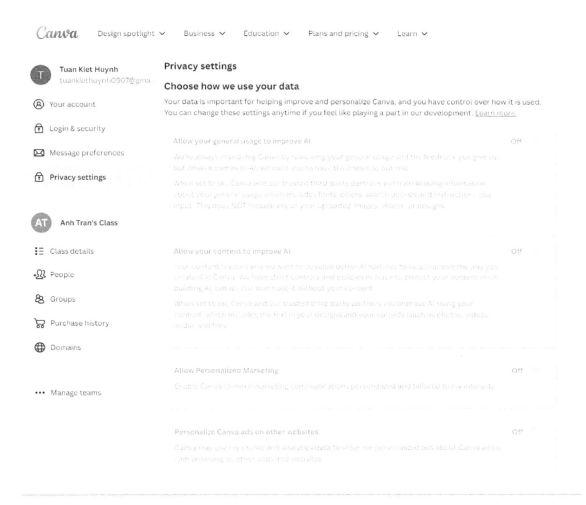

Your privacy settings determine who can see your profile and interact with your designs. This is particularly important if you're using Canva in a professional or team environment, where sensitive designs may need to be protected.

1. Public vs. Private Profiles: Canva allows you to set your profile as either public or private. A public profile makes it easier for potential collaborators or clients to find you. However, if you prefer to keep your designs and activities more confidential, a private profile may be a better option. You can adjust this setting in the privacy section of your account settings.

2. Controlling Access to Your Designs: Privacy settings also extend to the designs you create. Canva allows you to control who can view or edit your designs. You can make

designs private, share them with specific individuals, or allow public access if you're creating content for broad audiences.

3. Managing Team Permissions: If you're working within a team, you can control who has access to your designs. In the privacy settings, you can set permissions for team members, deciding who can view, edit, or comment on designs. This feature is especially useful for maintaining control over sensitive projects while still collaborating effectively.

Two-Factor Authentication (2FA)

Security is a top priority for any online platform, especially when it comes to protecting your creative work. Canva offers Two-Factor Authentication (2FA) to ensure your account remains secure.

1. Enabling Two-Factor Authentication: To enable 2FA, navigate to the "Security" section of your account settings. You can set up 2FA using a mobile authentication app or via email verification. This adds an extra layer of security, requiring you to provide a secondary code (in addition to your password) when logging into Canva.

2. Why 2FA is Important: Using 2FA significantly reduces the risk of unauthorized access to your account. It is particularly crucial if you store valuable design assets or collaborate with clients on confidential projects.

3. Managing Security Alerts: Canva also allows you to receive security alerts if there are suspicious login attempts. You can enable these notifications in your security settings, ensuring that you're always informed of any potential security threats.

Integrating Social Media Accounts

For users who frequently share designs on social media, integrating your Canva profile with your social accounts can save time and streamline your workflow.

1. Linking Social Accounts: In the "Integrations" section of your profile settings, you can link your Canva account to platforms like Facebook, Instagram, and Twitter. This allows you to post designs directly to social media without leaving the Canva interface.

2. Customizing Social Sharing Settings: Canva allows you to customize how your designs are shared. For instance, you can choose to add hashtags, captions, or location tags directly

from Canva. You can also set specific permissions for how your designs are used or displayed on social media.

3. Benefits of Social Integration: Linking your social accounts to Canva is particularly beneficial for businesses and social media managers. It simplifies the process of publishing content, ensuring that designs are posted efficiently and consistently across multiple platforms.

By taking the time to customize your Canva profile settings, you can create a more personalized and efficient workspace. Whether you're an individual designer or part of a larger team, these settings will help you stay organized, secure, and in control of your creative process.

1.3.2 Managing Team Collaboration

In today's highly collaborative working environments, Canva offers robust features to support team-based projects, allowing multiple users to work together seamlessly on designs. Whether you're a small business owner, a marketer, or just someone working on a group project, Canva's collaboration tools streamline the design process by making it easy to share designs, provide feedback, and manage access across teams. This section explores how you can make the most out of Canva's collaboration features by understanding the different roles available, the process for adding team members, and the tools Canva provides for a smooth team experience.

Understanding Roles and Permissions in Canva Teams

One of the most important aspects of managing collaboration in Canva is understanding how roles and permissions work. Canva offers several levels of permissions depending on the type of account you have and the level of control you want to give other users. These roles allow you to maintain control over who can edit, share, and manage your designs, ensuring that your projects are secure and manageable.

- Administrator (Admin): The Administrator role in Canva gives full control over the team's settings, including the ability to add or remove members, assign roles, and manage billing. Admins can also edit any design and access every feature available to the team.

- Template Designer: This role is especially useful in teams that need to create and maintain a consistent brand. A Template Designer can create templates that the rest of the team can use but cannot edit team settings or manage billing. This ensures that your team's designs stay cohesive while allowing for different levels of access.

- Member: Team members can create and edit designs, but their access is limited compared to administrators. They can use templates and make their own designs but do not have access to account settings or billing.

- Viewers: Viewers can see the designs shared with them but cannot make any edits. This role is particularly useful when you need to present work to stakeholders or clients who don't need editing access but should review the progress or final product.

Understanding and assigning the right roles in Canva ensures that team members have the appropriate level of access to get their work done while maintaining security and structure within the team. Before adding anyone to your team, it's important to consider their role in the design process and assign them the correct permissions to prevent unauthorized changes or confusion over access.

Inviting Team Members to Your Canva Workspace

Adding team members to Canva is straightforward and can be done with just a few clicks. The process will vary slightly depending on whether you're using a free or Pro account. Canva Pro users can create multiple teams and manage them all within the same dashboard, while Canva Free users are limited to one team.

Here's a step-by-step guide to inviting people to your Canva workspace:

1. Navigate to the Teams Tab:

From your Canva dashboard, find and click the "Teams" tab. If this is your first time creating a team, Canva will guide you through the process of setting up one.

2. Creating a New Team (For Pro Users):

Canva Pro users can create multiple teams. If you need to set up a new team, click "Create a New Team" and give your team a name that reflects the project or group you're working with.

3. Inviting Members:

Once you have a team set up, you can start adding members by clicking the "Invite People" button. Canva allows you to send invites via email. Simply enter the email addresses of the people you want to invite, and they'll receive a notification with a link to join your team. You can also invite team members via a shareable link.

4. Assigning Roles:

After inviting people, you can assign them roles based on their responsibilities within the team. For instance, if you're working with a marketing team, your designers might be "Members," while the marketing lead could be an "Administrator" to oversee the whole project.

5. Accepting Invitations:

Team members will receive an email with an invitation to join the Canva team. They will need to sign in or create a Canva account if they don't already have one. Once they accept the invitation, they'll have access to all team resources and designs, according to the role assigned.

6. Managing Team Members:

As the project evolves, you may need to change the roles of certain members or remove them from the team. From the Teams tab, you can see all your current team members, change their roles, or remove them from the group if needed.

Adding and managing team members ensures that collaboration runs smoothly, and everyone is on the same page regarding access and responsibilities.

Collaborating on Designs in Real-Time

One of Canva's most powerful features for teams is the ability to collaborate on designs in real time. This feature allows multiple team members to work on the same design simultaneously, offering a level of flexibility and immediacy that can save hours of back-and-forth communication.

How to Collaborate on a Design:

1. Sharing the Design:

When you open a design that you want to collaborate on, simply click the "Share" button in the top right corner of the screen. You'll be given options to invite specific team members

or to generate a shareable link. Be sure to set the appropriate permissions for the link—whether team members can view only, comment, or fully edit the design.

2. Real-Time Edits:

Once team members have access, they can open the design and start making changes. Any edits made by your collaborators will appear in real-time, allowing you to see their updates as they happen. Canva even provides a cursor that highlights the exact part of the design a team member is working on, ensuring that you don't accidentally overlap efforts.

3. Leaving Comments and Feedback:

Canva also allows for easy communication within designs through its comment feature. To leave feedback, click on any element in the design and type your comment in the side panel. Team members can respond to your comments, creating a clear dialogue about the project without needing to leave Canva. This is particularly useful for design approvals or brainstorming sessions, where several ideas need to be discussed and refined before finalization.

4. Version Control:

Another significant benefit of Canva's collaborative features is its built-in version control. Canva automatically saves versions of your designs, which means you can always revert to an earlier iteration if a mistake is made or if a new direction needs to be explored. This ensures that collaboration remains flexible and that no design progress is lost.

Tips for Effective Team Collaboration in Canva:

- Set Clear Expectations: Before jumping into a collaborative design session, make sure everyone understands their role in the process. Clear communication is key to ensuring that everyone contributes productively without stepping on each other's toes.

- Use Comments for Feedback: Rather than making changes directly to someone else's work, use Canva's comment feature to suggest adjustments. This avoids confusion and ensures that feedback is clear and actionable.

- Designate a Final Approver: In larger teams, it can be helpful to designate one person as the final approver of designs. This person can gather feedback from the group, make final tweaks, and ensure that the design aligns with the project's goals.

- Use Templates to Ensure Consistency: For teams working on multiple projects, creating and using templates ensures consistency across all designs. Templates provide a unified look and feel while speeding up the design process for everyone involved.

Managing and Organizing Team Projects

As the number of team members and projects grows, it's essential to have a system in place for organizing designs and keeping everything accessible. Canva provides several tools to help you manage your team's projects efficiently, ensuring that designs are easy to find, edit, and share.

Creating Folders for Organization:

Folders are a great way to keep designs organized, especially when working on multiple projects or with a large team. To create a folder, simply click the "Folders" tab from the Canva dashboard and select "Create New Folder." You can name the folder according to the project, department, or any other organizational structure that makes sense for your team.

Once you have folders in place, team members can save their designs directly into the appropriate folder, making it easy for others to access and contribute. For example, if you're working on a marketing campaign, you might have separate folders for social media graphics, email templates, and presentation materials. This structure not only saves time but also keeps the workflow efficient.

Using Projects for Larger Campaigns:

For larger, ongoing campaigns, Canva's "Projects" feature allows you to group related designs and resources together. This is especially useful for marketing or branding efforts where you might need to manage various elements like brochures, posters, logos, and digital assets simultaneously. By creating a project in Canva, you can keep all these related designs under one umbrella, making collaboration more straightforward and organized.

Sharing Design Resources with the Team:

In addition to sharing designs, Canva allows you to share folders, templates, and brand kits with your team. Sharing these resources ensures that everyone has access to the same assets and can work more efficiently. For example, sharing a folder of company logos or brand colors means team members don't have to search for these elements each time they start a new project.

By mastering the tools and techniques in this section, you will ensure smooth and effective collaboration with your team on Canva. From managing roles to sharing designs in real time, Canva's team features make it easy to work together and create stunning visuals, whether you're in the same office or working remotely from around the world.

CHAPTER II
Canva Interface Overview

2.1 The Design Workspace

2.1.1 The Toolbar and Its Functions

In Canva, the Toolbar is one of the most crucial features to master because it contains the primary tools needed for creating, editing, and enhancing your designs. Whether you're working with text, images, shapes, or templates, the toolbar provides quick access to the essential functions required to manipulate these elements effectively. Understanding each tool and its functionality will significantly improve your ability to design efficiently and produce professional-looking work.

Overview of the Toolbar Layout

When you open a new design in Canva, you'll immediately notice the toolbar located at the top of the design workspace. This horizontal strip houses various tools that allow you to modify the design elements on your canvas. Depending on the type of object you've selected—whether it's text, an image, a shape, or another element—the toolbar options change to suit that specific item, offering customization options tailored to the selected component.

At its most basic, the toolbar includes options for adjusting alignment, changing colors, applying effects, adding animations, and more. Let's break down each section of the toolbar and its corresponding functions, starting with the most commonly used tools.

Alignment Tools

One of the first groups of icons you'll notice in the toolbar is related to alignment. Canva provides multiple ways to align the objects on your canvas for a more organized and visually appealing design.

- Align Left, Center, and Right: These tools allow you to align text, images, and shapes to the left, center, or right within a specific frame or canvas. They are especially useful for creating symmetry or structuring elements in relation to each other.

- Align Top, Middle, and Bottom: If you're working with multiple objects on your canvas, these tools help you align them along the top, middle, or bottom edges. This ensures even spacing between items and a clean, professional look.

- Distribute Objects: Canva allows you to evenly distribute multiple objects horizontally or vertically on the canvas with just one click. This feature is incredibly helpful when you're working with numerous elements and want to maintain equal spacing between them.

Mastering the alignment tools can speed up your design process, especially when working with layouts that require precise placement of elements.

Font and Text Tools

When working with text, Canva provides a robust set of tools for customizing the look and feel of your written content. These text tools are located in the toolbar and appear whenever a text box is selected.

- Font Selection: Canva offers a vast library of fonts to choose from, both free and premium (for Pro users). The Font Selection dropdown allows you to browse through various font families, including serif, sans-serif, and decorative fonts. Canva's search function makes it easy to find the perfect font by entering keywords or browsing categories such as modern, classic, and elegant.

- Font Size: Once you've chosen a font, the Font Size tool lets you adjust the size of your text. Canva allows you to either select a pre-set size from a dropdown or manually input a specific size for more precision.

- Font Color: Canva's color tool is highly flexible, offering a palette of default colors, the ability to choose a custom shade using the color wheel, or inputting a specific hex code. This ensures that your text color aligns perfectly with your design's theme.

- Bold, Italic, Underline: These options allow you to apply basic formatting to your text. Bold makes the text heavier and more prominent, italic adds emphasis through a slanted type, and underline highlights important information. These tools are essential for creating text hierarchies and drawing attention to key messages.

- Text Alignment: Similar to alignment for objects, Canva allows you to adjust the alignment of text within its text box. You can choose to align your text to the left, center, or right of the text box, or justify it to ensure the text stretches evenly across the box.

- Line Height and Letter Spacing: These tools are particularly useful when you need to adjust the readability and overall aesthetic of your text. Line Height controls the space between lines of text, which can be increased for more open designs or decreased for compact layouts. Letter Spacing adjusts the distance between individual characters, providing more breathing room or creating a tighter, more uniform appearance.

- Text Effects: Canva also includes Text Effects, which allow you to apply a range of visual enhancements to your text. Options include shadows, glows, and outlines, which help make your text stand out against busy backgrounds or add a touch of style to your design.

Image Editing Tools

If you're working with images, Canva offers an array of powerful tools to modify, enhance, and fine-tune photos or illustrations.

- Filters and Adjustments: When an image is selected, the toolbar will present options for applying filters. Canva's Filters tool allows you to apply preset color and lighting effects, such as grayscale, sepia, or vignette. Additionally, the Adjustments tool gives you manual control over settings like brightness, contrast, saturation, and blur, allowing you to tweak the image to fit your design's theme.

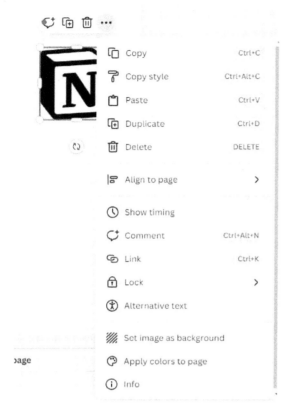

- Cropping and Resizing: The Crop tool is essential for trimming unwanted parts of an image or adjusting its focus. Canva also lets you resize images using the drag handles on the canvas, but for more precision, the toolbar offers manual input options for exact dimensions.

- Transparency: The Transparency slider allows you to adjust the opacity of an image. This tool is handy for creating subtle overlays, backgrounds, or ghosted images that blend seamlessly into the design.

- Flip and Rotate: These tools are useful for reorienting images and other objects. Flip allows you to reverse an image either horizontally or vertically, while Rotate provides options to adjust the orientation by fixed angles or to freely rotate the image.

Shapes and Lines

For non-text elements such as shapes and lines, Canva provides simple yet effective customization options in the toolbar.

- Shape Color: Similar to the font color tool, the Shape Color option allows you to select a color for any shape you've added to your design. You can use the color wheel to pick from millions of colors or input a specific hex code.

- Borders and Stroke Width: If your shape or line has a border, you can adjust the Stroke Width to make the border thicker or thinner. Canva also offers options for changing the style of the border, from solid lines to dashes or dots.

- Corner Rounding: Canva's Corner Rounding tool lets you adjust the sharpness or softness of a shape's edges. This is especially helpful when creating buttons, badges, or icons with rounded corners.

Position and Layering Tools

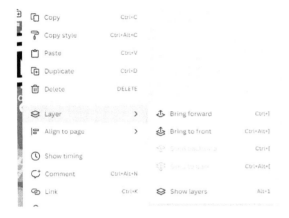

The toolbar also includes tools for controlling the position and layering of objects on your canvas, allowing you to move elements forward or backward relative to other objects.

- Positioning Tools: These allow you to move objects precisely around the canvas, whether you're aligning them to the top, bottom, center, or corners. Additionally, you can nudge elements using arrow keys for minute adjustments.

- Layering Options: Canva uses a stacking system for objects, where elements can be placed in layers. The Bring Forward and Send Backward options let you control which objects appear on top and which recede behind other elements.

Additional Tools in the Toolbar

- Group/Ungroup: This tool allows you to group multiple elements together, so you can move and adjust them as a single unit. You can always ungroup them later if individual adjustments are needed.

- Lock/Unlock: The Lock tool is extremely useful for fixing elements in place, ensuring that they don't accidentally move while you're working on other parts of the design.

- Duplicate: The Duplicate tool creates an exact copy of the selected element or group of elements. This is particularly helpful for maintaining consistency in your design without having to recreate items from scratch.

Summary of Toolbar Functionality

The toolbar in Canva is designed for ease of use while offering a broad range of customization options. By mastering each tool, from alignment and font manipulation to image editing and object positioning, you'll gain the flexibility needed to create designs that are not only visually compelling but also structured and balanced.

2.1.2 The Canvas and Layout Area

The canvas is at the heart of any design project in Canva. It is the blank space where all the elements—such as text, images, shapes, and illustrations—come together to create your final visual product. This section explores how to interact with the canvas, manipulate design elements, and use various tools and features that help refine your work.

Understanding the Canvas

In Canva, the canvas is the working area where your design takes shape. It represents the real-world size and dimensions of your project, whether it's a social media graphic, a presentation slide, or a printed document. When you start with a template or create a design from scratch, the canvas will display the exact proportions of your design, making it easy to envision how the final product will appear.

The canvas adapts to the type of project you are working on. For example, if you are designing an Instagram post, the canvas will be a square (1080x1080 pixels), while a presentation slide will be rectangular in landscape orientation (1920x1080 pixels). This flexibility allows you to work confidently, knowing that your design will maintain its integrity across various platforms.

The Role of the Canvas in Layout Design

The canvas isn't just a blank space—it serves as the foundation for layout design. Canva provides built-in tools such as grids, rulers, and margins that guide you in organizing your content effectively. These features are essential for maintaining balance and harmony in your designs. The layout is what ties together the various visual elements and ensures a cohesive, professional look.

Canva's layout tools are especially useful when working with multiple design elements. For example, the Snap to Grid feature helps align objects to key points on the canvas, ensuring that your text, images, and shapes are evenly distributed. Similarly, rulers and margins assist in maintaining consistent spacing, which is particularly important in printed designs like brochures or flyers.

Zooming In and Out

One of the key functionalities available in Canva's canvas is the ability to zoom in and out. This feature is especially useful when you're working on intricate designs or dealing with multiple layers of content. Zooming in allows you to focus on the finer details, such as ensuring that text spacing is correct or aligning elements to perfection. On the other hand, zooming out gives you an overview of the entire design, which is essential when assessing the overall balance and composition.

To zoom in or out, simply use the zoom slider located at the bottom right corner of the Canva interface, or use keyboard shortcuts. On most systems, holding "Ctrl" (Windows) or "Cmd" (Mac) and scrolling your mouse wheel will zoom the canvas in and out, respectively. Alternatively, you can select a specific zoom percentage (e.g., 50%, 100%, 200%) from the dropdown menu to get an exact view of your design.

It's important to remember that zooming does not affect the actual size of your design—it only changes your perspective while working within Canva. This means that you can safely zoom in to perfect small details without altering the final dimensions or proportions of the project.

Resizing and Adjusting the Canvas

At any point in your design process, you may need to adjust the size of your canvas. Canva makes this simple with its Resize feature, which allows you to change the dimensions of your project to fit different platforms or formats. This is especially useful if you need to create the same design for multiple purposes, such as resizing a flyer into a social media post or adjusting a poster into a presentation slide.

To resize your canvas, click the Resize button in the top toolbar. This opens a menu where you can select from pre-defined dimensions (such as Facebook posts, A4 paper size, or YouTube thumbnails) or enter custom dimensions based on your requirements. Canva Pro users also have access to the Magic Resize tool, which automatically adjusts the size of your design for multiple formats simultaneously, saving time and effort.

When resizing your canvas, Canva automatically adjusts the placement of your design elements to fit the new dimensions. However, you may still need to make minor tweaks to ensure that everything looks perfect. Elements like text boxes, images, and icons may shift or change proportionally, so double-check your layout after resizing to avoid any unintended overlaps or misalignments.

Using the Alignment Tools

In Canva, the layout and arrangement of design elements are critical to creating visually appealing content. One of the most powerful features of the canvas is the alignment tool. This feature ensures that all elements in your design are aligned perfectly, whether horizontally or vertically.

To access alignment tools, simply click on any element on the canvas, and you will notice alignment guides automatically appear. These are thin lines that help you place elements symmetrically or in relation to other objects. Canva's intelligent alignment guides snap your elements into place, ensuring even distribution and a polished look.

Additionally, Canva offers the Align button in the top toolbar, which provides precise control over element positioning. You can align objects to the left, center, or right, or distribute them evenly across the canvas. These options are invaluable when working with multiple elements that need to maintain equal spacing or when creating grid-based designs, such as brochures or presentations.

Using Canva's Layout Grids

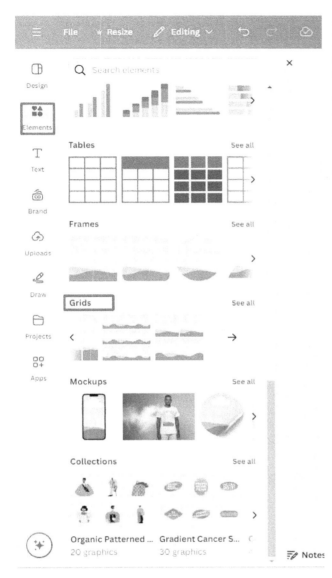

Grids are one of the most versatile layout tools in Canva. They allow you to structure your designs with clear visual separation and balance. Grids are pre-defined areas that divide the canvas into sections, making it easy to arrange your content in a cohesive and organized manner.

To add a grid, click on the Elements tab in the side panel, then scroll down to Grids. You can choose from a variety of grid layouts, ranging from single-column designs to complex multi-column layouts. Once selected, the grid will automatically fill the canvas, and you can drag and drop images or elements into each section.

Grids are especially useful for creating photo collages, blog headers, or multi-image social media posts. Each section of the grid can hold a separate image, and Canva will automatically resize your images to fit the allocated space. This ensures that all of your photos are uniform in size and spacing, creating a clean, professional look.

Moreover, Canva's grid system supports flexible customization. You can resize individual grid cells, adjust the spacing between columns, or even remove sections of the grid to suit your needs. This level of control makes grids a powerful tool for achieving both simple and complex layouts.

Working with Guidelines and Rulers

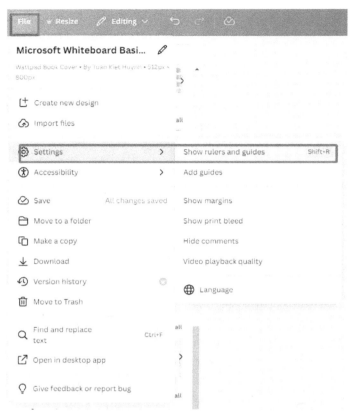

Rulers and guidelines are essential for achieving precision in your designs. Canva includes built-in rulers that appear along the top and side of the canvas, helping you measure the exact position of your design elements. You can also drag guidelines from the rulers onto the canvas to create reference points for alignment and spacing.

To enable rulers and guidelines, go to the File menu and select Show Rulers and Guides. This will activate the rulers on the canvas, allowing you to drag horizontal and vertical guidelines into place. These guides are not part of the final design; they serve as visual aids to help you align and distribute elements consistently.

Guides are especially helpful when you need to ensure that text boxes, images, and shapes are perfectly aligned across multiple sections of your design. For example, if you are creating a multi-page presentation, using guides ensures that your titles and subtitles are consistently placed on every slide.

Using Canva's Snap Feature

Another useful tool in Canva's canvas area is the Snap feature. This feature automatically detects and aligns elements based on their proximity to other objects on the canvas. As you move elements around, Canva will display dotted lines indicating alignment with other nearby elements or the center of the canvas. This allows you to position items quickly and precisely without needing to manually adjust them.

The Snap feature is especially beneficial when working with text boxes and images that need to be centered or aligned with other elements. For example, if you are designing a business card, Snap can help you ensure that your logo, name, and contact information are perfectly aligned, giving your card a professional appearance.

Organizing Multiple Layers

When you work with multiple design elements, each object is placed on its own "layer" within the canvas. Layers determine the stacking order of elements—whether they appear in front of or behind other objects. Canva provides tools to help you manage these layers efficiently, ensuring that your design remains organized and easy to edit.

To adjust the layer order of an element, right-click on it and choose Bring Forward or Send Backward. This will move the element up or down in the layer stack. Alternatively, you can use the Position button in the top toolbar to control layer placement.

Managing layers is particularly useful when you have overlapping elements, such as text on top of an image. For example, if you're designing a flyer with a background image and text overlay, you can ensure that the text remains visible by moving it to the front layer.

2.2 Layers, Grids, and Guides

When working on any design, especially more complex ones, having precise control over the placement and alignment of elements is crucial. Canva offers several tools to assist with this, including layers, grids, and guides. These features help designers organize their work, maintain alignment, and achieve a clean, professional look. In this section, we'll explore how you can use layers to organize your design elements, grids to arrange them symmetrically, and guides to ensure proper alignment.

2.2.1 Working with Layers

In graphic design, layers refer to the different levels at which you can place an object or element in your design. Think of layers as transparent sheets stacked on top of each other. Each element in your design—whether it's text, an image, or a shape—exists on its own layer. You can move layers around, reposition elements on different layers, and arrange them so they don't overlap in unintended ways.

While Canva doesn't have a dedicated "Layers" panel like other advanced design software such as Adobe Photoshop, the platform still allows you to simulate working with layers through careful control of object positioning and arrangement. Understanding how layers work in Canva will give you greater flexibility and control when building designs.

What Are Layers in Canva?

In Canva, every object you add to your design—whether it's text, images, icons, shapes, or illustrations—sits on its own "layer." These layers can overlap and interact with each other, depending on how they are arranged. For instance, you may place text on top of an image, a shape behind an illustration, or multiple overlapping photos to create a collage. Although Canva automatically organizes layers as you add elements, manually adjusting their arrangement can give you more control over how your design appears.

Every element can be brought to the front, sent to the back, or positioned between other elements. This is essentially how layers function in Canva. Knowing how to manage layers allows you to handle complex designs that require precise control over where each object is placed.

How to Arrange Layers in Canva

When designing in Canva, you may want to adjust the order of objects, sending some elements forward or backward to create the desired visual hierarchy. Canva offers simple tools to manage these layers without complicating the design process.

Here's how you can manage layers in Canva:

1. Select the Element: Click on the element you want to move. This could be a text box, an image, or a shape. Once selected, the element is highlighted, and a blue bounding box appears around it.

2. Right-click to Access Layer Options: Right-click on the selected element, and a menu will appear. This menu provides the basic options for arranging layers, including Bring to Front, Send to Back, Forward, and Backward. These options give you control over how elements are layered in relation to others.

- Bring to Front: This option moves the selected element to the topmost layer, making it the foremost element visible.

- Send to Back: This option moves the selected element behind all other elements, sending it to the background.

- Forward: This allows you to move the selected element one layer forward, bringing it closer to the front without fully positioning it above everything else.

- Backward: Similarly, this option moves the element one layer back, pushing it further behind other objects.

3. Shortcut Buttons for Layer Management: Canva also provides shortcut buttons for bringing elements forward or sending them backward. Once you select an element, these buttons appear in the top toolbar. They function the same as right-clicking but provide a quicker way to manage layers.

Practical Tips for Layer Management in Canva

Layer management can greatly improve your design's appearance and make the process more efficient. Here are some tips to help you work effectively with layers in Canva:

- Use Layers to Create Depth: If you're designing posters, presentations, or even social media graphics, playing with layers can give your design depth. For instance, you can place a translucent background behind text to make it stand out while keeping the image in the back partially visible.

- Group Elements to Simplify Layer Management: Grouping multiple elements together can help you manage layers more efficiently. To group elements, select all the objects you want to combine (hold the Shift key while clicking on multiple items), then click the Group button that appears on the top toolbar. Once grouped, these elements will behave as one layer. You can easily move, resize, or adjust the opacity of the group while keeping their internal arrangement intact.

- Lock Layers to Prevent Unintended Adjustments: In Canva, you can also lock an element, which freezes its position on the canvas. This is useful when you have finished working on certain elements and want to avoid accidentally moving them while working on other layers. To lock an element, select it, and click the Lock icon that appears in the top toolbar.

- Use Transparency for Layer Effects: If you want to create a softer effect in your design, you can adjust the transparency of a layer. For instance, an image or shape set at 50% transparency can serve as a subtle background for text. To change an element's transparency, select it and click the Transparency icon in the top toolbar, then adjust the slider.

Examples of Layer Management in Different Designs

Here are a few scenarios where effectively managing layers can enhance your design:

- Creating a Flyer: You might use an image as the background and overlay text to convey your message. Additionally, a semi-transparent shape behind the text can improve readability without fully obscuring the background image. In this case, the background image is the bottom layer, the semi-transparent shape is the middle layer, and the text is the top layer.

- Designing Social Media Graphics: A popular approach in social media design is to have an eye-catching image as the background, with bold text layered on top. You could also add an icon or logo in the corner, adjusting its position with the layer tools to ensure it appears over the image but behind the main text.

- Building Presentations: In presentations, layers can be useful for emphasizing certain points. You might want to place bullet points or images behind the main text to add visual interest without overpowering the message.

Common Challenges with Layers

While Canva makes layer management relatively simple, there can still be some common challenges that arise:

- Accidentally Selecting the Wrong Layer: When working with multiple overlapping elements, you might accidentally select the wrong layer, especially when smaller objects are involved. To avoid this, try zooming in on the design or temporarily move obstructing elements out of the way.

- Difficulty Aligning Layers Precisely: With more complex designs, aligning layers precisely can be a challenge. Canva's snap-to-grid feature can help with this, ensuring that elements align properly with each other. We'll discuss this more in the next section, but having a basic understanding of grids and alignment tools will make working with layers easier.

2.2.2 Utilizing Grids and Guides for Alignment

When it comes to creating professional designs in Canva, precise alignment is essential. Proper alignment helps ensure that all elements in your design appear balanced, visually appealing, and easy to read. Grids and guides are critical tools that help designers align images, text, and other elements perfectly on the canvas. Whether you're a beginner or a seasoned designer, mastering grids and guides will elevate the quality of your designs.

The Importance of Alignment in Design

Before diving into how grids and guides function, it's important to understand why alignment matters so much in design. Properly aligned elements create a sense of harmony and order. When objects and text are placed without careful alignment, the design can feel disorganized or visually overwhelming, making it harder for the viewer to process the information.

Some benefits of effective alignment include:

- Clarity and Readability: Elements that are aligned well are easier for the audience to understand.

- Professional Appearance: Symmetry and balance often indicate careful attention to detail, which can give your design a more polished, professional look.

- Visual Hierarchy: Alignment helps guide the viewer's eye to important areas of the design. By aligning key elements, you can create a visual flow that naturally directs the audience's attention where you want it.

Now that we understand why alignment is important, let's explore the tools Canva provides to achieve this: grids and guides.

What Are Grids and Guides?

Grids and guides are invisible tools that help you structure your design. They act like scaffolding to ensure all elements are placed correctly in relation to one another.

- Grids are a framework of intersecting horizontal and vertical lines that divide the canvas into equal parts. They help break down the design area into manageable sections, making it easier to arrange elements consistently across the layout.

- Guides are specific lines you can add manually to align elements precisely. Unlike grids, which are uniform across the entire canvas, guides can be placed exactly where you need them, allowing for greater flexibility in alignment.

These tools are crucial for creating clean and structured designs, especially when you have multiple elements such as text, images, icons, or buttons on your canvas.

How to Use Grids in Canva

Using grids in Canva is quite simple and incredibly effective for achieving consistent alignment. Let's walk through the process of using grids in your design.

1. Adding a Grid to Your Design

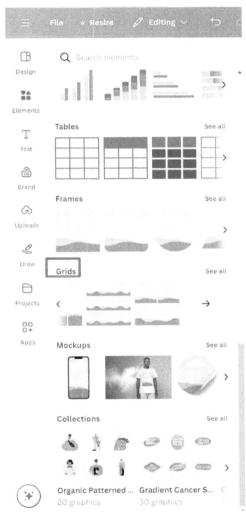

To add a grid in Canva:

1. Open Your Design: Start by opening an existing design or creating a new one.

2. Navigate to the Elements Tab: On the left-hand sidebar, you'll see an option labeled "Elements." Click on it.

3. Search for Grids: Type "grids" into the search bar. Canva will show several grid options, ranging from simple single-section grids to more complex multi-section grids.

4. Choose a Grid Layout: Select the grid that best fits your design needs. For example, if you're designing a photo collage, you might choose a multi-section grid to hold various images.

5. Drag and Drop: Once you select a grid, drag it onto your canvas. It will automatically adjust to the size of your design.

2. Adjusting and Customizing Your Grid

Once the grid is on your canvas, you can resize it by clicking on the corners and dragging it to fit the space. Canva's grids are very versatile; you can adjust the number of rows and columns depending on the layout you're aiming for. Grids are particularly helpful when working with images, as they allow you to neatly position and crop photos within each section.

3. Snapping Elements to the Grid

One of the best features of Canva's grid system is its "snap to grid" functionality. When you move an element (like an image or text box), Canva will automatically align it to the nearest grid line. This ensures that your elements stay perfectly aligned without needing to adjust their position manually.

How to Use Guides in Canva

Unlike grids, which are more structured, guides allow for freeform alignment. Canva's guides are useful when you want to align elements that don't necessarily fit into a strict grid layout.

1. Adding Guides to Your Design

To add guides in Canva:

1. Open the Ruler: If the ruler is not already visible on your canvas, go to the top of your workspace and click "File," then select "Show Ruler." Once the ruler is activated, you'll see measurements along the top and left edges of your canvas.

2. Drag a Guide onto the Canvas: Click on the ruler and drag your cursor onto the design area to create a guide. Horizontal guides are dragged from the top ruler, while vertical guides are dragged from the left ruler.

3. Positioning the Guide: You can place guides wherever you need them. They are flexible and can be moved by clicking and dragging them to your desired position.

2. Snapping Elements to Guides

Just like grids, guides also feature a "snap" function. When you move an element near a guide, Canva will automatically snap it to the guide, ensuring perfect alignment. This is especially helpful when you want to align text boxes or images with precision, even if they are located in different areas of the canvas.

3. Removing Guides

If you no longer need a guide, simply click on it and drag it off the canvas to remove it. This won't affect the rest of your design but will give you more space to work.

Practical Uses of Grids and Guides

Grids and guides can be used for a variety of design projects, ranging from simple one-page layouts to complex, multi-element designs. Below are a few practical examples of when and how to use these tools.

1. Designing a Photo Collage

When creating a photo collage, grids make it easy to position multiple images without them overlapping or appearing uneven. You can select a grid layout with the right number of sections, drop each photo into its respective grid, and Canva will automatically align and crop them to fit perfectly.

2. Creating Business Cards

For business cards, guides are especially helpful for aligning text with other elements such as logos or icons. You can use a guide to ensure that all text is uniformly positioned, making the card appear clean and organized.

3. Designing Presentations

In presentations, consistency is key. By using grids, you can maintain the same layout across multiple slides, ensuring that headings, images, and bullet points are placed in the same position on each slide. This consistency improves readability and gives your presentation a professional look.

4. Creating Infographics

Infographics typically contain a lot of information, so it's crucial to keep everything aligned for clarity. Guides can help ensure that each section of the infographic is evenly spaced and properly aligned, making it easier for viewers to digest the information.

Tips for Effective Use of Grids and Guides

To get the most out of Canva's grids and guides, here are a few tips:

- Plan Your Layout in Advance: Before diving into the design, sketch out where you want your elements to be. This will help you choose the right grid or place your guides more effectively.

- Use Grids for Symmetry: If your design requires symmetry, such as a photo gallery or menu layout, grids are your best friend. They ensure each section has the same dimensions and spacing.

- Use Guides for Flexibility: Guides are great for more flexible layouts where strict symmetry isn't necessary, such as aligning text boxes or placing logos on different sides of the canvas.

- Snap for Precision: Take advantage of Canva's snap feature to align elements precisely to the grid or guide without manually adjusting their positions.

Conclusion

Mastering grids and guides in Canva is essential for creating professional, well-organized designs. These tools help you maintain alignment, ensuring that your final product is both visually appealing and easy to navigate. By using grids and guides effectively, you can enhance the structure and readability of your designs, ultimately improving their overall impact.

2.3 Using the Template Library

Canva offers a vast library of templates designed to suit a wide variety of needs. Whether you're creating a presentation, a social media post, or a business card, Canva provides pre-made templates to jumpstart your design process. This feature is especially helpful for beginners, as it eliminates the need to start from scratch and gives users a professional foundation to work from.

One of the most convenient aspects of Canva's template library is its organization by categories, allowing users to quickly find the most suitable design for their specific project. In this section, we'll walk you through how to search for templates by category, giving you the tools to efficiently locate and customize designs that align with your goals.

2.3.1 Searching for Templates by Category

1. The Importance of Categories in Canva

When it comes to design, different projects require different aesthetics and functionalities. Canva has recognized this need by grouping its templates into categories. This means you can find a template designed specifically for the type of content you're creating, whether it's a social media post, flyer, invitation, or resume. These categories are highly relevant because each one takes into account the purpose and audience for that type of content. For example, a template for a birthday invitation will have a playful, celebratory feel, while a business proposal template will feature a more professional and formal design.

By using categories, you can save time, avoid decision fatigue, and ensure that your design aligns with the specific purpose for which it's intended. Canva's system eliminates the need for browsing through hundreds of unrelated templates, allowing you to focus only on those that are suitable for your project.

2. Accessing Canva's Template Categories

Finding templates by category is a straightforward process in Canva. Once you've logged into your Canva account and are on the main dashboard, the template search bar will appear prominently at the top of the page. Right below this search bar, you'll find a selection of category tiles that display various popular categories like "Presentations," "Social Media," "Videos," and more.

To dive deeper into the available templates, you can do the following:

- Click on a category tile: Canva's homepage offers tiles for popular categories. Clicking on one of these tiles will lead you to a library of templates curated specifically for that category. For example, if you click on "Social Media," you'll be presented with templates designed for Instagram posts, Facebook banners, Twitter headers, and more.

- Use the search bar: Another way to explore templates by category is to type a specific project type into the search bar. Typing keywords like "Flyers" or "Business Cards" will filter out templates unrelated to your search and display relevant results. The search bar also gives suggestions for more specific subcategories, which can make your search even more precise.

After accessing the appropriate category, you will see a multitude of options neatly organized for your convenience. In the following sections, we'll explore the most popular Canva categories and how to efficiently search within them.

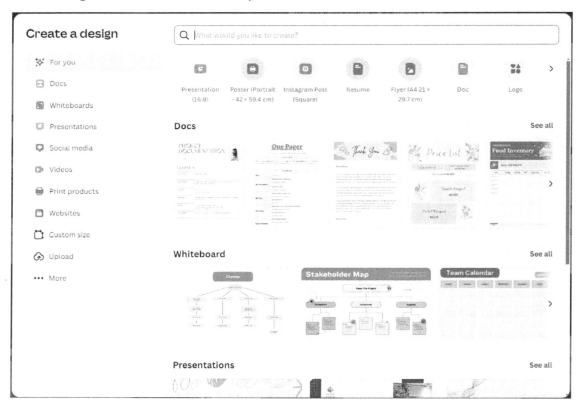

3. Popular Template Categories in Canva

- Presentations

Canva offers an extensive collection of templates for presentations, which are perfect for everything from business meetings to school projects. These templates are designed with different themes, ranging from minimalist and corporate to creative and colorful. To search for a presentation template, you can simply click on the "Presentation" category on the homepage or type "presentation" into the search bar.

Once inside the presentation category, you can filter your search by specific themes such as "Business," "Educational," or "Pitch Deck." These additional filters allow you to narrow down your search to match your specific presentation style. Templates in this category typically feature multiple slides, each with distinct layouts for text, images, and charts, making them ready for customization.

- Social Media

Social media templates are some of the most frequently used in Canva. They cater to platforms like Instagram, Facebook, Twitter, Pinterest, and LinkedIn. Clicking on the "Social Media" category will lead you to a variety of templates designed for specific post types and platforms. Canva has made this process incredibly intuitive by clearly marking the dimensions of each template, ensuring that your design will perfectly fit the platform's format.

For instance, you can find templates for Instagram stories, Facebook event covers, and YouTube thumbnails, each tailored to the optimal size and resolution for that platform. If you're working on a specific campaign or marketing project, searching for themes such as "sale," "announcement," or "holiday" will help you find templates with seasonal or promotional designs.

- Videos

The rise of video content has made Canva's video templates increasingly popular. In the "Videos" category, you can browse templates for Instagram Reels, TikTok videos, YouTube intros, and more. Canva provides both static and animated video templates, giving you the option to include dynamic elements in your designs.

If you're creating content for a specific platform, you can filter video templates by platform to ensure the right dimensions and formats. Additionally, searching for keywords like "advertisement," "tutorial," or "explainer" will help you find video templates suited for your project's purpose.

- Marketing Materials

For users focused on business, Canva's "Marketing" category includes templates for flyers, brochures, posters, and business cards. These templates are essential for branding and promotional purposes, offering a professional look for companies of any size. Searching within this category using specific terms like "real estate," "restaurant," or "event" will yield templates designed specifically for those industries or occasions.

Each marketing template can be customized with your own text, images, and branding, allowing you to create professional promotional materials in just a few minutes. Canva's drag-and-drop functionality makes it easy to swap out placeholder text and images, enabling even non-designers to produce polished materials.

- Documents

Canva also excels at helping users create professional documents, such as resumes, reports, and business proposals. In the "Documents" category, you'll find templates structured for professional presentation, with clearly defined sections for headers, body text, charts, and graphs. This category is ideal for those looking to create polished, easy-to-read documents without the need for advanced design software like Adobe InDesign or Microsoft Word.

Searching for templates within this category can be particularly helpful for specific document types, such as "resume," "proposal," or "newsletter." Each document template is fully customizable, allowing you to adapt the design to your personal or professional style.

4. Filtering Templates for Greater Precision

While searching for templates by category is an excellent starting point, Canva also provides filtering options to further refine your search results. After selecting a category, you will typically see additional filtering tools on the left-hand side of the page. These filters allow you to sort templates by various factors such as color, style, and theme.

Here's how you can use filters to your advantage:

- Color: If your brand or project requires a specific color scheme, you can filter templates based on their dominant colors. This can be particularly useful for branding purposes, as it ensures that your template aligns with your brand's color palette.

- Style: Canva offers a range of styles, from minimalist to bold and creative. By filtering for a particular style, you can ensure that the template matches the aesthetic tone of your project.

- Theme: You can also search for templates that match specific themes, such as "holiday," "retro," or "modern." This is helpful when creating seasonal content or projects with a specific design aesthetic in mind.

Using filters in combination with category searches helps narrow down the vast array of template options, making it easier for you to find exactly what you need.

5. Customizing Templates to Fit Your Needs

Once you've selected a template from your chosen category, the next step is customization. Canva's templates are highly flexible, allowing you to adjust virtually every element to fit your project's needs. Customization options include editing text, changing fonts, swapping images, adjusting colors, and resizing elements.

- Text: Most templates will come with placeholder text that you can easily replace. When editing text, you can choose from Canva's extensive library of fonts to match your design style. You can also adjust font size, color, and alignment to better suit the look of your project.

- Images: Canva allows you to replace template images with your own photos or choose from their vast library of stock images. Images can be cropped, resized, or edited directly within the platform.

- Colors: Changing the color scheme of a template to match your brand or personal preferences is simple. Canva provides a color picker tool, allowing you to customize the template's color palette with just a few clicks.

- Layout Adjustments: If you need to change the layout of the template, you can drag and drop elements within the design workspace. Canva's snapping grid makes it easy to align elements precisely, ensuring that your design remains visually balanced.

6. Best Practices for Searching Templates

To make the most out of Canva's template library, consider the following best practices:

- Be Specific with Keywords: When using the search bar, try to be as specific as possible with your search terms. If you're looking for a template for an event flyer, for instance, typing "event flyer" rather than just "flyer" will yield more relevant results.

- Use Filters Wisely: Applying multiple filters can narrow your search too much. Use just enough filters to refine your search but not so many that you end up with too few results.

- Explore Related Categories: If you don't find the perfect template in your chosen category, consider exploring related categories. For example, templates for "Invitations" may also be suitable for "Events," so it's worth exploring multiple options.

- Check Template Details: Before committing to a template, check its details to ensure it meets the dimensions and formatting requirements for your project. This is especially important for print templates, where resolution and size can affect the final product.

By mastering the process of searching for templates by category, you'll unlock a world of possibilities in Canva. The platform's intuitive organization and vast selection of professionally designed templates make it easy for anyone, regardless of their design experience, to create beautiful and effective visuals. Whether you're working on a personal project or a professional campaign, Canva's template library is your gateway to high-quality design with minimal effort.

2.3.2 Customizing Pre-made Templates

Canva's pre-made templates are a fantastic way to start designing, especially for beginners or those short on time. These templates offer pre-structured designs for various purposes such as social media posts, presentations, business cards, posters, and more. However, a key strength of Canva lies in its flexibility. Pre-made templates are just the foundation, and you can completely customize them to suit your needs, preferences, or brand identity.

In this section, we'll explore how to modify and personalize pre-made templates to create unique, professional designs that stand out. Whether you're tweaking a template for branding purposes or crafting a design that reflects your individual style, Canva provides a variety of tools to help.

1. Selecting the Right Template

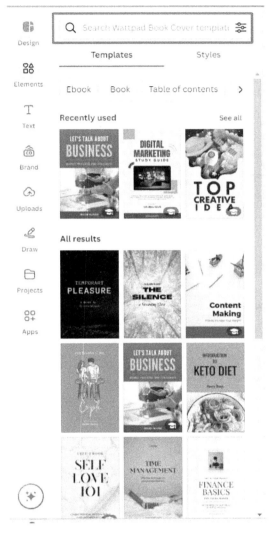

Before diving into customization, the first step is selecting the right template for your project. Canva offers thousands of templates, categorized by themes like presentations, social media, marketing, personal, and business needs.

- Search by Keyword: To quickly find a relevant template, you can use the search bar. For instance, if you're creating a flyer, simply type "flyer" into the search bar, and Canva will display various templates suited for that purpose.

- Filter by Category: Canva allows you to filter templates based on different categories such as "Business," "Marketing," or "Social Media." This makes it easier to narrow down your choices.

- Consider Your Brand or Theme: Keep in mind your brand colors, fonts, and overall aesthetic when selecting a template. You can always customize these later, but starting with a template that aligns with your design goals will make the process smoother.

Once you've chosen your template, click on it to open the design workspace.

2. Editing Text in Templates

One of the easiest and most impactful ways to customize a pre-made template is by editing the text. Pre-made templates come with placeholder text, such as "Your Title Here" or "Lorem Ipsum." Replacing this text with your own words helps convey your specific message.

- Selecting Text: Click on the text box you want to edit. Once selected, you'll notice a text toolbar appears at the top of the workspace.

- Changing Font Styles: Canva provides a wide range of fonts, from playful and decorative fonts to clean, professional typefaces. You can replace the default font by selecting the font dropdown in the toolbar. Canva also allows users to upload custom fonts if you're on a Canva Pro account, ensuring your designs align with your brand identity.

- Adjusting Text Size: In many cases, the template's default text size may not be appropriate for your message. Increase or decrease the size of the text using the size dropdown in the toolbar, or manually adjust the text box's boundaries to resize the font proportionally.

- Color Customization: Canva offers an intuitive way to change text color. Select the text, then click on the text color button on the toolbar. You can choose from the pre-set palette, add your own custom colors, or apply your brand colors if you have a Brand Kit set up.

- Aligning Text: Whether you prefer your text left-aligned, center-aligned, or right-aligned, the alignment tool in the toolbar allows you to change the positioning of your text within its text box. Proper alignment ensures readability and gives your design a polished look.

3. Replacing and Customizing Images

Images play a crucial role in the visual appeal of any design. Canva templates typically include pre-set images or placeholders, but you can easily swap them with your own visuals or those from Canva's extensive library.

- Replacing Images: To replace an image, click on it and choose the "Replace" option. You can either upload your own image from your device or select one from Canva's library. If you're using your own image, make sure it's high-quality to avoid pixelation. Canva's image library offers both free and premium stock photos, covering a wide range of topics, themes, and styles.

- Cropping and Resizing: After uploading a new image, you may want to adjust how it appears in the design. Canva allows you to crop and resize images easily. Simply click on the image, select the "Crop" tool from the toolbar, and adjust the image as needed. You can also resize the image by dragging the corners to maintain its proportions.

- Applying Filters: To give your image a distinct style, consider applying filters. Canva offers several pre-set filters, or you can manually adjust settings such as brightness, contrast, and saturation to match the overall tone of your design.

- Image Frames and Shapes: If your template includes framed images, you can replace the images while keeping the frame intact. Canva offers a wide selection of frames, ranging from simple rectangular shapes to circular, geometric, and abstract designs. You can customize the frame's appearance by changing its border color or size.

4. Adjusting Layouts and Elements

Beyond text and images, Canva templates often include various design elements such as shapes, icons, and patterns. These can be customized or rearranged to better suit your vision.

- Modifying Shapes and Icons: If a template includes shapes or icons, you can easily alter them. Click on the shape or icon, and use the toolbar to change its color, resize it, or even replace it with another element from Canva's library.

- Restructuring the Layout: Templates provide a basic layout, but sometimes you may need to move elements around to create more space or adjust the design flow. Click and drag any element to reposition it within the canvas. Holding down the "Shift" key while moving elements helps maintain alignment.

- Grouping and Ungrouping Elements: Some templates feature grouped elements, meaning several design components are linked together to make editing easier. To move or modify multiple elements at once, click on the grouped item. You can also ungroup elements if you need to adjust each part individually. This flexibility is essential for making precise customizations.

5. Customizing Colors

Color schemes in templates are designed to be visually appealing, but you can always adjust the colors to match your branding or personal preference. Canva allows full control over the color of any element in a template.

- Changing Color Palettes: Click on any element with color (such as backgrounds, shapes, or text), then use the color picker to choose a new color. Canva offers both pre-set color palettes and the option to input custom hex codes for exact color matching.

- Applying Gradient Effects: While most Canva templates come with solid colors, you can add gradient effects for a more dynamic appearance. Choose a gradient color from the "Elements" tab, and adjust the colors and direction to fit your design.

- Using the Brand Kit: If you're working on designs for a business or personal brand, Canva Pro's Brand Kit feature allows you to save your brand colors, fonts, and logos. This ensures consistency across all your designs and simplifies the process of customizing templates with your brand identity.

6. Enhancing Templates with Additional Elements

Even after customizing the existing elements in a template, you may want to add more to enhance your design. Canva offers a wide variety of additional elements that you can insert to make your design truly unique.

- Adding Icons and Illustrations: Canva's "Elements" tab provides access to a huge library of icons, illustrations, and vectors. You can search by theme or keyword to find elements that complement your design. Icons can be resized, recolored, and positioned anywhere in the design.

- Inserting Shapes and Lines: Adding shapes or lines can help define sections of your design, guide the viewer's eye, or simply enhance the visual structure. Use shapes to create emphasis, or add lines to separate content in an organized way.

- Including Decorative Elements: For creative designs like invitations or social media posts, you might want to add decorative elements such as flourishes, patterns, or doodles. Canva's library is packed with unique decorative assets to enhance your design.

7. Finalizing and Exporting Your Customized Design

Once you've finished customizing your template, it's time to prepare your design for download, printing, or sharing online.

- Previewing Your Design: Before exporting, use the "Preview" feature to ensure that everything looks perfect. Double-check alignment, text size, and image quality.

- Downloading in the Right Format: Canva allows you to download designs in various formats, including PNG, JPEG, PDF, and even MP4 for video. Choose the format based on your needs. For high-quality prints, PDF Print is the best option, while PNG works well for digital displays.

- Sharing and Collaborating: If you're working with a team, Canva offers collaboration tools that allow you to share your design for feedback or co-editing. You can provide others with view or edit access, making it easy to collaborate in real-time.

CHAPTER III
Designing with Canva Tools

3.1 Working with Text

Text is one of the most essential elements of design, whether you're creating a presentation, social media post, or business card. The way you present text can greatly impact how your message is received, and Canva provides a range of tools to help you make text both aesthetically pleasing and easy to read. This section will guide you through the key features that Canva offers for working with text, including adding, editing, choosing fonts and styles, applying effects, and utilizing formatting options to enhance your designs.

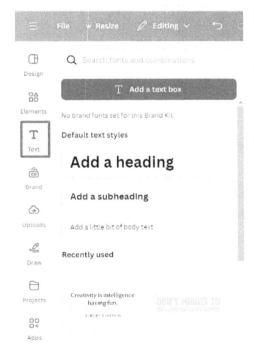

3.1.1 Adding and Editing Text

Adding and editing text in Canva is a straightforward process, but mastering the features that accompany these actions will give you more control over your design. Let's break it down into steps and explore each option in detail.

Step 1: Adding Text Boxes

When you start a design in Canva, you'll likely want to add text to communicate your message. Whether it's a heading, subheading, or body text, adding a text box is the first step. Here's how you do it:

1. From the toolbar on the left-hand side of your design screen, click on the "Text" button. You'll see a panel that offers three main options:

- Add a heading – For bold and large text, usually used for titles or main headings.

- Add a subheading – Slightly smaller text for subtitles or section titles.

- Add a body of text – Best for longer text content such as paragraphs or detailed information.

You can also click anywhere on your design and simply press the "T" key on your keyboard. Canva will automatically add a new text box at the location where you clicked.

2. Adjusting text size: After adding your text box, Canva allows you to manually adjust the size of the text. You can use the corner handles to resize the text box itself, which will also change the text's size, or you can choose a specific font size from the text editing toolbar at the top.

Step 2: Editing Text

Once your text box is in place, you can type directly into it. You'll also have access to various editing tools that can make your text stand out or align with the theme of your design.

1. Selecting text: To edit existing text, click on the text box, and then click on the text you want to modify. A cursor will appear, allowing you to type or delete as needed. You can also drag to highlight specific words or sections for formatting changes.

2. Basic formatting options: Above your design workspace, you'll see the text toolbar, which offers various formatting options:

- Font – Canva offers a wide selection of fonts, from playful and decorative to more professional, clean fonts. Scroll through the font options or type the name of a specific font in the search bar.

- Font Size – You can either choose from preset sizes in the dropdown menu or manually type a number to specify your desired size.

- Text Alignment – You can align your text to the left, center, or right, depending on your design layout. Canva also offers justification for a balanced look.

- Text Color – Click on the color box to change the font color. Canva provides a default color palette, and you can also add custom colors by typing in a hex code or selecting from the color wheel.

3. Adjusting text position and spacing: Canva makes it easy to precisely position your text. Simply click and drag the text box to move it around the canvas. Canva's gridlines will

appear as you drag, helping you align text centrally or at key points in your design. You can also use the arrow keys on your keyboard for fine adjustments.

4. Text Spacing: If you want to adjust the spacing between letters or lines in your text, click on the "Spacing" button located in the text toolbar. Here you can adjust:

- Letter spacing – The distance between individual characters.

- Line height – The space between lines of text within the same text box.

5. Undo and redo options: If you make a mistake or want to experiment with different text styles, you can use the undo and redo buttons at the top of the workspace to revert or reinstate your changes quickly.

Step 3: Managing Multiple Text Elements

In many designs, you'll likely use multiple text boxes. Whether you have a heading, subheading, and body text or multiple captions on different areas of a design, Canva allows you to manage these easily.

1. Grouping and ungrouping text elements: When you have multiple text elements that you want to keep together, grouping them can be helpful. This is done by selecting the text boxes (hold Shift and click on each box) and then clicking the "Group" button at the top right of the toolbar. Grouping allows you to move and resize all the elements as one. If you want to modify one of the elements later, you can ungroup them by clicking "Ungroup."

2. Locking text layers: If you have finalized a section of your text and don't want to accidentally move or edit it, you can lock it in place by clicking the lock icon in the top-right corner of the text box. Locked elements remain static until you unlock them.

Step 4: Organizing and Aligning Text

An often-overlooked aspect of working with text is alignment and organization. Canva offers several tools that make it easy to ensure your text is aligned, spaced evenly, and structured visually.

1. Snap to gridlines: As you move a text box around your canvas, Canva's gridlines automatically appear, helping you align your text with other elements. This can ensure consistency in your design, particularly when working with multiple text sections.

2. Use the position tool: Canva's position tool can help align text boxes horizontally or vertically in relation to the entire design or other elements. This is located in the upper-right toolbar under the "Position" option.

Step 5: Applying Text Hierarchy

Text hierarchy refers to the arrangement of text elements in such a way that it indicates their importance. In Canva, you can create a clear visual hierarchy by varying font sizes, weights, and colors for headings, subheadings, and body text.

1. Headings and Subheadings: Make sure your main heading is bold, large, and eye-catching, while the subheadings are smaller and less prominent. This contrast guides the viewer's eye from the most important information to the supporting details.

2. Body text: Body text should be legible and unobtrusive. It's often best to keep the font size between 10-16 points for readability, and avoid overly decorative fonts in this section.

3. Using color for emphasis: In addition to size, you can use color to highlight key points. For example, you might use a bold color for the heading and a more neutral one for body text. Just be cautious of using too many colors, which can create a cluttered look.

Now that you understand the basics of adding and editing text, you can begin to experiment with the wide range of options Canva provides to create striking and well-organized designs. In the following sections, we'll dive deeper into choosing fonts, applying text effects, and exploring more advanced formatting techniques to bring your designs to the next level.

3.1.2 Choosing Fonts and Styles

Fonts are a fundamental part of design. The right font can set the tone, convey a message, and impact the readability of your content. In Canva, choosing and pairing fonts is both an art and a science, offering you an incredible array of possibilities to create visually appealing designs. This section will explore the process of choosing fonts, understanding font categories, pairing fonts effectively, and utilizing styles to enhance your design.

Understanding Font Categories

Fonts fall into several main categories, each with distinct characteristics. In Canva, you have access to fonts from these categories, allowing you to match the style of your design with the mood and message you're trying to convey. Here's a breakdown of the main font categories:

1. Serif Fonts

Serif fonts are the traditional fonts characterized by the small lines, known as "serifs," attached to the ends of their letters. Examples include Times New Roman, Georgia, and Playfair Display. These fonts are often associated with formal, elegant, and classic designs. They are frequently used in print media, such as books, magazines, and newspapers, because they are highly readable in long-form text.

When to use: Serif fonts work well in formal designs or where a sense of tradition, sophistication, or reliability is needed. They are great for headers in professional reports, invitations, or websites that want to convey a sense of authority and trustworthiness.

2. Sans-Serif Fonts

Sans-serif fonts, as the name implies, do not have the small lines (serifs) attached to the ends of the letters. They are modern, clean, and typically easier to read on screens. Examples include Arial, Helvetica, and Montserrat. Their simplicity makes them versatile, and they're often used in digital designs such as websites, apps, and modern marketing materials.

When to use: Sans-serif fonts are perfect for projects that need a clean and contemporary look, such as tech-related content, startups, or blogs. They can be used in headings and body text for a minimalist and sleek appearance.

3. Script Fonts

Script fonts are designed to mimic handwriting. They are flowing, cursive, and often add a personal, elegant touch to your design. Examples include Pacifico, Lobster, and Great Vibes. These fonts work best in small doses as they can be harder to read in large blocks of text.

When to use: Script fonts are ideal for invitations, logos, or branding materials where you want to add a personal, creative flair. They are perfect for weddings, elegant events, or any occasion where formality meets creativity. However, use them sparingly as they can easily become overwhelming in larger quantities.

4. Display Fonts

Display fonts are decorative fonts intended for large headlines or titles. They are eye-catching and attention-grabbing, often used in posters, banners, or branding materials. Examples include Bebas Neue, Oswald, and Impact. These fonts can be highly stylized, from bold and blocky to intricate and ornate.

When to use: Display fonts are perfect for creating visual hierarchy in large headlines, posters, or advertisements where you want to draw immediate attention. Since they are more ornamental, they should not be used in body text due to their complexity and reduced readability at smaller sizes.

5. Monospace Fonts

Monospace fonts are fonts in which each letter and character occupy the same amount of space. Examples include Courier and Consolas. They are commonly associated with typewriters or coding environments and provide a uniform, organized appearance.

When to use: Monospace fonts are great for creating designs related to coding, tech, or anything that requires a clean, unvaried look. They are also useful for presenting technical information, such as code snippets or data tables.

Choosing the Right Font for Your Project

Choosing the right font starts with understanding the message you want to convey. Ask yourself these questions:

1. What's the purpose of your design?

Different fonts evoke different emotions. A playful, bold font might work well for a children's party invitation, while a sleek sans-serif font would be better suited for a corporate presentation.

2. Who is your audience?

Consider who will see your design. A script font might be too fancy for a general audience but perfect for a bridal boutique. A tech startup might want to opt for a clean sans-serif font to communicate modernity and innovation.

3. What's your design's tone?

Is it formal, casual, playful, or serious? Fonts set the tone for your design. A serif font like Garamond can convey authority, while a playful handwritten font like Pacifico gives off a more relaxed, informal vibe.

4. How much text will be used?

If you have large blocks of text, you'll want to opt for fonts that are highly readable, such as sans-serif fonts like Helvetica or serif fonts like Georgia. For short, impactful statements, you can experiment with more decorative or bold fonts.

Font Pairing Techniques

Choosing one font is only part of the equation. Many designs benefit from pairing two or more fonts to create contrast and visual interest. Canva makes it easy to experiment with different combinations, but here are some general rules to keep in mind when pairing fonts:

1. Contrast is Key

When pairing fonts, aim for contrast in style and weight. Pair a bold, strong heading font with a lighter, more neutral body font. For example, a serif font like Playfair Display in the headings can be paired with a sans-serif font like Lato in the body text. This contrast makes your design visually appealing while maintaining readability.

2. Limit to Two or Three Fonts

Too many fonts can make your design feel cluttered and disorganized. Sticking to two fonts—one for headings and one for body text—often works best. If you need more variety, consider adding a third font for accents or subheadings, but avoid overloading your design with different styles.

3. Match the Mood

Fonts should complement each other in tone and mood. If you're using a playful script font for a title, make sure the body font shares a similar tone. For example, pairing a playful font like Pacifico with a modern sans-serif font like Montserrat creates a cohesive and balanced look.

4. Use Typeface Families

Some fonts come in a range of weights and styles, known as a typeface family. For example, a font like Raleway has multiple weights (thin, light, regular, bold, etc.), allowing you to create variety within a single font family. This ensures consistency while adding enough variety to differentiate between headings, subheadings, and body text.

5. Avoid Conflicting Styles

Be cautious when mixing highly decorative fonts. Two ornate or complex fonts can compete for attention, making the text hard to read. Instead, balance an ornate font with a simpler, more neutral one to avoid clashes.

Utilizing Font Styles and Variants

In Canva, fonts often come with several variants—bold, italic, underline, and sometimes more. Understanding how to apply these styles effectively can help you emphasize important parts of your design without overwhelming the viewer. Here's how to use font styles to your advantage:

1. Bold

The bold style adds weight to a font, making it perfect for headings or key statements you want to emphasize. Bold fonts grab attention and stand out against lighter text. Use bold styles sparingly in body text to highlight important words or phrases without sacrificing readability.

2. Italic

Italics are used for emphasis or to add a stylistic flair to your design. They are often used in quotes, citations, or to give a design a more personalized touch. Be careful not to overuse italics, as they can reduce readability in large amounts of text.

3. Underline

Underlines can be used to highlight links or key points in your design. However, they can also clutter the design if overused. Use underlining primarily for calls to action or important references rather than general emphasis.

4. All Caps

Using all uppercase letters can create a strong, impactful message. This style works well for headings, logos, or statements where you want to convey boldness. However, using all caps for long sections of body text can make it harder to read, so it's best reserved for short, punchy phrases.

Exploring Canva's Font Library

Canva offers an extensive font library, giving you access to hundreds of fonts for free and even more with a Canva Pro subscription. You can filter fonts by style, category, and popularity, making it easier to find the right font for your project.

1. Searching for Fonts

Canva allows you to search for fonts by name, style, or use case. You can start by typing the name of a font, or explore categories like "Modern," "Handwritten," or "Serif" to find something that matches your design's tone.

2. Canva Pro Fonts

With a Canva Pro subscription, you unlock access to exclusive fonts that can take your design to the next level. Canva Pro fonts often include additional weights, styles, and decorative elements that can enhance your work.

3. Custom Fonts

Canva also allows you to upload your own fonts if you have a specific typeface that aligns with your brand or project. This is especially useful for businesses or designers who need consistency across their marketing materials.

Conclusion: Choosing Fonts with Confidence

Choosing fonts and styles in Canva is more than just picking something that looks good. It's about ensuring your design is readable, conveys the right message, and aligns with the mood of your project. By understanding the different categories of fonts, practicing effective font pairing, and utilizing Canva's powerful font tools, you'll be able to create designs that stand out and communicate your message clearly.

In the next section, we will explore how to apply text effects and formatting options to further enhance the appearance of your text in Canva designs.

3.1.3 Text Effects and Formatting Options

When designing with Canva, text plays an essential role in conveying messages and establishing the overall tone and feel of your design. Canva provides a wide range of formatting options and text effects that allow you to customize your text in a way that grabs attention, complements your design, and reflects your branding or messaging.

In this section, we will explore various ways to elevate your text using effects and formatting options. Whether you are creating a simple invitation, a professional presentation, or a visually dynamic social media post, Canva's text tools can help you achieve the exact look and feel you desire.

Applying Basic Formatting

Before diving into text effects, it's important to familiarize yourself with basic text formatting tools in Canva. These tools give you control over essential aspects such as font size, color, alignment, and spacing.

1. Font Size:

Adjusting the size of your text is crucial for ensuring readability and emphasis. Canva allows you to increase or decrease the font size with a simple slider or by entering a specific value in the size box. Larger text sizes are ideal for headings, while smaller sizes work best for body text or captions. It's important to maintain a hierarchy between your text elements, so headings stand out and body text remains easy to read.

2. Font Color:

Canva's color picker provides a broad spectrum of colors to apply to your text. You can choose from preset color palettes, manually pick a color from the color wheel, or input specific hex codes for precise branding. Additionally, Canva offers suggestions based on your design's theme or color scheme, making it easy to ensure your text colors complement the overall design.

3. Alignment:

Aligning text properly enhances readability and visual balance. Canva provides several alignment options, including left, center, right, and justified alignment. Depending on your design, you may choose different alignments. For example, center-aligned text is often used for invitations or posters, while left-aligned text is preferred for more formal documents like resumes or presentations.

4. Spacing:

Canva also gives you control over letter spacing (the space between individual characters) and line height (the space between lines of text). Adjusting letter spacing can make your text feel more open and legible, while increasing line height can improve readability, especially for long paragraphs.

5. Text Transformations:

Canva provides basic text transformation options, such as changing your text to all uppercase or lowercase. This can be useful when you want to emphasize certain words or headings.

Exploring Canva's Text Effects

Now that you've mastered basic formatting, let's move on to text effects, which allow you to add personality and flair to your text. Text effects can make your design more visually dynamic and engaging.

1. Text Shadow:

Adding a shadow to your text can give it depth and make it stand out from the background. Canva allows you to adjust the shadow's color, blur, direction, and intensity, giving you full control over how subtle or dramatic the shadow effect appears. For instance, using a soft, blurred shadow can create a subtle lift effect, while a bold, high-contrast shadow can make your text pop off the page.

2. Lift:

The "Lift" effect is similar to a shadow but subtler. It creates a light shadow directly under the text, giving it a lifted appearance without the need for complex adjustments. This is ideal for adding depth without overpowering your design with strong shadows.

3. Outline:

Outlined text is a bold and eye-catching effect where the text is hollowed out, and only its outline is visible. Canva lets you control the thickness and color of the outline, allowing for creative freedom. This effect is particularly useful for retro or poster-style designs where the text needs to be bold but minimal.

4. Glitch:

The glitch effect distorts the text with a digital-style shift, creating an edgy, modern look. This effect is perfect for designs that aim to convey a futuristic, tech-driven, or avant-garde aesthetic. The glitch effect also allows for color customization, adding even more versatility.

5. Neon:

The neon effect adds a glowing, electric look to your text, mimicking the appearance of neon lights. You can choose the glow's intensity and color, creating a striking look that works well for bold posters, social media graphics, or advertisements that need to draw immediate attention.

6. Echo:

The echo effect layers multiple copies of your text in different colors and positions, creating a dynamic, 3D appearance. This effect works well when you want your text to look playful or vibrant. Canva allows you to adjust the echo distance and color to achieve the exact look you want.

7. Curve:

Canva's curve text effect allows you to bend your text along a curve or circle. This is particularly useful for designing logos, badges, or any design that requires circular text. You can control the degree of the curve, making it tighter or more open depending on your needs. This effect adds a professional touch to designs where straight lines of text wouldn't be as visually appealing.

8. Background:

The text background effect adds a solid or semi-transparent background behind your text, creating contrast between the text and the rest of your design. This effect is perfect when you need to ensure text readability over a busy or complex image background. Canva allows you to adjust the background color, transparency, and padding to suit your design's needs.

Combining Effects for Unique Results

One of Canva's strengths is its ability to layer multiple effects to create truly unique text treatments. For example, you can combine a shadow with a neon effect to create a glowing text that has depth and a 3D feel. Alternatively, you could pair an outline effect with a glitch effect for a cutting-edge, retro look.

Experimenting with combinations of effects can lead to creative breakthroughs in your designs. However, it's important to strike a balance and ensure that your text remains legible and fits the overall tone of your design. Overusing effects can make your text harder to read and detract from the design's message.

Formatting for Different Devices and Platforms

When applying text effects and formatting, consider where your design will be viewed. Designs intended for social media, mobile devices, or printed materials may require different formatting choices. For example, heavily stylized text with complex effects may look great on a computer screen but could become difficult to read on a small mobile device.

Canva allows you to preview your designs in various formats, so take advantage of this feature to ensure that your text is optimized for all viewing platforms. Simple, clean formatting often works best for mobile and web-based designs, while more elaborate effects can shine in print and larger displays.

Best Practices for Using Text Effects

While Canva's text effects offer a wide range of creative possibilities, there are some best practices to follow to ensure your text looks professional and effective:

1. Less is More:

Avoid overloading your design with too many text effects. While it's tempting to use every available effect, keeping your design simple and clean will often result in a more polished and readable final product.

2. Match the Effect to the Message:

The text effect you choose should align with the message or tone of your design. For example, the neon effect may work well for a nightclub poster but would feel out of place in a formal business presentation.

3. Ensure Readability:

No matter how many effects you apply, readability should always be your top priority. If the effects are making the text difficult to read, consider scaling back or choosing simpler formatting options.

4. Consistency is Key:

In multi-page designs or designs with multiple text elements, it's important to maintain consistency. Using the same text effects across all elements can create a cohesive and professional look.

By mastering Canva's text effects and formatting options, you can create visually compelling designs that capture attention and communicate your message effectively. Whether you are designing for social media, print, or presentations, these tools give you the flexibility to customize your text to suit any design scenario.

3.2 Adding and Customizing Images

Images are one of the most important elements of design. They have the power to convey emotions, deliver messages, and grab attention instantly. Canva, being a design platform that emphasizes visual content, offers various ways to add and customize images to enhance your projects. In this section, we will walk through how to add images from various sources and customize them to fit your design needs.

3.2.1 Uploading and Inserting Images

Images play a crucial role in modern-day design, and Canva makes it incredibly easy to upload and incorporate them into your projects. Whether you're using personal images, stock photos, or logos, Canva's user-friendly platform offers flexibility to insert images into your designs seamlessly. Below, we will cover how to upload images from your device, use Canva's extensive image library, and integrate external image sources like cloud storage or URLs.

Uploading Images from Your Device

To begin working with images in Canva, one of the first things you'll want to do is upload images from your computer or mobile device. This allows you to incorporate personal photographs, logos, or any custom graphics into your design. Canva supports various image formats, including JPEG, PNG, and SVG, ensuring you can upload images in formats that maintain high quality.

Here's how you can upload an image from your device:

1. Click on the "Uploads" Tab: On the left-hand sidebar of your design workspace, you'll see an option labeled "Uploads." Click on it to open the upload panel.

2. Select "Upload Files": Within the "Uploads" section, you'll see a button labeled "Upload Files." Click on this button to access your device's file explorer.

3. Choose Your Image: Navigate to the folder where your image is stored. Select the image file you wish to upload and click "Open." Canva will then upload the image to your design workspace.

4. Drag and Drop onto the Canvas: Once the image has been uploaded, it will appear under the "Uploads" tab. You can drag and drop it directly onto your canvas, and Canva will automatically size it to fit within the project's layout.

5. Adjust the Image Size and Position: After placing the image on your canvas, you can easily resize it by clicking and dragging the corner handles. Position the image anywhere within the layout by simply dragging it to your desired location.

Uploading images from your device gives you the freedom to integrate custom visuals into your design effortlessly. Whether it's a logo for a business card or a family photo for a personalized greeting card, Canva supports a smooth upload process. Moreover, images you upload remain stored in your Canva account, meaning you can reuse them across multiple projects without the need to re-upload.

Uploading Images from Cloud Storage

In addition to uploading images directly from your device, Canva offers the option to upload files from various cloud storage platforms. This feature is particularly useful if you store your images on Google Drive, Dropbox, or other online storage services. Canva's integration with these platforms streamlines the design process, as you can access all your images without needing to download them locally.

Here's how to upload images from cloud storage:

1. Click on the "Uploads" Tab: Similar to uploading from your device, you'll begin by navigating to the "Uploads" tab on the left-hand sidebar.

2. Select "Cloud Storage": Below the "Upload Files" button, you will find an option to connect cloud storage platforms. Canva supports Google Drive, Dropbox, and OneDrive. Click on the respective platform that stores your images.

3. Authorize Access: The first time you use a cloud storage platform, Canva will prompt you to authorize access. This process is secure and allows Canva to access only the files you choose to upload. Follow the on-screen prompts to grant Canva permission to access your files.

4. Select Your Image: After authorization, a file explorer for your cloud storage will open. Navigate to the image you want to upload, select it, and click "Open." Canva will then upload the image to your workspace.

5. Insert the Image: Once uploaded, the image will appear in your "Uploads" tab, where you can drag it onto your canvas as you would with any locally uploaded image.

The ability to upload images from cloud storage makes Canva even more flexible, particularly for users who work on multiple devices or collaborate on shared folders. This feature also eliminates the need to manage local file storage, as all your images can remain in the cloud.

Using Canva's Image Library

While uploading your images is important, Canva offers an extensive image library with millions of photos, illustrations, and graphics that you can use. Canva's image library is a valuable resource, especially for users who don't have their own images but still want to produce professional-quality designs.

To add an image from Canva's library:

1. Click on the "Elements" Tab: On the left-hand sidebar of the design workspace, click on the "Elements" tab. This section contains various elements, including images, icons, shapes, and more.

2. Search for Images: Canva's image library is categorized for ease of use. You can either browse the categories or use the search bar at the top to find specific images. For example, if you're designing a travel poster, you can search for terms like "beach," "mountains," or "vacation."

3. Preview and Select an Image: Once you find an image you like, hover over it to preview how it looks in a larger format. Click on the image to insert it into your design.

4. Adjust the Image as Needed: Once the image is on your canvas, you can resize, reposition, and crop it as necessary to fit your design. Canva also allows you to apply filters and adjustments, giving you the flexibility to match the image's tone with the overall theme of your design.

Canva offers both free and premium images in its library. Free images can be used without any additional cost, while premium images (marked with a crown symbol) require a Pro subscription or a one-time purchase. If you're on a budget, there are plenty of high-quality free images available, covering nearly every design need.

Embedding Images from URLs

Another useful feature Canva provides is the ability to embed images directly from URLs. This feature is particularly beneficial if you want to use images that are hosted online, such as stock photos from licensed websites or specific product images from a client's website.

Here's how you can embed an image from a URL:

1. Go to the "Uploads" Tab: As with other uploading methods, start by navigating to the "Uploads" tab in the left-hand sidebar.

2. Select "URL Upload": Below the "Upload Files" button, you will see an option to upload from a URL. Click on this to open the URL input box.

3. Paste the Image URL: In the input box, paste the direct URL of the image. It's important to note that this must be a direct link to the image file itself, not a webpage. The URL should typically end in .jpg, .png, or another image file extension.

4. Insert the Image: After pasting the URL, click "Upload." Canva will retrieve the image and insert it into your "Uploads" section. From here, you can drag and drop it into your design as with any other image.

Embedding images via URL is useful for quick design tasks when you want to use web-hosted content without downloading it. However, ensure that you have permission to use the image in your design, especially if it is copyrighted material.

Inserting Stock Photos

Canva also partners with stock photo providers like Pexels and Pixabay to give users access to an even larger pool of free and paid images. These stock photo sources are integrated directly into Canva, making it easy to search for and insert professional-quality images without leaving the platform.

Here's how to insert stock photos:

1. Click on the "Photos" Tab: In the left-hand toolbar, click on the "Photos" tab. This section contains a collection of stock photos sourced from various libraries.

2. Search for Stock Images: Use the search bar to find specific stock images by keywords. Canva's stock photos are categorized, so you can also browse by themes such as "nature," "food," "business," etc.

3. Choose and Insert the Image: Once you find a suitable stock photo, click on it to insert it into your design. Canva allows you to adjust, crop, and enhance the image as needed to fit the project.

By leveraging stock photos, you can quickly find high-quality images that enhance your design without the need to take or create photos yourself. Canva's stock photo integration saves time and provides designers with a professional edge.

By understanding the different ways to upload and insert images into Canva, you can truly unlock the creative potential of your projects. Whether you're working with personal photos, cloud storage, stock images, or web-based images, Canva offers flexible and intuitive tools to help you integrate visuals effortlessly.

3.2.2 Using Canva's Image Library

When it comes to designing in Canva, images play a critical role in enhancing the visual appeal of your projects. Whether you're creating a presentation, social media post, flyer, or any other type of design, the right image can amplify your message and help you connect with your audience. Fortunately, Canva's extensive image library makes finding and using the perfect images a seamless process. This section will guide you through everything you need to know about utilizing Canva's vast collection of images, including searching, filtering, and customizing them to fit your design.

Overview of Canva's Image Library

Canva's image library is a treasure trove of high-quality images that span various categories, styles, and themes. From photos to illustrations, Canva offers a wide range of visual assets that can be used across a multitude of design projects. With millions of free and premium stock images available, Canva caters to diverse creative needs.

The platform's image library includes:

- Stock Photos: These are high-resolution images captured by professional photographers, perfect for adding realism and aesthetic appeal to your designs.

- Illustrations and Icons: These are vector-based images that are useful for adding artistic and symbolic elements to your work.

- Textures and Patterns: You can find various textures like wood, fabric, and metal, as well as patterns that can be used for backgrounds or layering.

Whether you're working on a corporate presentation or a fun social media post, Canva's library has something for every occasion.

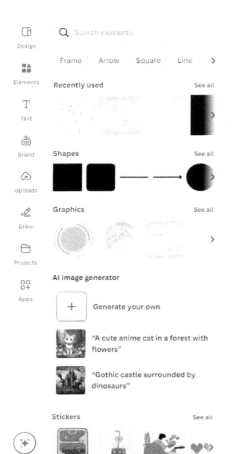

How to Access Canva's Image Library

Accessing Canva's image library is straightforward:

1. Open Your Design: Once you're in your Canva workspace, open the design you want to add an image to.

2. Select the 'Elements' Tab: On the left-hand side of the Canva interface, you'll see various tabs such as Text, Videos, and Elements. To access the image library, click on the Elements tab.

3. Search for Images: Within the Elements tab, you'll find a search bar. You can type keywords or phrases related to the type of image you're looking for. For example, if you're designing a beach-themed social media post, you might type in "beach," "waves," or "sunset."

Once you press enter, Canva will display a variety of images related to your search term, sourced from both free and premium stock libraries.

Navigating the Image Categories

If you're not sure what you're looking for, Canva allows you to explore various image categories, making the search process easy and efficient. Some of the main categories include:

- Nature: Ideal for projects involving landscapes, wildlife, and natural elements.

- Business: Perfect for corporate presentations, office scenes, and professional settings.

- Technology: Great for anything related to digital devices, software, and modern advancements.

- Lifestyle: Includes a wide array of images reflecting day-to-day activities, hobbies, and social interactions.

- Food and Drink: Excellent for restaurant menus, food blogs, or anything culinary-related.

Simply clicking on any of these categories will present you with a curated selection of images that match your design theme.

Filtering Images in Canva's Library

Canva's image library offers several filters to help you find the most suitable images for your project. You can refine your search results by using filters based on:

- Image Type: Choose between photos, illustrations, icons, or textures.

- Orientation: You can select whether you want vertical, horizontal, or square images, depending on your design needs.

- Price: Filter by free or premium images. Canva Pro users have access to a much larger selection of premium content.

- Color: This feature allows you to search for images that contain specific colors, which is especially useful for maintaining brand consistency or fitting a certain aesthetic.

For example, if you're creating a social media post for a health-related brand and need images that match your brand's color palette, you can filter by the colors green and white to find relevant images. To apply these filters:

1. Perform a search based on your keyword.

2. On the top right of the search results page, click the Filters button.

3. Adjust the filters according to your requirements.

4. Click Apply Filters to narrow down the results.

These filters make the process of finding the perfect image fast and efficient, allowing you to stay focused on your design.

Customizing Canva's Images

Once you've selected an image from Canva's library, you can customize it in several ways to make it work seamlessly with your design. Canva offers a range of editing tools that allow you to modify and enhance images directly within the platform.

Here are some of the key image customization options available:

Resizing and Cropping

Images can often be resized and cropped to fit the specific dimensions of your design. Canva makes this easy:

- Resizing: Click on the image, then drag the corners to resize it proportionally. You can also hold the Shift key to resize the image without maintaining the aspect ratio.

- Cropping: Click on the image and select the Crop button from the toolbar. This will allow you to trim the image to focus on a particular area. You can manually adjust the crop window by dragging the corners.

Image Adjustments

Canva offers a range of image adjustment options that allow you to tweak the brightness, contrast, and saturation of your images. These adjustments are particularly useful when you want to create a specific mood or atmosphere in your design.

- Brightness: Modify the brightness of the image to make it lighter or darker. Increasing the brightness can make the image look more vibrant, while decreasing it can give it a more subdued, moody effect.

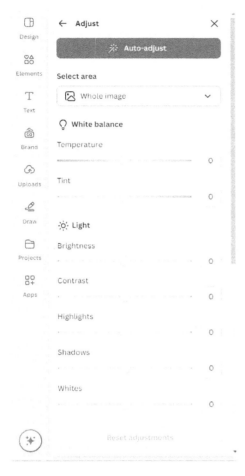

- Contrast: Adjusting the contrast affects the difference between the lightest and darkest areas of an image. A higher contrast will make the image pop, while a lower contrast will give it a softer, more blended look.

- Saturation: Increase or decrease the saturation to make the colors more vivid or more muted, depending on the tone you want to convey.

These tools allow you to bring out the best in your images and ensure they complement the rest of your design elements.

Filters and Effects

One of Canva's most popular features is its wide array of filters and effects, which can dramatically alter the appearance of your images. To apply a filter:

1. Click on the image to select it.

2. Choose the Filter button from the top toolbar.

3. Browse through the preset filters to find one that suits your design.

You can also adjust the intensity of the filter using a slider. Some common filter categories include:

- Classic: Simple, everyday filters for enhancing photos.

- Vintage: Filters that give your images a nostalgic, old-school feel.

- Dramatic: High-contrast filters that add intensity and emotion to your image.

- Soft: Filters that smooth out details and create a dreamy, ethereal quality.

In addition to filters, Canva offers advanced effects like blur, vignette, and pixelate. You can even apply a duotone effect to create striking images with two contrasting colors.

Transparency

Another handy customization tool is the transparency slider. This feature allows you to adjust the opacity of an image, making it partially transparent. This can be particularly useful when creating layered designs where text or other elements need to sit on top of an image without overpowering it.

To adjust the transparency:

1. Select the image.

2. Click on the Transparency button in the toolbar.

3. Use the slider to set the desired level of opacity.

This effect works well for creating subtle backgrounds, watermarking images, or giving your designs a more dynamic, layered look.

Flipping and Rotating Images

Canva also allows you to flip or rotate images to better fit the composition of your design. This feature is especially useful when you want to mirror an image or create symmetry.

To flip or rotate an image:

1. Click on the image to select it.

2. In the toolbar, click the Flip button and choose either Flip Horizontal or Flip Vertical. You can also use the Rotate option to turn the image clockwise or counterclockwise.

This simple tool can help you make small adjustments that drastically improve the balance and layout of your design.

Conclusion

Canva's image library, combined with its easy-to-use customization tools, allows you to elevate your designs with professional-quality visuals. By taking advantage of the extensive search features, filters, and editing options, you can quickly find and modify images that perfectly suit your project's needs. Whether you're a beginner or an experienced designer, mastering Canva's image library will open up new creative possibilities and make your designs stand out.

3.2.3 Cropping, Resizing, and Adjusting Images

One of the key skills you need when working with images in Canva is the ability to crop, resize, and adjust images to suit the design you're working on. These are basic but highly essential techniques to ensure that your visuals are both effective and aesthetically pleasing. Whether you're designing a flyer, creating a social media post, or working on a presentation, proper image manipulation allows you to craft professional-looking designs with ease. Let's dive into how you can master these skills using Canva.

Cropping Images

What is Cropping?

Cropping an image involves trimming away unwanted parts of it, allowing you to focus on a specific area. This is useful when you want to highlight certain elements of a photo or remove unnecessary background distractions. In Canva, the cropping tool is intuitive and simple to use.

How to Crop Images in Canva

1. Select the Image: Click on the image you want to crop. The image will be highlighted, and a toolbar will appear at the top of the screen.

2. Click on the Crop Button: In the toolbar, you'll see an option labeled "Crop." Clicking this will bring up handles around the edges of your image.

3. Adjust the Crop: Drag these handles inward or outward to adjust the cropped area. Canva allows you to drag from any corner or edge, giving you precision in determining which parts of the image to keep and which to remove.

4. Finalize the Crop: Once you're satisfied with the area selected, click "Done" or press Enter. Your cropped image will now appear in your design, focusing only on the parts you chose.

Why Crop Images?

Cropping is particularly helpful when your image contains unwanted elements or background noise. Imagine a picture of a group of people where you only need one person featured in the design. By cropping, you can isolate that person, making them the focal point of your layout.

You can also use cropping to shape the image into unconventional formats. For example, cropping into a square or circular shape can give your design a modern, sleek appearance.

Tips for Cropping Effectively:

- Rule of Thirds: When cropping, consider aligning the subject of your image according to the rule of thirds. This compositional technique divides your image into a 3x3 grid, and placing your subject along these lines or at their intersections creates a balanced, visually appealing design.

- Don't Over-Crop: Avoid cropping too close to the subject. Leaving some breathing space around the subject will make the image look more natural and comfortable within the design.

- Consider Symmetry: For certain designs, maintaining symmetry through cropping can create a clean, professional look. For example, when centering objects or people, an even amount of space on all sides can enhance the design's harmony.

Resizing Images

What is Resizing?

Resizing refers to altering the dimensions of an image, either making it larger or smaller, while maintaining the same content. Canva makes resizing images straightforward, giving you full control over the dimensions of your images within your design.

How to Resize Images in Canva

1. Select the Image: Just like cropping, begin by selecting the image you want to resize.

2. Resize by Dragging: Once the image is selected, resize handles will appear at the corners and edges. Simply click and drag these handles to enlarge or reduce the size of the image. To maintain the image's aspect ratio (so it doesn't look distorted), hold down the Shift key while resizing.

3. Type in Exact Dimensions: If you want more precision, Canva allows you to input exact dimensions for your image. Select the image, and in the toolbar, you can manually enter width and height values. This is especially helpful for projects where the image needs to fit specific design specifications.

Maintaining Image Quality

When resizing images, it's essential to consider the impact on the quality. Enlarging an image too much can cause pixelation, making it appear blurry or grainy. Canva's image library contains high-quality, scalable images that maintain clarity when resized, but if you upload your own images, ensure they are of sufficient resolution to avoid degradation when enlarged.

Why Resize Images?

Resizing is useful when your image needs to fit within a certain space or align with other design elements. For instance, social media posts often require specific dimensions, and resizing ensures that your image aligns with platform standards.

Tips for Resizing Effectively:

- Maintain Aspect Ratio: Always try to resize images proportionally to avoid stretching or compressing them unnaturally. Distorted images can make your design look unprofessional.

- Use Canva's Built-In Size Guides: Canva provides size presets for various social media platforms, print products, and more. These guides help you resize images appropriately for different uses without guesswork.

Adjusting Images

Beyond cropping and resizing, Canva provides powerful adjustment tools that allow you to fine-tune the visual qualities of your images. These adjustments can significantly enhance your design, making your images look more vibrant, balanced, and cohesive within the overall layout.

Basic Adjustments in Canva

1. Brightness: You can control how light or dark your image appears by adjusting the brightness. Increasing brightness will make an image look lighter, while reducing it will darken the image.

2. Contrast: Contrast refers to the difference between the light and dark areas of your image. Boosting contrast can make details pop, while lowering it will soften the image.

3. Saturation: This controls the intensity of colors in your image. Increasing saturation makes colors more vibrant, while reducing it results in a more muted or grayscale effect.

4. Blur: Canva also provides a blur slider, which allows you to soften the focus of your image. This can be useful for backgrounds or when trying to create a specific visual effect.

5. Tint and Temperature: The tint adjustment lets you alter the color cast of your image, adding more warmth (orange) or coolness (blue). Similarly, the temperature tool allows you to adjust how warm or cool the image appears overall.

How to Adjust Images in Canva

1. Select the Image: Choose the image you want to adjust by clicking on it in your design.

2. Access Adjustment Settings: In the toolbar, you will see an option labeled "Adjust." Click on this, and a panel with sliders for brightness, contrast, and other settings will appear.

3. Make Adjustments: Use the sliders to tweak the image properties. Each slider can be moved to the left (to reduce the effect) or to the right (to increase the effect). For example, moving the brightness slider to the right will brighten the image, while moving it to the left will darken it.

4. Preview Changes: Canva allows you to see your changes in real-time. You can undo any adjustments by either clicking the reset button or manually readjusting the sliders.

5. Finalize the Adjustments: Once you're satisfied with the adjustments, click away from the image or press Enter to apply the changes.

Why Adjust Images?

Adjusting images can help integrate them into the overall aesthetic of your design. For example, if your design has a vintage theme, lowering the saturation and adding a slight tint can make the image blend seamlessly. Conversely, increasing brightness and contrast might be more suitable for a modern, high-energy design.

Tips for Adjusting Images Effectively:

- Consistency is Key: If you're working with multiple images in a single design, try to adjust them similarly to maintain a cohesive look. This ensures that no single image feels out of place.

- Don't Overdo It: While adjustments can enhance your design, over-adjusting can lead to unnatural results. Subtlety often yields better results, especially when dealing with contrast and saturation.

- Use Adjustments to Set the Mood: The adjustments you make to an image can influence the emotional tone of your design. A warmer image may feel more inviting, while cooler tones can evoke a sense of calm or professionalism.

Conclusion

Mastering the art of cropping, resizing, and adjusting images in Canva is an essential skill for creating stunning, effective designs. These techniques allow you to control how images appear in your layouts, helping you craft visuals that communicate your message clearly. By understanding when and how to crop for focus, resize for fit, and adjust for mood, you'll elevate the quality of your designs, ensuring they stand out whether you're creating for personal, professional, or social media use.

In the next section, we will explore 3.3 Creating Shapes and Illustrations, which further enhances your ability to design visually appealing content in Canva.

3.3 Creating Shapes and Illustrations

3.3.1 Using Canva's Built-in Shapes

Shapes are one of the most essential elements of design. They provide structure, emphasis, and visual interest to a design. Canva offers an extensive collection of built-in shapes that cater to various design needs. Whether you're creating a flyer, a social media post, or a presentation, the proper use of shapes can dramatically enhance your design's overall look and feel. In this section, we'll explore how to find, use, and customize Canva's built-in shapes to create impactful designs.

Why Shapes Matter in Design

Shapes are more than just visual elements; they play a significant role in how we perceive a design. By using shapes effectively, you can:

- Create Hierarchy: Shapes help organize content and guide the viewer's eye through the design. For example, a circle or rectangle can be used to highlight a key message or call to action.

- Balance and Structure: Shapes contribute to the visual balance of a composition, making it more aesthetically pleasing. The careful placement of squares, lines, or other geometric shapes can help distribute content evenly.

- Add Visual Appeal: Shapes break up monotony and make designs more engaging. By integrating a mix of shapes, your design will appear more dynamic and professional.

With Canva's vast library of built-in shapes, you can quickly incorporate these essential elements into your design. Let's dive into the process of using Canva's built-in shapes.

Accessing Canva's Built-in Shapes

Using shapes in Canva is simple and straightforward. Follow these steps to locate and insert shapes into your design:

1. Open a Design: Start by opening an existing project or creating a new one. If you're new to Canva, you can select a template or choose a blank canvas from the homepage.

2. Locate the Shapes Menu: On the left side of the Canva editor, you'll see a vertical toolbar. Click on the 'Elements' tab, which contains a variety of design elements, including shapes, icons, and illustrations.

3. Search for Shapes: Once inside the 'Elements' menu, scroll down to the 'Shapes' section or type "shapes" in the search bar. Canva provides various shape categories, such as circles, squares, triangles, stars, and custom shapes like arrows, hearts, and speech bubbles.

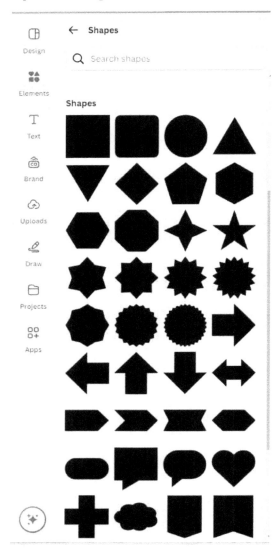

4. Choose a Shape: Browse through the available shapes and click on one to add it to your design. You can also hover over a shape to see a preview before adding it.

Types of Shapes Available in Canva

Canva offers a wide array of shapes, ranging from simple geometric forms to more intricate custom designs. Here's an overview of the most common types of shapes you can find in Canva:

1. Basic Shapes:

- Circles, Squares, and Triangles: These are the foundational shapes in design and can be used in various ways. Circles are often used to highlight content or create a soft, balanced look, while squares and rectangles add structure and symmetry to a layout. Triangles can be used to create directional movement or to point out specific elements in your design.

2. Lines and Borders:

- Straight and Curved Lines: Canva provides various lines, from thin, straight lines to more decorative, curved options. Lines are useful for dividing content, creating underlines for text, or drawing attention to specific areas of your design.

- Borders and Frames: Borders can be applied around text, images, or the entire canvas to give your design a finished, polished look. Frames, on the other hand, are versatile elements that can be used to contain photos, creating a neat and organized appearance.

3. Custom Shapes:

- Icons and Symbols: Beyond basic geometric shapes, Canva's library includes a wide range of icons and symbols. These include arrows, hearts, speech bubbles, stars, and more. Icons are great for adding emphasis and creating a playful or informative tone in your design.

- Abstract Shapes: Canva also offers abstract shapes that can add a modern, artistic touch to your design. These include wave-like lines, irregular polygons, and complex geometric patterns.

Customizing Built-in Shapes

Once you've added a shape to your design, Canva provides a variety of tools to customize it. Here's how you can manipulate shapes to suit your design:

1. Resizing Shapes:

- Click on the shape you've added to your design. A border with handles will appear around it. Drag any of the corners to resize the shape proportionally, or drag the side handles to stretch or compress the shape horizontally or vertically.

- Pro Tip: Hold the Shift key while resizing to maintain the shape's original proportions. This is especially useful when working with circles and squares to prevent them from becoming distorted.

2. Changing Shape Colors:

- To change the color of a shape, click on it, and a color tile will appear in the toolbar at the top. Clicking the color tile will open Canva's color palette, allowing you to choose from default colors or add custom ones using hex codes or the color wheel.

- You can also apply gradients or use Canva's brand colors if you're working with a specific palette.

3. Rotating Shapes:

- Rotate shapes by clicking on the rotate icon that appears when you select a shape. Drag it clockwise or counterclockwise to rotate the shape to the desired angle. You can also enter a specific rotation degree by typing it into the rotation field in the toolbar.

4. Flipping Shapes:

- Canva allows you to flip shapes horizontally or vertically. Select your shape, then click the 'Flip' button in the top toolbar. You can choose to flip your shape either horizontally (left to right) or vertically (top to bottom).

5. Layering Shapes:

- Canva's built-in shapes can be layered to create depth and dimension. Select a shape, then use the 'Position' tool in the toolbar to move it forward or backward in relation to other elements in your design.

- Pro Tip: Try layering different shapes with varying opacity levels to create interesting effects. For example, overlapping circles with lower opacity can create a modern, transparent design element.

Using Shapes in Layout Design

Incorporating shapes into your layout can significantly improve the overall visual impact of your design. Here are a few design tips to help you make the most out of Canva's built-in shapes:

1. Create Contrast with Shapes:

- Use contrasting shapes to make your design more dynamic. For example, pair circular elements with sharp-edged squares or triangles to create visual interest. Contrast also applies to color – combining bright shapes with muted backgrounds can make your design stand out.

2. Use Shapes for Text Emphasis:

- Shapes like speech bubbles, banners, and rectangles are perfect for highlighting important text or call-to-action buttons. Place your message inside a shape to draw attention and make the text stand out from the rest of the design.

3. Create Patterns and Repetitions:

- Repeating shapes throughout a design can create a sense of harmony and consistency. Use repeating circles, squares, or lines to form patterns that guide the viewer's eye across the layout. This technique works well for backgrounds or borders.

4. Balance Your Layout:

- Shapes are key to achieving balance in your composition. Use symmetrical shapes like squares and circles to evenly distribute elements across the design. If your design feels heavy on one side, consider adding shapes to the opposite side to create equilibrium.

Practical Examples of Shape Usage in Canva Designs

1. Flyer Design: Use rectangles and lines to structure sections of text, and place a circle in the center to highlight the event name or date.

2. Social Media Post: Layer several transparent shapes to create a modern, abstract background. Use a square or rectangle for the main text block.

3. Business Card: Create a minimalist design by placing a company logo inside a circle, and use a line beneath the contact information for a clean, professional look.

4. Infographic: Combine arrows, circles, and rectangles to create a flow chart or visual hierarchy that makes the information easy to follow.

Final Thoughts

Canva's built-in shapes are versatile tools that can transform any design into something unique and eye-catching. By understanding the various types of shapes available and learning how to customize them, you can create professional-looking designs with ease. Whether you're highlighting key information, adding structure, or simply making your design more visually appealing, shapes are a crucial component in the Canva design toolkit.

This section has covered the fundamentals of using Canva's built-in shapes, but don't be afraid to experiment and combine shapes in new ways. With practice, you'll discover even more creative possibilities to elevate your designs.

3.3.2 Applying Icons and Illustrations

Icons and illustrations are key elements in visual design. Whether you're creating a social media post, a business card, or a presentation slide, the use of icons and illustrations can enhance the communication of your message. Icons serve as visual shorthand, making your design more accessible and easier to understand, while illustrations add creativity and artistry, making your work visually appealing and engaging.

In Canva, the process of applying icons and illustrations is seamless, offering a wide range of customization options. Let's explore the different ways you can use these elements to elevate your designs.

What are Icons and Illustrations in Design?

Before diving into the tools and features that Canva offers for applying icons and illustrations, it's important to understand what these terms mean in the context of design:

Icons are simplified visual symbols that represent concepts, actions, objects, or ideas. They are used extensively in digital and graphic design to replace or supplement text. Icons can be universally recognizable, like the envelope symbol for an email or a magnifying glass for a search function, or they can be custom-designed to fit a particular brand's style. They are highly versatile and can be used to create lists, call attention to key points, or even serve as decorative elements in a design.

Illustrations, on the other hand, are more complex and detailed visual elements, often created to convey a story or bring a specific creative vision to life. Unlike icons, which are typically minimalist, illustrations can range from simple drawings to intricate art pieces. They add a personal and unique touch to designs, making them ideal for creating themed content, educational materials, or storytelling visuals.

Both icons and illustrations are crucial in design for their ability to convey meaning without relying on words. With the right application, these visual elements can dramatically improve the effectiveness of your design.

Using Canva's Icon Library

One of Canva's standout features is its extensive icon library, which provides access to thousands of ready-to-use icons that can be integrated into your projects with just a few clicks.

Accessing the Icon Library

To access Canva's icon library, follow these steps:

1. Open a new or existing project in Canva.

2. From the side toolbar on the left, click on the Elements tab.

3. Scroll down until you find the Icons section. Alternatively, you can type specific keywords into the search bar, such as "phone," "arrow," or "heart," to locate specific icons relevant to your project.

The icon library is searchable, so whether you're looking for basic geometric shapes, symbols representing technology, or thematic icons for a holiday or event, you can quickly find what you need.

Customizing Icons in Canva

Once you've selected an icon, you can customize it in various ways to fit your design. Canva provides several customization options:

1. Resizing Icons: Icons in Canva can be resized without losing quality. Simply click on the icon and drag the corner handles to make it larger or smaller. Unlike images, icons in Canva are vector-based, meaning they maintain clarity no matter how large or small you make them.

2. Changing Colors: Most icons in Canva are fully customizable in terms of color. After clicking on an icon, you'll see a color option in the toolbar at the top of the screen. You can change the icon's color to match your brand or the theme of your design. For multi-colored icons, Canva allows you to change individual parts of the icon, giving you total control over the design.

3. Rotating Icons: If you need to adjust the orientation of an icon, Canva allows you to rotate it freely. Click on the icon, and use the rotation handle to turn it to the desired angle. This can be particularly useful for creating dynamic designs or emphasizing certain elements.

4. Layering Icons: Just like other elements in Canva, icons can be layered on top of each other or other design elements. This is useful when you want to combine icons with text, images, or shapes. The layering feature allows you to send icons backward or bring them forward, giving you flexibility in arranging elements for a balanced composition.

5. Transparency Settings: Canva also allows you to adjust the transparency of icons. This feature is useful when you want to blend an icon into the background or create a subtle effect. To adjust transparency, click on the icon and use the transparency slider located in the toolbar.

6. Flipping Icons: In addition to resizing and rotating, you can also flip icons horizontally or vertically. This is useful when you want to mirror an icon's direction or achieve symmetry in your design. The flip option can be found in the toolbar at the top of the editor.

By customizing icons, you can create consistent and professional designs that are aligned with your message and style. Whether you're using them as stand-alone elements or combining them with other visuals, Canva's tools allow you to achieve the exact look you're going for.

Working with Canva's Illustration Library

In addition to icons, Canva's illustration library offers a wealth of creative possibilities. From simple line drawings to complex scenes, Canva provides access to a wide variety of illustrations that can add flair and personality to your design projects.

Accessing Illustrations in Canva

Accessing Canva's illustration library is just as easy as finding icons:

1. Click on the Elements tab from the side toolbar.

2. Scroll down to the Illustrations section, or type keywords into the search bar to find a specific style or theme.

Canva's illustrations cover a broad range of topics and styles, from flat designs and cartoons to more detailed, hand-drawn art. Whether you need a playful illustration for a children's event flyer or a professional-looking visual for a business presentation, Canva's library has something to fit the bill.

Customizing Illustrations in Canva

Just like icons, illustrations in Canva are highly customizable:

1. Resizing Illustrations: Canva allows you to resize illustrations without losing image quality. Drag the corner handles to adjust the size to fit your design. Because illustrations in Canva are vector-based, they maintain their crispness at any size.

2. Changing Colors: Many illustrations in Canva allow for color customization. Depending on the illustration, you may be able to adjust each individual color element to fit your design's color scheme. To change the colors of an illustration, click on the color box in the toolbar and choose your desired hue from the palette or input a hex code for more precise branding.

3. Positioning and Layering: Like icons, illustrations can be layered on top of other design elements, such as images, text, or shapes. You can move them forward or backward in the layer stack to create the desired layout. This is particularly useful when you want illustrations to interact with other elements, such as having them appear behind text or overlap other visuals for a more dynamic composition.

4. Rotating and Flipping Illustrations: You can rotate and flip illustrations in Canva just like any other element. This flexibility allows you to adapt the illustration to your design's layout or visual style.

5. Adjusting Transparency: Canva's transparency slider works for illustrations as well. Adjusting transparency is helpful for creating overlays or blending illustrations with backgrounds, especially when you want to create a more subtle or layered effect in your design.

Combining Icons and Illustrations for Effective Design

While icons and illustrations serve different purposes, combining them effectively can take your designs to the next level. Here are a few tips for integrating both elements seamlessly:

1. Consistency is Key: When using both icons and illustrations in the same design, aim for consistency in style. If your illustrations have a minimalist, flat design, use icons that share the same aesthetic. Mismatched styles can create visual dissonance and make the design feel cluttered.

2. Balance and Contrast: Use icons to highlight key points or organize information, while illustrations can be employed to add personality and creativity. For example, in an infographic, icons can be used to represent data points, while illustrations add a thematic or artistic flair.

3. Space Management: Both icons and illustrations should be used sparingly and with purpose. Overloading a design with too many visual elements can detract from the main message. Always keep white space in mind and ensure that each element has enough breathing room.

4. Color Harmony: When combining icons and illustrations, ensure that the colors complement each other. Canva's color palette tool can help you maintain a harmonious color scheme across all visual elements, creating a cohesive look.

Practical Examples of Applying Icons and Illustrations

To better understand the real-world application of these elements, here are a few practical examples of how icons and illustrations can be used in Canva designs:

1. Social Media Posts: Use icons to represent actions like "Share," "Like," or "Comment," while incorporating illustrations that align with the post's theme (e.g., a hand-drawn coffee cup for a café promotion).

2. Presentations: Icons can be used to visualize statistics or concepts in bullet points, while illustrations add flair to slide backgrounds or cover pages.

3. Flyers and Posters: Incorporate illustrations for the main theme (e.g., a festival scene for an event flyer) while using icons to direct attention to contact information or website links.

4. Infographics: Icons are perfect for labeling sections of an infographic, while illustrations help tell the story or visually represent the theme of the content.

Conclusion

Icons and illustrations are powerful tools that can transform your designs from ordinary to extraordinary. In Canva, the ability to customize these elements gives you endless creative possibilities. Whether you're working on a simple design or a more complex project, applying icons and illustrations in thoughtful, purposeful ways will not only make your work more visually appealing but also help communicate your message more effectively.

The next time you're creating a design in Canva, don't hesitate to explore its vast library of icons and illustrations and experiment with different combinations, colors, and effects. With the right approach, these elements will not only complement your work but elevate it to a professional level.

3.4 Working with Colors and Themes

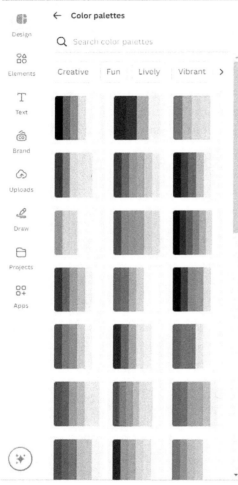

Color is one of the most powerful elements in any design. It communicates emotions, defines moods, and conveys a message to your audience long before they read your text or focus on your visuals. In Canva, working with colors is not just about picking random hues from a palette, but about understanding how colors work together and how they can influence the effectiveness of your design.

In this section, we'll explore how to choose, apply, and manage color palettes in Canva, and discuss the importance of color harmony, branding, and accessibility in the process.

3.4.1 Choosing Color Palettes

Choosing a color palette might seem like a simple task, but it's an essential part of the design process. The right color palette can enhance your message, while the wrong one can confuse your audience or make your design feel disjointed. This section will walk you through the basics of selecting a color palette in Canva and help you understand the role of color theory in making your designs stand out.

Understanding Color Theory

Before diving into Canva's color tools, it's important to have a basic understanding of color theory. Color theory involves the science and art of using color, and it's a foundational skill for any designer. It helps you understand the relationships between colors and how they can be combined to create harmony or contrast in your designs.

- Primary Colors: These are red, blue, and yellow. They are the building blocks of all other colors and cannot be created by mixing other colors.

- Secondary Colors: These are green, orange, and purple, and are made by mixing two primary colors.

- Tertiary Colors: These are created by mixing a primary color with a secondary color.

Beyond these basic categories, color theory also considers aspects like hue (the base color), saturation (the intensity of the color), and value (how light or dark the color is). Understanding these elements will help you manipulate colors effectively in Canva.

One of the most critical aspects of color theory is the color wheel, which arranges colors in a circle, showing the relationships between them. Here are some common color schemes you can use in Canva based on the color wheel:

- Monochromatic: Using variations in lightness and saturation of a single color. This is ideal for clean and elegant designs.

- Analogous: Colors that are next to each other on the color wheel (e.g., blue, green, and teal). This creates harmony and a serene look.

- Complementary: Colors that are opposite each other on the color wheel (e.g., red and green). These colors create contrast and vibrancy.

- Triadic: Three colors evenly spaced around the color wheel (e.g., red, yellow, and blue). This creates a balanced yet vibrant look.

- Tetradic (Double Complementary): Four colors that form two complementary pairs. This scheme offers plenty of contrast and diversity but can be challenging to balance.

Choosing Colors in Canva

Canva makes it easy to experiment with and apply these color schemes. Here's how you can start selecting your palette:

1. Accessing Color Palettes

In Canva, when you are working on a design, the color tool is located on the toolbar at the top of your workspace. When you click on a design element, such as text, shapes, or backgrounds, you'll see a color square that opens a color menu. This menu provides options to select pre-set colors, input custom hex codes, or choose from Canva's palette suggestions.

2. Using Pre-made Palettes

Canva offers a wide variety of pre-made color palettes that are based on different themes such as "Bold," "Calm," "Retro," or "Warm." These palettes are great for users who may not have a strong sense of color harmony but want to ensure their design looks polished and cohesive. You can find these in the "Colors" section of the editor, usually suggested when working on any new template.

3. Creating a Custom Color Palette

To make your design truly unique or on-brand, you can create a custom color palette. Canva lets you do this by adding custom colors using a hex code (a six-digit code that represents specific colors) or by using the color picker tool to sample colors from an image or other elements in your design.

Using the Color Picker Tool

One of Canva's most useful features is the color picker tool, which allows you to select any color from an image or an existing element in your design. This is especially helpful if you're working with images or logos and want to match your design elements to those specific colors. To use the color picker tool:

1. Select the element you want to change the color of.

2. Open the color menu from the toolbar.

3. Click the "+" sign to create a new color.

4. Use the eyedropper icon to hover over the color you wish to sample from your image or design.

Matching Colors to Your Brand

If you are designing for a brand, consistency in color usage is key. Canva's Brand Kit tool (available in Canva Pro) allows you to store your brand colors, fonts, and logos for easy access. This is incredibly useful if you're creating multiple designs and want to ensure that all of them maintain a cohesive look.

To use the Brand Kit tool:

1. Navigate to the Brand Kit section in Canva's dashboard.

2. Add your brand colors by entering the hex codes.

3. Once your palette is saved, it will be available in the color menu of any design, ensuring quick and consistent application across all your projects.

Exploring Color Psychology

Color does more than make your design visually appealing—it also conveys emotions and meaning. This is known as color psychology, and it's a powerful tool for ensuring your design resonates with your audience. Here are some common associations with different colors:

- Red: Energy, passion, urgency (often used in sales).

- Blue: Calmness, trust, professionalism (often used by corporations and financial institutions).

- Yellow: Optimism, happiness, warmth (often used to grab attention).

- Green: Growth, health, nature (often used by environmental or health brands).

- Purple: Luxury, creativity, mystery (often used by beauty or high-end brands).

- Black: Elegance, sophistication, power (often used in luxury branding).

Understanding the psychological impact of colors can help you choose the right palette for your audience and purpose. For example, if you're designing for a wellness brand, soft greens and blues might be more appropriate than bold reds and blacks.

Creating Accessible Color Palettes

When choosing your colors, it's also important to consider accessibility. People with visual impairments, such as color blindness, may have difficulty distinguishing between certain colors, especially if there is insufficient contrast. Canva makes it easy to check the accessibility of your design by providing guidelines for color contrast.

To create an accessible palette, follow these tips:

1. Use High Contrast: Ensure that there is enough contrast between your text and background. Canva provides color contrast indicators to help you make informed choices.

2. Avoid Certain Color Combinations: People with red-green color blindness, for example, may have difficulty distinguishing between those two colors. Try using a combination of hues, patterns, or textures to make your designs more distinguishable.

3. Test with Accessibility Tools: There are online tools available (such as the WebAIM Contrast Checker) that allow you to input your hex codes and check the contrast ratio for compliance with accessibility standards. This ensures that your design is inclusive and usable by all audiences.

Incorporating Trends into Your Color Palette

While timeless design principles are important, keeping up with color trends can give your designs a modern and relevant edge. Every year, companies like Pantone announce a "Color of the Year," which often influences trends in design, fashion, and branding. Canva stays up-to-date with these trends and often includes new, on-trend palettes in its library for users to experiment with.

Using trend-based colors can make your designs feel fresh, but be cautious of overusing them—trends can change quickly, and what looks modern today may feel outdated in a few months. For long-term projects or branding, it's usually better to stick with classic color combinations that will stand the test of time.

Practical Applications of Color Palettes

Here are some examples of how different color palettes can be used in Canva for specific projects:

1. Social Media Posts: Bright and bold colors can help your posts stand out on a crowded feed. Experiment with complementary or triadic color schemes to create eye-catching visuals.

2. Presentations: For business presentations, consider using a monochromatic or analogous color scheme for a clean, professional look that doesn't distract from your message.

3. Invitations: For invitations (e.g., weddings or parties), soft pastels or muted colors can create an elegant and inviting atmosphere.

4. Logos: For logos and branding, it's important to choose colors that reflect the essence of the brand and can be consistently applied across different media, both print and digital.

Final Thoughts on Choosing Color Palettes

Choosing the right color palette is more than just picking your favorite colors—it's about creating a design that resonates with your audience, enhances your message, and stays true to your brand or purpose. In Canva, the tools are at your fingertips to experiment, play, and refine your palette until you find the perfect combination.

As you continue to design with Canva, you'll grow more comfortable with color selection and develop your own unique style. Remember to balance creativity with intention, and always consider the broader impact your color choices may have on those who view your design.

3.4.2 Applying Themes to Your Design

Themes play a pivotal role in design, serving as a foundation that unifies and connects various elements of your project, ensuring consistency and harmony throughout. In Canva, applying themes allows you to create visually coherent content, whether for personal projects or professional branding. In this section, we'll explore how to apply themes in Canva, understand the importance of cohesive design elements, and how to tailor themes to different types of projects.

Understanding Themes in Canva

In Canva, a theme consists of a predefined set of fonts, colors, and design elements that work together to form a visually unified look. Whether you're creating a presentation, social media post, or marketing collateral, using a consistent theme helps maintain brand identity and reinforces your message.

Canva offers a range of pre-built themes and templates across various categories, from social media and marketing materials to event invites and educational presentations. These themes are crafted by professional designers and offer a great starting point for users who want a polished design without building from scratch.

However, applying a theme doesn't mean you're locked into a rigid design. Canva provides flexibility by allowing users to modify aspects of the theme—colors, fonts, layout—to suit their specific needs while maintaining overall cohesion.

Steps to Apply a Theme in Canva

1. Select a Template with a Theme

Canva's extensive library of templates is often organized by themes. To start, choose a template that fits the overall purpose of your project. You can find these by browsing the template library or by searching for specific categories such as Presentation, Instagram Post, Business Card, etc. Templates come with predefined themes that are ready to be applied and customized.

2. Customize the Theme's Colors

After selecting a template, you can customize the theme's colors to align with your brand or personal preferences. Themes often come with suggested color palettes, but Canva allows users to modify these colors to suit their needs.

- To change the color palette:

Click on any element within the design, such as a background or text box, and then click on the color box in the toolbar. From here, you can either select from the preset color palette or use the color wheel to pick specific shades. For branding purposes, Canva's Brand Kit feature (available in Canva Pro) allows users to store and apply their brand colors across all designs, ensuring consistency.

- Best Practices for Color Customization:

When customizing a theme's colors, ensure that the shades complement each other. The general rule of thumb is to use a primary color (the dominant color in your design), a secondary color (for supporting elements), and an accent color (for highlights or to draw attention to specific features). Avoid overloading the design with too many colors, as it can overwhelm the viewer and reduce visual impact.

3. Adjust the Fonts and Typography

Typography is an essential component of a theme, as fonts convey tone and readability. Canva's themes come with selected fonts that reflect the style and purpose of the design, but these fonts can be adjusted to better suit your content.

- To modify fonts:

Click on any text element, and the font toolbar will appear. You can choose from a variety of fonts provided by Canva or upload custom fonts (available with Canva Pro). When selecting or customizing fonts, ensure that the typography remains legible and appropriate for the tone of your message.

- Combining fonts effectively:

For a well-balanced design, it's often advisable to stick to two fonts—one for headings and another for body text. This contrast creates visual interest without overwhelming the viewer. Consider pairing a bold, decorative font for headlines with a more readable sans-serif or serif font for the body text.

4. Aligning Visual Elements with Your Theme

Themes include visual elements such as icons, shapes, and illustrations, which Canva provides in abundance. These elements are vital in maintaining the visual flow of the design. Once a theme is selected, you can further modify or replace these elements as long as they align with the overall style.

- Incorporating icons and shapes:

Canva's library offers a variety of icons and shapes, which can be resized, recolored, and positioned to complement your theme. Make sure these elements enhance the design without distracting from the main message. For example, if you're creating a modern, minimalist design, avoid adding too many ornate icons.

- Using consistent styles:

If your theme employs flat icons, make sure you continue using flat icons for consistency. Similarly, if you're working with 3D-style illustrations, maintain that style throughout the design. This attention to detail will make your final product look polished and professional.

5. Applying Backgrounds and Textures

Canva's themes often come with predefined backgrounds and textures that complement the color palette and overall aesthetic. You can use these as-is or replace them with backgrounds that better suit your project.

- To modify the background:

Click on the background of your design and choose the Background tab in the toolbar. Canva offers solid colors, gradients, textures, and image backgrounds. For designs like invitations or posters, textured or patterned backgrounds can add depth and interest. However, be cautious with busy patterns, as they can distract from the main message.

- Balancing text and background:

If using a detailed background, ensure that the text remains legible by using contrasting colors or overlaying the text on a solid shape. Canva allows users to adjust the transparency of the background to make the text stand out more.

6. Enhancing the Theme with Photos

Photos are a powerful way to enhance the emotional impact of a design. Many Canva themes incorporate placeholders for images, and Canva's image library provides millions of stock photos you can use.

- Choosing the right images:

Select images that resonate with the tone and message of your design. For example, a professional business presentation may use clean, minimalist images, while a lifestyle blog post may use bright, vibrant images. Consistency is key—make sure the images fit the overall aesthetic of the theme.

- Customizing image appearance:

Canva allows users to apply filters, adjust brightness and contrast, and even crop images to fit the design. Subtle adjustments can help align the images with the theme, ensuring a harmonious look. For instance, if the theme uses muted colors, consider applying a similar filter to all images.

7. Maintaining Visual Consistency

One of the primary reasons for applying a theme is to create a visually consistent design. Consistency reinforces brand identity and enhances the viewer's experience by making the design more cohesive.

- Ensuring consistency across all design elements:

Use the same colors, fonts, and visual styles throughout your design. If you're working on a multi-page project like a presentation, ensure that each slide follows the same theme. This not only makes the design look professional but also helps communicate your message more effectively.

8. Leveraging Canva's Brand Kit for Theme Consistency

Canva Pro users have access to the Brand Kit feature, which allows for seamless application of themes across all designs. The Brand Kit lets you store your brand's colors, logos, fonts, and other visual elements, making it easier to maintain consistency across various projects.

- Using the Brand Kit for future projects:

Once you've customized a theme to fit your needs, you can save these settings in your Brand Kit. This makes it easier to apply the same theme across different types of content, such as social media posts, presentations, or advertisements.

The Importance of Themes in Branding

For businesses and content creators, themes are not just about aesthetics; they are crucial for establishing a recognizable brand identity. Applying themes ensures that all your visual materials—whether it's a business card, a social media graphic, or a promotional flyer—look cohesive and reflect your brand's personality.

Conclusion: Themes for Every Purpose

Themes in Canva provide a structured, visually appealing foundation for your designs. Whether you're a beginner or an experienced designer, applying a theme helps maintain consistency, enhances professionalism, and reduces the time spent on design decisions. Remember, while themes offer a great starting point, feel free to customize them according to your personal or brand-specific needs to create unique and impactful designs.

CHAPTER IV
Advanced Canva Features

4.1 Using Canva's Photo Editing Tools

One of Canva's most powerful features is its photo editing tools. These tools allow users to adjust, enhance, and transform images to fit the specific aesthetic needs of their design projects. Whether you're working on social media graphics, presentations, posters, or any other type of design, mastering Canva's photo editing tools can elevate your visual content to the next level.

Canva's photo editing suite is user-friendly, designed for both beginners and experienced users. It offers a wide range of functions, from basic adjustments like brightness and contrast to more advanced features like filters, effects, and image overlays. In this section, we'll explore how to use these tools effectively, starting with filters and adjustments.

4.1.1 Filters and Adjustments

Filters and adjustments in Canva provide a simple yet impactful way to transform the appearance of your images. Filters are pre-made settings that apply a specific look or mood to your image with one click, while adjustments allow you to fine-tune various image properties to achieve the perfect effect. This section will dive deep into how to use filters and make manual adjustments to your photos to achieve your desired outcome.

What Are Filters in Canva?

Filters in Canva are essentially pre-set combinations of adjustments designed to enhance or alter the overall appearance of an image. They can instantly change the tone, mood, or

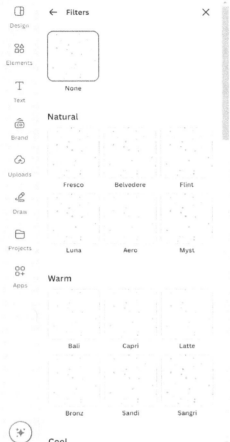

style of your image by altering the color palette, brightness, contrast, and saturation. Filters are a quick and effective way to add a cohesive look to your designs, especially when working with multiple images that need to share the same aesthetic.

Canva offers a wide range of filters, each named to reflect the look it will apply to the image. For instance, filters like "Retro" will give your image a nostalgic, old-fashioned look, while "Summer" might brighten the colors, enhancing the vibrancy to make the image feel more lively and warm. These filters save time by eliminating the need to manually adjust individual settings.

Applying Filters in Canva

To apply a filter in Canva, follow these simple steps:

1. Select Your Image: Click on the image you wish to edit. This will bring up a toolbar at the top of the Canva workspace.

2. Choose the Filter Button: Once you've selected the image, locate the "Filter" button on the toolbar. Clicking this will open the filter options.

3. Browse Filter Options: Scroll through the various filter options available. You'll see a preview of how each filter will affect your image.

4. Adjust the Intensity: After choosing a filter, Canva allows you to adjust the intensity of the filter. This is done via a slider, enabling you to increase or decrease the filter's strength to suit your needs.

Using filters strategically can help unify the color scheme of a design or evoke a specific emotion or theme, such as making an image look warm and inviting, or cool and professional. However, it's essential to ensure that the filter you choose aligns with the overall message of your design.

Customizing Filters

One of the standout features in Canva is the ability to customize filters after applying them. This allows for even more flexibility and control over the final look of your image. For example, after selecting a filter, you can manually tweak settings like brightness, contrast, and saturation to ensure that the filter complements your design perfectly.

Let's say you apply the "Retro" filter to give your image a vintage feel. However, you feel the brightness is too low for the overall composition. You can easily increase the brightness while keeping the other aspects of the filter intact. This feature ensures that you have creative freedom and can fine-tune your images to your liking.

What Are Image Adjustments in Canva?

While filters provide a quick and easy way to enhance your images, Canva's adjustment tools allow for more granular control. Adjustments give you the ability to manually alter the specific characteristics of your image, including brightness, contrast, saturation, blur, and vignette effects. This is ideal when you want to make subtle changes to enhance an image or if you're trying to correct a specific issue, such as an image that is too dark or washed out.

Here's a breakdown of the main adjustment options:

- Brightness: Adjusts the overall lightness or darkness of an image.

- Contrast: Increases or decreases the difference between light and dark areas in an image, enhancing shadows and highlights.

- Saturation: Controls the intensity of the colors in the image, allowing you to create either more vibrant or more muted tones.

- Blur: Adds a soft blur effect to your image, which can be useful for creating a focal point or softening the background.

- Vignette: Darkens the edges of an image, drawing attention to the center.

How to Use Image Adjustments

To manually adjust an image in Canva, follow these steps:

1. Select Your Image: Click on the image to bring up the editing options.

2. Click the "Adjust" Button: In the toolbar that appears, you will see the option to "Adjust." Clicking this will open the adjustment panel.

3. Use the Sliders: Each adjustment option is controlled via a slider. Move the slider left or right to decrease or increase the effect.

4. Fine-Tune Your Image: Experiment with different adjustments to achieve the desired look. For example, if your image appears too dark, increasing the brightness and slightly enhancing the contrast can make the image more visually appealing.

Brightness and Contrast

The brightness adjustment increases or decreases the overall light levels of your image. A well-balanced brightness setting is key to making your image look natural. Increasing brightness can help bring out details in a darker photo, while decreasing it can make an overexposed image more balanced. It's essential to avoid making the image too bright or too dark, as this can reduce the overall quality.

Contrast, on the other hand, adjusts the difference between the darkest and lightest areas of an image. High contrast can make an image pop by intensifying shadows and highlights, while low contrast creates a softer, more muted look. Adjusting contrast is particularly useful when trying to add drama or depth to an image. However, be mindful not to overdo it, as too much contrast can make an image look unnatural.

Saturation

Saturation controls the intensity of colors in an image. Increasing saturation makes colors more vibrant, which is great for creating lively, eye-catching designs. However, reducing saturation can be effective when aiming for a more subtle, muted aesthetic. Desaturated images, or those with reduced color intensity, can evoke a sense of calm or nostalgia.

Saturation adjustments are particularly useful in social media graphics or marketing materials where bold, vibrant colors are often more engaging. But, just like with brightness and contrast, moderation is key. Oversaturating an image can make it appear unrealistic or overly processed.

Blur and Vignette

The blur tool can be used for both artistic and practical purposes. You can add a blur effect to soften the overall appearance of an image, or strategically blur parts of an image to create a focal point. This is especially useful in presentations or marketing materials where you want to highlight a specific element, such as a product or logo, while keeping the rest of the image subtle.

Vignette, meanwhile, is a more specific tool that darkens the edges of an image, drawing attention to the center. This effect is perfect for creating a sense of focus on the subject of your image. It's commonly used in portrait photography, but it can be applied to any image where you want to emphasize the center and make the outer edges less noticeable.

Practical Tips for Using Filters and Adjustments

When applying filters and adjustments, there are a few key tips to keep in mind to ensure your images look polished and professional:

1. Consistency is Key: When working with multiple images in a design, apply the same filter or a similar adjustment style to maintain visual consistency. This is particularly important for projects like social media campaigns, where uniformity can enhance brand recognition.

2. Less is More: It's easy to get carried away with adjustments, but subtlety is often more effective. Small tweaks to brightness, contrast, or saturation can significantly enhance an image without making it look over-processed.

3. Use Adjustments to Fix Issues: If an image is too dark or the colors seem washed out, adjustments are your go-to tool for correction. However, be mindful of the quality of the original image. Sometimes, low-resolution images may become pixelated when heavily adjusted, so always start with high-quality images when possible.

4. Experiment and Revert: Canva allows you to experiment with different filters and adjustments without committing to them immediately. If you're not happy with the result, you can easily revert the changes. Don't be afraid to try out various combinations until you find the perfect look for your design.

By mastering Canva's filters and adjustment tools, you can dramatically improve the quality and impact of your designs. Whether you're creating vibrant social media posts or sleek business presentations, understanding how to manipulate these elements will give your designs a professional edge.

4.1.2 Applying Effects and Enhancements

Applying effects and enhancements in Canva is an essential skill that can significantly elevate your design's overall appearance. While Canva's default settings and templates already offer a visually appealing foundation, the addition of specific effects can help make your designs more unique and professional. Understanding how to apply these enhancements gives you greater control over the tone, style, and impact of your visuals.

In this section, we will explore the different effects and enhancements that Canva offers, how to apply them to your images and other design elements, and tips for maximizing their potential to suit different types of projects. From subtle filters that alter the mood of your image to advanced adjustments like transparency, shadowing, and blending, you'll learn how to take your designs to the next level.

Understanding Canva's Effects Panel

The effects panel in Canva is where all the magic happens. You can access it by selecting an image or an element on your canvas and clicking on the "Effects" option from the top toolbar. This panel provides a wide range of effects and adjustments, allowing you to refine and enhance your design with just a few clicks.

The primary categories in the effects panel are:

- Filters

- Adjustments

- Special Effects

- Shadows

- Glow and Neon

- Transparency

Let's dive deeper into each of these categories to understand their functions and how you can use them effectively.

Filters: Establishing Mood and Atmosphere

One of the easiest ways to give your images a professional, polished look is by applying filters. Filters in Canva work similarly to those found in popular photo-editing apps like Instagram, where a pre-set group of adjustments is applied to the entire image to create a particular style or mood.

- Black and White Filters: These filters convert your images into monochrome, creating a dramatic, classic, or even nostalgic feel. They are perfect for designs where you want to emphasize texture and contrast without the distraction of color.

- Vivid and Color-Enhanced Filters: These filters boost saturation and contrast, making colors pop. They are excellent for social media posts, product photography, or anything where vibrant visuals are crucial to grabbing attention.

- Warm and Cool Filters: Warm filters introduce yellow and orange tones to your image, giving it a sun-kissed, cozy appearance, while cool filters emphasize blues and greens, adding a refreshing and clean feel.

How to Apply Filters:

1. Select the image or background you want to apply the filter to.

2. Click on the "Effects" tab and select "Filters."

3. Browse the available filter options. As you hover over each one, you'll see a live preview on your canvas.

4. Adjust the intensity of the filter using the slider provided. This allows you to control how strong or subtle the effect will be.

Adjustments: Fine-Tuning Your Image

If filters are like broad brushstrokes, adjustments give you the fine-tuned control to tweak individual aspects of your image. Canva's adjustment tools allow you to manipulate brightness, contrast, saturation, and more to get your image looking exactly how you want it.

- Brightness: This controls the light levels of your image. Increasing brightness can make an image feel lighter and more airy, while decreasing it can create a more dramatic or moody atmosphere.

- Contrast: Contrast determines the difference between the light and dark parts of an image. High contrast will make shadows darker and highlights brighter, giving your image a punchier look. Lower contrast softens the difference between lights and darks, creating a more muted and subtle design.

- Saturation: This adjustment increases or decreases the intensity of colors. If your image feels dull, increasing the saturation can make the colors pop. Reducing saturation can give your design a more washed-out or vintage feel.

- Blur: The blur tool is handy for softening parts of your image or creating depth of field effects. Blurring the background while keeping the subject in focus can draw attention to key areas of your design.

- Vignette: Adding a vignette darkens the edges of your image, drawing attention toward the center. This effect is often used in portrait photography but can be applied creatively in any design to emphasize focal points.

How to Use Adjustments:

1. Select the image or design element.

2. Click on "Effects" and navigate to the "Adjust" section.

3. Use the sliders for each option (brightness, contrast, etc.) to tweak the image as desired. You'll see the adjustments take place in real-time.

Special Effects: Adding Flair and Creativity

Canva offers a variety of special effects that allow you to creatively enhance your designs. These effects go beyond basic filters and adjustments, adding unique touches that can make your project stand out.

- Duotone: This effect allows you to overlay two colors on your image, replacing the existing color scheme with a more artistic look. You can choose from Canva's preset duotone combinations or create your own. Duotone is great for branding, especially when you want to align images with your brand colors.

- Pixelate: Pixelation is often used for creating a retro or digital look. It breaks your image into blocks of color, resembling low-resolution graphics from old video games. This effect can be used to create artistic abstracts or even hide sensitive parts of an image.

- Liquify: The liquify effect distorts the image to give it a wavy, fluid appearance. It's best used for abstract designs or when you want to add an artistic twist to your visuals.

- Glitch: The glitch effect creates a distorted, "broken" appearance with split colors and misalignment. This effect is often associated with tech or futuristic themes and can be used to add a sense of dynamic movement or tension to your design.

How to Apply Special Effects:

1. Select the image or element.

2. Go to the "Effects" panel.

3. Choose a special effect like Duotone, Pixelate, or Glitch.

4. Customize the effect parameters where applicable. For instance, with duotone, you can select the specific colors to apply.

Shadows: Creating Depth and Dimension

Shadows can add realism, depth, and dimension to your designs, making elements like text and objects pop from the background. Canva provides several shadow effects that you can apply to any element or image.

- Drop Shadow: This is the most commonly used shadow effect. It simulates the shadow cast by an object, giving the impression that it's lifted off the canvas. You can adjust the direction, distance, and blur of the shadow to suit your design.

- Glow and Neon Shadows: These add a glowing outline around an object, often used for a more stylized, modern effect. The neon shadow, in particular, works well for designs where you want to create a futuristic or vibrant atmosphere.

How to Apply Shadow Effects:

1. Select the element (text, image, or shape) that you want to add the shadow to.

2. Navigate to the "Effects" panel and choose "Shadow."

3. Customize the shadow's color, blur, angle, and distance using the sliders.

Transparency: Blending Elements Seamlessly

Transparency in Canva allows you to adjust the opacity of any element, making it see-through to varying degrees. This feature is especially useful when you want to blend text or images subtly into the background or layer multiple elements for complex designs.

For example, lowering the transparency of an image can be a great way to use it as a background for text, ensuring the text remains readable without the image being too distracting.

How to Adjust Transparency:

1. Select the element you want to adjust.

2. Click on the transparency icon in the top-right toolbar (it looks like a small checkerboard).

3. Use the slider to adjust the transparency level.

Combining Effects for Maximum Impact

One of the most powerful aspects of Canva is that you can combine multiple effects and adjustments to create unique, customized designs. For example, you could:

- Apply a duotone effect to give your image a pop of color.

- Add a drop shadow to the text to create depth.

- Adjust the transparency of an overlay for a subtle, layered look.

By experimenting with different combinations of filters, adjustments, and special effects, you can create highly personalized designs that stand out from the crowd.

Best Practices for Using Effects and Enhancements

- Don't Overdo It: Less is often more. While Canva provides a wide array of effects, it's essential not to go overboard. Too many effects can clutter your design and detract from its overall impact. Aim for subtlety and cohesion.

- Match Effects with Your Design Purpose: The effects you choose should align with the message or tone of your design. For instance, a vintage filter might be perfect for a nostalgic photo but inappropriate for a sleek, modern product ad.

- Keep Branding in Mind: If you're designing for a brand, ensure the effects you apply are consistent with the brand's aesthetic. You can even use Canva's Brand Kit feature to maintain uniformity across all your designs.

- Experiment and Play: One of the best ways to learn Canva's effects and enhancements is through experimentation. Play around with different settings, combinations, and styles to discover what works best for your specific needs.

By mastering Canva's effects and enhancements, you can take your designs from good to great. With just a few clicks, you can transform a basic image or layout into something truly eye-catching and professional. Whether you're creating social media posts, presentations, or marketing materials, the right effects can make all the difference in ensuring your design captures attention and communicates your message effectively.

4.2 Designing with Frames and Grids

Designing with frames and grids in Canva is an essential skill that enhances the structure, organization, and visual appeal of your designs. Grids help to ensure that elements are aligned and positioned consistently, while frames allow for precise image cropping and masking. This section delves into how you can creatively utilize frames and grids to elevate your Canva projects, providing a foundation for creating more professional and visually pleasing compositions.

4.2.1 Creating Collages with Grids

Collages are a popular form of visual storytelling, often used in marketing materials, social media posts, and presentations. A collage allows you to present multiple images within a single layout, helping you convey more information or tell a more comprehensive story. With Canva's grids feature, creating professional-looking collages is easy, even for those with little design experience.

What Are Grids?

Grids in Canva are pre-set structures that divide your design space into multiple sections, allowing you to place different images, text, or elements into each segment. These grids can be simple, with a few squares or rectangles, or they can be more complex, consisting of many smaller sections. Grids automatically align images and elements within their designated areas, making them a powerful tool for creating neat, organized designs.

Grids act as containers for content. When you drag and drop an image into a grid section, Canva automatically fits the image into that space. You can adjust the image's positioning within the grid, but the boundaries of the grid remain constant, which helps to maintain the overall structure of your design.

The Benefits of Using Grids in Collages

Using grids offers several advantages when creating collages, especially when compared to manually aligning individual images:

- Precision and Alignment: Grids ensure that all images and elements are perfectly aligned, creating a cleaner and more professional look.

- Consistency: With grids, you can maintain a consistent size and spacing between images, which enhances the visual harmony of your design.

- Time Efficiency: Grids save time because you don't need to manually position and resize each element. Simply drag and drop your images into the grid, and Canva will handle the rest.

- Versatility: Grids can be used in a variety of ways, from simple two-photo layouts to intricate multi-image collages. You can also combine grids with other elements like text, shapes, or frames to create unique designs.

How to Create a Collage Using Grids in Canva

Creating a collage with grids in Canva is straightforward, thanks to the intuitive drag-and-drop interface. Below is a step-by-step guide to help you create a beautiful collage using Canva's grid feature.

Step 1: Open a New Design

First, open Canva and select the design type that fits your project. Canva offers a variety of design types, such as posters, social media posts, presentations, and more. The design type you choose will determine the dimensions of your canvas. For collages, it's common to use a square format, like Instagram posts, but you can choose any layout that suits your needs.

Step 2: Search for Grids in the Elements Tab

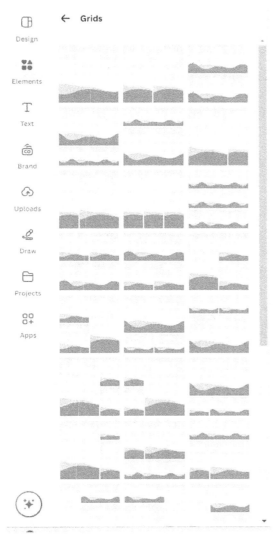

On the left-hand side of your Canva dashboard, you'll see a panel with various tools and options. Click on the "Elements" tab to access a library of design elements. In the search bar at the top of the Elements tab, type "grid" and press Enter. This will display a wide range of grid options, from simple two-column grids to more complex multi-image grids.

Canva offers various grid configurations, such as:

- Single-column and multi-column grids: Ideal for clean, linear designs.

- Circular or geometric grids: Perfect for creative, playful collages.

- Mosaic-style grids: Useful for eclectic or abstract designs.

Scroll through the options and choose a grid that best fits your design vision.

Step 3: Drag and Drop the Grid onto Your Canvas

Once you've selected a grid, drag it onto your design canvas. The grid will automatically resize to fit the canvas, but you can manually adjust its size by clicking and dragging the edges of the grid. The number of sections in the grid will depend on the template you selected, and you can resize individual grid sections by clicking on the dividing lines and dragging them to adjust their width and height.

Step 4: Add Images to the Grid

Now that your grid is in place, it's time to fill each section with images. You can either upload your own images by clicking on the "Uploads" tab and selecting images from your device, or you can choose from Canva's vast library of stock photos.

To add an image to a grid section, simply drag and drop the image into the desired grid cell. Canva will automatically resize the image to fit the section, but you can reposition the image within the grid by double-clicking on it. This will open the image adjustment tool, allowing you to move the image around within the boundaries of the grid cell.

Step 5: Adjust Image Properties

After placing your images into the grid, you may want to make some adjustments to ensure that your collage looks balanced and cohesive. Canva offers a variety of tools for adjusting images, including cropping, rotating, and flipping options. To access these tools, click on an image within the grid, and a toolbar will appear at the top of the screen.

Here are a few adjustments you might consider:

- Zooming In or Out: Double-click on the image within the grid to open the image cropping tool. From here, you can zoom in or out to highlight different parts of the image.

- Repositioning: Drag the image within the grid cell to change its focus. For example, if your image contains a central subject, you can reposition it to ensure that it remains the focal point.

- Applying Filters: Canva provides various filters and adjustments to enhance your images. You can access these options by selecting the image and clicking on the "Edit Image" button. From here, you can apply pre-set filters or manually adjust settings like brightness, contrast, and saturation.

Step 6: Customize the Collage with Text and Elements

Once your images are in place, you can further customize your collage by adding text or additional design elements. Click on the "Text" tab in the left-hand panel to add headings, subheadings, or body text to your collage. Canva offers a variety of fonts and text styles, allowing you to match the typography with the overall theme of your design.

You can also enhance your collage with additional elements like shapes, lines, or icons. Simply return to the "Elements" tab and search for any additional graphics that you want to incorporate into your design. These elements can be placed on top of or between grid sections to add visual interest or provide context to your collage.

Step 7: Final Adjustments and Finishing Touches

Before finalizing your collage, take a moment to review the overall design. Make sure that the images are balanced, the colors are cohesive, and the layout aligns with your original vision. If necessary, make final adjustments to the grid spacing, image positions, or added elements.

At this stage, you can also experiment with different backgrounds, frames, or borders to complete your collage. Canva allows you to change the background color or texture by selecting the "Background" tab on the left-hand panel and choosing from the available options.

Step 8: Download and Share Your Collage

Once you're satisfied with your collage, you can download it by clicking the "Share" button in the top-right corner of the Canva interface. From here, you can select the file format (JPEG, PNG, or PDF) and download the collage to your device. Canva also provides options for sharing your design directly on social media or via email.

You can choose to save the collage in high-resolution for printing purposes or in a web-friendly format for online sharing. Canva also offers the option to create print products like posters or photo books directly from your collage design.

Creative Ideas for Collages with Grids

Creating a grid-based collage offers limitless creative possibilities. Here are a few ideas to inspire your next project:

- Travel Photo Collage: Use a grid to showcase highlights from a recent trip. Include images of landmarks, landscapes, and memorable moments, and add captions to tell the story of your adventure.

- Before-and-After Comparison: Create a collage that highlights a transformation, such as a home renovation or fitness progress. Use a simple two- or three-column grid to show the "before" and "after" images side by side.

- Mood Boards: Collages are perfect for creating mood boards or inspiration boards. Use a grid to arrange images, colors, and textures that represent a particular theme or aesthetic.

- Event Highlights: Capture the best moments from an event, such as a wedding, birthday party, or corporate event, by creating a collage of candid shots, posed photos, and key moments.

Conclusion

Grids in Canva make it easy to create stunning collages that are both visually appealing and well-organized. Whether you're designing for personal projects, social media, or professional presentations, grids offer a quick and efficient way to arrange multiple images in a cohesive layout. By mastering the art of collage-making with grids, you can elevate your Canva designs to a whole new level of creativity and professionalism.

4.2.2 Using Frames for Image Masks

Frames in Canva serve as a powerful tool for designers looking to present images in a structured, aesthetically pleasing way. When combined with the concept of image masking, frames allow users to place images within pre-defined shapes, creating a visually appealing effect that enhances the overall design. This section will guide you through the use of frames as image masks, exploring their potential applications, customization options, and tips for mastering this technique.

What Are Frames in Canva?

Frames in Canva are pre-made placeholders that can be used to insert images or videos into specific shapes or areas of your design. Essentially, they act as containers for visual elements. The beauty of frames is their versatility—Canva offers a wide range of frame shapes and designs, from basic rectangles and circles to more complex forms like stars, letters, and abstract shapes.

When you place an image into a frame, Canva automatically adjusts the image to fit the frame's dimensions. This can help create a polished look without needing manual cropping or resizing. However, the real magic of frames lies in their ability to act as "image masks," meaning the image is confined within the boundaries of the frame, no matter how large or small it is.

The Concept of Image Masks

In design, an image mask refers to the process of placing an image within a specific shape or outline, hiding any parts of the image that fall outside the shape's borders. This creates a focused, organized appearance, which can make even a complex image blend seamlessly into your overall design.

Image masking is particularly useful when working with designs that need a clean, professional look, such as social media graphics, presentations, or business cards. By using frames as image masks in Canva, you can transform ordinary images into dynamic elements that stand out.

Choosing the Right Frame for Your Design

The first step in using frames for image masks is selecting the right frame for your project. Canva offers a wide variety of frames, and choosing the appropriate one depends on the overall theme and purpose of your design. Here are a few considerations:

1. Purpose of the Design:

If you're creating a business card, for example, you might want to use simple, professional frames like squares or circles to maintain a clean look. On the other hand, if you're designing a playful social media post, you could experiment with fun shapes like stars, hearts, or custom shapes.

2. Image Composition:

Think about how the content of your image will fit within the frame. For example, if your image is portrait-oriented, it might look better in a rectangular or oval frame. Likewise, images with central focal points work well in circular frames to draw attention to the middle.

3. Consistency with the Overall Design:

It's important to ensure that the frame complements the rest of your design. Using highly stylized or ornate frames in a minimalist design could create visual dissonance. Make sure the frame style aligns with the overall aesthetic.

Step-by-Step: Using Frames for Image Masks in Canva

Let's break down the process of using frames as image masks in Canva:

Step 1: Adding a Frame to Your Design

To start using frames, navigate to the "Elements" tab on the left-hand side of the Canva workspace. Scroll down until you find the "Frames" section. You can either browse through the available options or type "frames" into the search bar for quicker access. Canva offers a diverse selection of frames, from basic geometric shapes to letters and numbers, even abstract designs.

Once you've found a frame that suits your design, click on it to add it to your workspace. You can resize and reposition the frame to fit your layout.

Step 2: Inserting an Image into the Frame

Once your frame is in place, it's time to insert an image. You can either upload your own image by going to the "Uploads" tab or choose one from Canva's extensive image library by searching through the "Photos" tab.

To place the image inside the frame, simply drag and drop the image onto the frame. Canva will automatically mask the image within the shape of the frame. You can then adjust the positioning of the image inside the frame by double-clicking it. This will bring up a cropping tool, allowing you to move the image around until it's positioned just the way you want.

Step 3: Adjusting Image Size and Position

After placing your image into the frame, you might want to adjust the image size or reposition it to fit the frame perfectly. Double-click on the image within the frame to open the image adjustment view. Here, you can drag the image around inside the frame to find the perfect placement. If the image is too large or too small, you can resize it by clicking and dragging the corners of the image box.

Take note of the frame's boundary. Any part of the image that extends beyond the frame will not be visible, which makes this feature incredibly useful for creating focused, impactful designs.

Customizing Your Frames

Frames offer more than just basic image placement—they can be customized to enhance your design. Here are a few ways to make the most of Canva's frame customization features:

1. Borders and Shadows:

You can add borders or shadows to your frames to give them a more distinct look. To do this, select the frame and navigate to the "Effects" tab, where you can apply shadow effects to make the frame pop. Adjust the intensity, direction, and blur to suit your design.

2. Background Colors:

If your frame contains transparent sections, you can fill the background with a solid color or gradient. Simply click on the frame, go to the "Background" tab, and choose your desired color.

3. Layering Frames:

You can use multiple frames layered on top of each other to create intricate designs. This technique works especially well when designing collages or mood boards. Combine different shapes and sizes of frames to create depth and texture in your layout.

Practical Applications of Frames as Image Masks

Now that you understand how to use frames as image masks, let's explore some practical ways you can implement this technique in your designs:

1. Social Media Graphics:

Frames can help elevate your social media posts by adding structure and focus to images. For instance, using circular frames for profile pictures or square frames for post layouts can give your designs a clean, modern look.

2. Presentations:

Incorporating frames into presentations can help break up the monotony of slides filled with text. Use frames to highlight important images or figures, giving your audience a visual break while maintaining a professional appearance.

3. Marketing Materials:

Whether you're designing flyers, brochures, or posters, frames can make your marketing materials more visually appealing. By using frames to mask images in specific shapes, you can create a cohesive, branded look that stands out from standard rectangular images.

4. Photo Collages:

Canva's frames are ideal for creating photo collages, whether for personal use or professional projects. You can combine multiple frames of different shapes and sizes to create a dynamic collage that tells a story or highlights a specific theme.

Tips for Mastering Frames and Image Masks

- Experiment with Overlays: Don't be afraid to layer different frames on top of each other to create unique compositions. Play with transparency and opacity to give your designs added depth.

- Maintain Image Quality: Always ensure that the images you use in frames are high-resolution. Poor-quality images can detract from your design, especially when using intricate or detailed frames.

- Use Symmetry and Alignment Tools: Canva provides alignment tools that help you keep your frames symmetrical and evenly spaced. Use these tools to ensure your design looks polished and professional.

Conclusion

Using frames for image masks in Canva is a powerful way to take your designs to the next level. Whether you're working on social media graphics, marketing materials, or personal projects, mastering this technique will allow you to create visually striking designs that stand out. By experimenting with different frame shapes, customizing their appearance, and carefully selecting the images you place within them, you can craft professional, dynamic designs with ease.

In the next section, we will explore another advanced Canva feature—Adding Animations and Interactivity—which will help you create more engaging and interactive designs.

4.3 Adding Animations and Interactivity

In today's digital world, creating static designs may not always be enough to capture the audience's attention. With the growing need for engaging content, adding animations and interactive elements to your designs can significantly boost their appeal. Canva offers an intuitive and powerful set of animation tools that make it easy for beginners and professionals alike to breathe life into their graphics.

Animations can add a dynamic flair to presentations, social media posts, videos, and even websites. Whether you're looking to animate text, elements, or the entire design, Canva provides a variety of options to make your work stand out. In this section, we'll explore how you can animate various design elements and incorporate interactivity into your projects.

4.3.1 Animating Text and Elements

Animating text and elements in Canva is a straightforward process that can elevate a design from static to dynamic. Whether you're preparing a presentation, a social media post, or a video, animation helps convey messages more effectively by drawing attention to key points or making transitions more engaging. Let's dive into the steps and best practices for adding animations to your designs.

What is Animation?

Before we begin, it's important to understand what animation means in the context of design. Animation refers to the movement or transformation of objects (such as text, shapes, or images) over time. Canva allows users to add simple animations to text and design elements, giving them motion to create an engaging, professional-looking output.

Animations can range from subtle fades and slides to more dynamic movements like bouncing or spinning. The key is to use these animations purposefully—enhancing the design without overwhelming the viewer.

Steps to Animating Text and Elements in Canva

Step 1: Selecting the Text or Element

To begin animating, click on the text box, image, or any other element you want to animate. This selection activates the toolbar, where animation options become available.

Step 2: Access the Animation Options

Once you've selected your element, look at the top of your Canva workspace, where the editing tools are located. You'll find the "Animate" button in the toolbar (usually to the right, near the effects and adjustments options). Click on this button to reveal Canva's range of animation options.

Step 3: Choose an Animation Style

Canva offers a wide array of animation styles categorized into three main types:

1. Basic Animations: These are simple movements that transition the text or elements onto the screen. Examples include fade, rise, pan, and slide. Basic animations are ideal for a clean, professional look.

2. Dynamic Animations: These offer more energy and motion. Examples include bouncing, spinning, and pulsating. Dynamic animations can be used sparingly to add excitement to certain elements of your design.

3. Continuous Animations: These are looping animations that create movement throughout the design. Continuous animations work best when you want certain elements to remain animated throughout a video or presentation.

After selecting a category, scroll through the available animations, and hover over each one to preview how it will look when applied to your text or element.

Step 4: Customize Animation Settings

Canva allows for limited customization of animation settings such as speed and timing, which gives you control over how quickly or slowly the animation occurs. For example, you can choose to make text fade in gradually or elements slide in rapidly.

To adjust the speed, click on the small gear icon that appears alongside the animation style once it's been applied. This will open a window where you can drag sliders to change the timing of the animation.

Step 5: Apply to Other Elements

Once you're satisfied with your animation, you can apply it to other elements by either repeating the process or selecting multiple elements at once before clicking on the "Animate" button. This allows you to animate multiple items simultaneously.

Step 6: Preview Your Animation

Before finalizing your design, it's important to preview how the animations work in context. Canva provides a "Play" button in the top right corner of the screen. Clicking on this will play the entire design with all animations, allowing you to see how everything moves together. Make any adjustments as necessary to ensure that the animations enhance your design without distracting from the main message.

Tips for Effective Use of Animation

Animation, when used properly, can greatly improve the overall impact of your design. However, over-animating or using distracting movements can detract from your message. Here are some tips for getting the most out of Canva's animation features:

1. Use Animations Sparingly

Less is often more when it comes to animation. A few well-placed animations can draw attention to key points, but too much movement can be overwhelming. Stick to animating only the most important elements, such as headlines or calls to action.

2. Match the Animation to Your Design's Tone

Different types of animations can evoke different feelings. For example, a simple fade-in animation might convey a calm, professional tone, while a bouncing or spinning animation can give your design a more playful, energetic vibe. Be sure to choose an animation style that aligns with the overall message and tone of your design.

3. Consider Animation Timing

The timing of animations can affect how your design is perceived. Fast animations can create a sense of urgency, while slower animations can be more elegant and graceful. Adjust the timing to suit the mood you're trying to convey.

4. Be Mindful of the Purpose

Animations should serve a purpose—whether it's highlighting a key message, transitioning between ideas, or simply adding visual interest. Avoid adding animations just for the sake of it; instead, think about how they can enhance the user experience.

5. Test Across Devices

If you're designing for social media, presentations, or websites, it's important to test your animations across different devices (desktop, tablet, and mobile). Canva's preview option can help you gauge how your animations look on different screen sizes.

Common Animation Styles in Canva

Now that we've covered the basics of how to add animations, let's explore some of the common animation styles in Canva and how to use them effectively:

1. Fade

The fade animation is one of the most subtle and commonly used effects in Canva. It makes an element gradually appear or disappear, creating a smooth transition. The fade effect is perfect for text or images that you want to introduce softly without drawing too much attention.

2. Pan

The pan effect makes an element move horizontally or vertically across the screen. It's great for adding a sense of direction or movement and can be especially useful in presentations when you want to draw attention to different sections.

3. Rise

Rise is an upward animation where an element appears to "rise" onto the screen. This effect works well for introducing headings or important text, as it adds a sense of prominence and gravity.

4. Bounce

Bounce is a dynamic and playful animation where elements appear to bounce onto the screen. While fun, it's important to use this animation style sparingly, as too much bouncing can be distracting. This effect is great for playful designs like children's party invitations or casual social media posts.

5. Slide

The slide animation moves elements horizontally or vertically across the screen, much like the pan effect. However, slide is often more fluid and quicker in its movement. This animation can be useful for transitioning between sections in presentations or guiding the viewer's attention from one point to another.

Best Practices for Animating Text

When it comes to animating text, there are several additional considerations to keep in mind. Text is often the primary conveyer of information, so the way it moves on-screen can greatly impact the readability and perception of your design.

1. Keep it Legible

Always ensure that the text remains legible throughout the animation. This means avoiding excessive movement that makes the text difficult to read, especially for longer sentences. A simple fade or rise effect is often the most effective choice for text.

2. Use Animation to Emphasize Key Points

Animations can be a great way to emphasize important points in your text. For example, animating a headline separately from the body text can draw attention to it, ensuring that viewers see your main message first.

3. Maintain Consistency

When animating multiple text elements, it's important to maintain consistency in the type and style of animations. Using the same animation for headlines across different slides or posts creates a cohesive, polished look.

By utilizing Canva's animation tools, you can add a dynamic layer of interactivity and engagement to your designs. Whether you're enhancing a social media post with bouncing text or adding subtle motion to a professional presentation, these tools offer flexibility and creativity for every type of project. With practice and thoughtful use, animation can significantly elevate the impact of your designs, helping you capture your audience's attention and convey your message more effectively.

4.3.2 Designing Interactive Presentations

Canva's interactive presentations bring a new dimension to traditional slide decks. Beyond static images and text, adding animation and interactivity transforms your presentations into a dynamic experience that captures and maintains audience attention. Whether you're presenting in person or virtually, Canva's versatile platform enables users to create visually appealing and engaging presentations without needing advanced design skills. In this section, we will explore how to design these interactive presentations effectively, covering the tools available within Canva and best practices for usage.

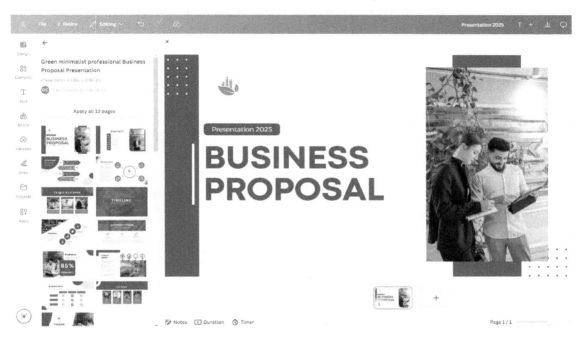

Understanding Interactive Presentations

Interactive presentations are more than just slides that move from one to the next. They enable users to incorporate multimedia elements, clickable objects, animations, and transitions, which make the presentation more engaging. With Canva, you can add links to navigate between slides or even external content, use animations to draw attention to specific points, and include video clips and audio to convey your message more effectively.

Interactive presentations are perfect for:

- Business pitches where you want to keep investors focused on key points.

- Training sessions that require engagement through clickable exercises or embedded resources.

- Virtual classrooms or e-learning modules where learners can interact with the content in a meaningful way.

Steps to Creating an Interactive Presentation in Canva

To help you get started, let's walk through the steps of creating an interactive presentation using Canva.

Step 1: Choosing the Right Template

Canva offers a wide range of presentation templates, including many designed for interactivity. When starting a new project, search for "interactive presentations" in Canva's template library. These templates often come pre-configured with animations and layouts that make it easier to add multimedia content. However, if you prefer, you can start with a blank presentation and add your own interactive elements.

Tips for Choosing a Template:

- Keep Your Audience in Mind: If you are designing for corporate settings, choose a template with a clean, professional layout. If your presentation is for creative or educational purposes, you can experiment with more vibrant colors and playful designs.

- Consider the Number of Slides: Ensure that the template you choose has an appropriate number of slides to suit your content. It's easier to remove unnecessary slides than to add and modify layouts later.

Step 2: Structuring Your Content

Once you have your template, start by structuring your presentation content. Consider the logical flow of information. Interactive presentations often break away from the linear progression of traditional slides. With the ability to navigate between slides using hyperlinks, you can create a more modular experience. Here's how to plan for interactive content:

- Non-Linear Navigation: Include a home slide that links to various sections within the presentation. This is particularly useful for long presentations, allowing viewers to navigate back and forth easily.

- Clickable Menus: Add clickable buttons on each slide that allow users to jump to specific topics, sections, or external content.

- Summary Slides: You can create a summary slide at the end of each section that links back to key points, reinforcing the most important takeaways.

Step 3: Adding Clickable Links and Buttons

One of Canva's most powerful features for creating interactivity is the ability to add clickable elements to your presentation. These can be buttons, icons, or even images that link to another slide or external content (e.g., a website or video).

To Add a Clickable Link:

1. Select the element (text, image, or shape) you want to make clickable.

2. Click on the link icon in the toolbar above.

3. In the pop-up window, choose whether you want the link to navigate to another slide within the presentation or to an external URL.

4. Test the link by entering presentation mode to ensure it works as expected.

Best Practices for Links:

- Keep it Obvious: Ensure that clickable elements are easy to identify, typically through visual cues like buttons or highlighted text.

- Internal vs External Links: Use internal links for navigation within the presentation, and reserve external links for additional resources, videos, or references.

- Limit Distractions: Avoid overloading your presentation with too many external links, as this can distract from your main content. Prioritize only the most relevant additional resources.

Step 4: Integrating Multimedia Elements

An interactive presentation thrives on multimedia. Canva allows you to easily embed videos, audio, and images to make your presentation more engaging. Multimedia elements can break up large blocks of text, highlight key ideas, or provide additional context.

Adding a Video:

1. Select the slide where you want to embed a video.

2. Click on the "Elements" tab in the left-hand menu and search for "videos."

3. Choose from Canva's stock video library, or upload your own video by clicking on the "Uploads" tab.

4. Drag and drop the video onto your slide and resize or reposition it as necessary.

5. You can also set the video to play automatically when the slide appears by adjusting the video settings in the toolbar.

Adding Audio:

1. Navigate to the slide where you want to include audio.

2. Click on the "Elements" tab, and search for "audio" if you want to use stock sounds.

3. Alternatively, upload your own audio file under the "Uploads" tab.

4. Drag and drop the audio file onto the slide. Once added, the audio will automatically play when the slide appears.

Best Practices for Multimedia Integration:

- Limit Video Length: Keep embedded videos short and to the point, ideally no more than 2-3 minutes per video. Longer videos can disengage viewers and may increase the file size, making the presentation harder to share.

- Ensure Compatibility: Ensure that the multimedia elements you include are compatible with your audience's viewing platform. Not all users may have the bandwidth or software to easily view heavy video or audio files.

- Provide Alternate Content: For critical information, consider providing alternate content such as text summaries for videos or transcripts for audio clips. This is especially useful for accessibility purposes.

Step 5: Applying Animations and Transitions

Animations and transitions can add flair to your presentation, helping emphasize key points or guiding the audience through a complex narrative. Canva's animation tools are simple but effective for adding movement to text, images, or entire slides.

To Add Animations:

1. Select the element (text, image, or shape) you wish to animate.

2. Click on the "Animate" button in the toolbar.

3. Choose from a variety of animation effects, such as "Fade," "Pan," or "Bounce."

4. Adjust the duration and speed of the animation to fit your presentation style.

Using Slide Transitions:

1. Navigate to the slide where you want to apply a transition.

2. Click on the "Animate" button for the entire slide.

3. Choose a transition effect, such as "Slide," "Dissolve," or "Block."

4. Preview the transition by entering presentation mode.

Best Practices for Animations:

- Use Animation Sparingly: While animations can make your presentation more dynamic, overusing them can distract your audience. Apply them to key elements rather than every object on the slide.

- Timing is Crucial: Ensure that animations are not too slow or too fast. Use a pace that allows the audience to absorb the content without feeling rushed or overwhelmed.

- Consistency: Maintain a consistent animation style throughout the presentation to ensure a smooth, professional flow.

Step 6: Testing and Reviewing the Presentation

Before presenting, always take time to review and test your interactive presentation. This ensures that all clickable links work, multimedia plays correctly, and animations flow smoothly. You can do this by entering presentation mode and navigating through the slides as your audience would.

Key Points to Check:

- Navigation: Ensure all links are functional and direct the viewer to the correct slide or external page.

- Media Playback: Test that videos and audio play as intended, with proper synchronization to the content.

- Performance: Ensure that your presentation runs smoothly on different devices, especially if you plan to share it online. Large files with heavy multimedia can sometimes cause lag or slow loading times.

Step 7: Presenting and Sharing Your Interactive Presentation

Once your interactive presentation is ready, Canva offers several options for presenting and sharing it. You can present directly from Canva by entering full-screen presentation mode, or you can export the presentation in various formats.

Presenting in Canva:

- Click the "Present" button in the top-right corner of the screen to enter full-screen mode.

- Use arrow keys or clickable links to navigate between slides.

- For interactive presentations, you can let the audience control navigation or guide them through the slides yourself.

Exporting the Presentation:

- If you need to share your presentation with others, you can export it as a PDF, PowerPoint file, or MP4 video, depending on the level of interactivity required.

- For maximum interactivity, share a direct Canva link that allows viewers to navigate the presentation themselves.

By following these steps, you can create compelling and engaging interactive presentations that not only capture your audience's attention but also make your message more impactful. With Canva's intuitive tools, designing these dynamic presentations becomes a straightforward process, even for beginners.

4.4 Collaborating and Sharing Designs

4.4.1 Sharing Projects with Others

In today's interconnected world, sharing designs and collaborating with others has become an essential part of the creative process. Canva excels in providing tools that make it simple to collaborate on designs, whether you're working with a team, clients, or friends. The platform offers various methods to share projects with others, ensuring that you can tailor the level of access and interaction based on the needs of your collaborators.

Why Share Projects?

There are many reasons why you might want to share your Canva designs with others. Perhaps you're part of a design team and need to collaborate on a project, or maybe you want feedback from a client or a colleague. Sharing your designs can also be an effective way to teach others, demonstrate concepts, or gather input on a design before finalizing it.

In addition to collaboration, sharing your Canva projects can streamline workflows, enhance creativity through group input, and save time. With Canva, you no longer need to email files back and forth or worry about compatibility issues between different design software. Everything is accessible online, and changes happen in real time, making the collaboration process seamless.

Methods of Sharing Projects

Canva provides several options for sharing your projects. Depending on the level of access you want to grant others, you can share a design as an editable project, a view-only file, or a downloadable link. Let's explore each of these methods in detail.

Sharing via Link

One of the most straightforward ways to share your Canva project is by generating a shareable link. Canva allows you to create a link that you can send to others via email, messaging platforms, or any other communication channel. There are two main options when sharing via a link:

- View-only link: With this option, recipients can view your design but cannot make any changes. This is ideal for situations where you want to share your work for feedback or approval without risking unwanted edits. For example, if you're sharing a draft design with a client or a supervisor, a view-only link allows them to see the design in full detail and offer their feedback without altering your work.

- Editable link: An editable link gives recipients the ability to make changes to the design. This is particularly useful in team settings where multiple people need to collaborate on the same project. By sharing an editable link, you can invite others to add their own text, images, and elements to the design. You also have the option to control the level of access for each person, ensuring that only authorized individuals can make edits.

To share your Canva project via a link, follow these steps:

1. Open the design you want to share.

2. Click the "Share" button located in the top right corner of the design screen.

3. In the sharing menu, you'll see the option to generate a shareable link. Choose whether you want to create a view-only or editable link.

4. Once the link is generated, you can copy it and send it to others via email, messaging apps, or social media platforms.

Setting Permissions for Shared Designs

When sharing designs with others, especially when giving them access to edit, it's important to set the appropriate permissions. Canva allows you to control who can view or edit the design, ensuring that you retain control over your project.

Permissions can be set based on the following options:

- Anyone with the link: This is the most open permission setting. If you select this option, anyone who has the link can view or edit the design, depending on the link type you choose. While this is convenient, it can also pose risks if the link is shared beyond your intended recipients. It's recommended to use this setting when you're sharing with a large group or don't mind the design being accessible to many people.

- Specific people: If you want to restrict access to certain individuals, you can specify the email addresses of the people you're sharing the design with. This ensures that only those individuals can access the design, providing an extra layer of security. This is particularly useful when working on sensitive projects or when collaborating with clients who require confidentiality.

Once you've set the desired permissions, Canva will allow you to track who has access to the design and what level of access they have. You can modify or revoke permissions at any time, giving you full control over your design's distribution.

Collaborating in Real-Time

One of Canva's most powerful features is the ability to collaborate in real-time. This means that multiple people can work on the same design simultaneously, making changes and updates that are visible to everyone in real-time. Whether you're in different locations or working on the same design from different devices, Canva ensures that your work is always up-to-date and accessible to your collaborators.

When you share a design with others using an editable link, they can join the project and make changes in real-time. Canva will display the initials of the people who are currently working on the design, so you can see who is active in the project. This feature is particularly useful in team environments where multiple people need to contribute to the design process.

For example, if you're working on a marketing campaign with a team, the graphic designer can work on the visuals while the copywriter simultaneously adds text. This real-time collaboration speeds up the workflow and allows for immediate feedback and adjustments. Moreover, you can leave comments directly on the design, making it easy to communicate ideas, suggestions, or corrections with your collaborators.

Sharing Designs with Clients

If you're a designer working with clients, Canva's sharing features can be incredibly helpful for managing client feedback and approvals. When sharing designs with clients, you can choose between a view-only link or an editable link, depending on the level of involvement you want the client to have.

For example, if you want the client to review the design but not make any changes, a view-only link is the best option. The client can provide feedback through other channels, such as email or comments on the design, and you can make the necessary changes.

If your client prefers to have more hands-on involvement in the design process, you can share an editable link. This allows the client to make small adjustments, such as changing text or swapping images, while you retain control over the overall design. This can be especially useful in industries like marketing or branding, where clients may want to make last-minute tweaks before final approval.

Collaboration Beyond the Design: Sharing the Brand Kit

For businesses or teams that rely on consistent branding across multiple projects, Canva's Brand Kit feature allows for easy sharing and collaboration. A Brand Kit is a collection of logos, fonts, and color palettes that define a company's visual identity. By sharing the Brand Kit with your team or clients, you can ensure that all designs adhere to the same branding guidelines, maintaining consistency across all projects.

To share a Brand Kit, you need a Canva Pro account. Once the Brand Kit is set up, you can share it with team members, allowing them to access the assets and apply them to their own designs. This is particularly useful for marketing teams, design agencies, and businesses that need to maintain a cohesive brand identity across various platforms.

Sharing Projects for Team Collaboration

If you're working as part of a team, Canva's collaboration features extend beyond individual projects. With a Canva for Teams account, you can set up a team workspace where everyone has access to shared designs, templates, and assets. This centralized workspace makes it easy for team members to collaborate on multiple projects simultaneously, ensuring that everyone has the resources they need to create cohesive designs.

In a team workspace, you can assign roles and permissions to each member, ensuring that everyone has the appropriate level of access. For example, you can give designers full editing access while limiting access for other team members to view-only or comment-only. This ensures that the design process is streamlined and that everyone's contributions are managed effectively.

Additionally, team members can leave comments directly on the design, allowing for real-time feedback and discussion. This eliminates the need for lengthy email chains or external communication tools, making the collaboration process more efficient.

Sharing for Feedback and Approval

Another important aspect of sharing Canva designs is gathering feedback and securing approval. Canva's sharing features make it easy to present designs for review and receive input from multiple stakeholders. By sharing a view-only link, you can invite others to review the design and provide feedback without giving them access to make changes.

Alternatively, you can use Canva's commenting feature to gather feedback directly within the design. Recipients can click on any part of the design and leave comments, which are visible to all collaborators. This feature is particularly useful when working with clients, managers, or team members who need to review and approve designs before they are finalized.

4.4.2 Commenting and Editing with Teams

Collaboration is one of Canva's most powerful and practical features, especially for teams working on projects that require multiple perspectives or inputs. Canva has optimized its platform for ease of use in collaborative environments, making it an excellent tool for both small businesses and large teams. This section explores how to use Canva's collaboration tools effectively, focusing specifically on the commenting and editing features, which streamline the feedback and approval process.

Understanding Team Collaboration in Canva

Before diving into the details of commenting and editing, it's essential to understand the basic structure of collaboration in Canva. When working in a team, Canva allows you to invite multiple collaborators to a single design project. Each team member can either be given editing privileges or restricted to view-only access, depending on their role in the project.

Canva's real-time collaboration capabilities allow multiple users to work on the same design simultaneously. This functionality mirrors tools like Google Docs, where changes made by one team member are instantly visible to others, facilitating smooth and dynamic collaboration. In collaborative projects, effective communication is critical, and Canva's commenting system is designed to promote clarity, efficiency, and direct feedback.

How to Enable Commenting

Commenting in Canva can be done on any part of the design canvas, allowing team members to provide precise feedback without ambiguity. To enable commenting on a project:

1. Share the Design: First, ensure the design is shared with team members. You can do this by clicking the "Share" button at the top-right corner of the interface. You will be prompted to enter the email addresses of your collaborators, and from here, you can control their access level—either allowing them to edit or limiting them to viewing and commenting.

2. Open the Comment Panel: Once the design is shared, you'll notice a small speech bubble icon on the toolbar, usually located at the top-right of the screen. Clicking on this will open the comment panel where you can see and manage all comments.

3. Add Comments: To add a comment to a specific element in the design, click directly on the object you wish to comment on. A small text box will appear where you can type your feedback. This feature is especially helpful in providing specific, actionable advice, such as adjusting the size of an image, changing font colors, or repositioning text elements.

Using Comments Effectively in Design Projects

Comments are most effective when they are clear, constructive, and specific. Here are some tips for using Canva's commenting feature to its fullest potential:

1. Be Specific: When giving feedback, avoid vague comments such as "This doesn't look right." Instead, say something more actionable like, "Can we increase the size of the logo by 20% for better visibility?"

2. Use Contextual Comments: Take full advantage of the ability to attach comments to specific elements in the design. This is much more effective than leaving general feedback, as it directs your team's attention to the exact area that needs improvement.

3. Stay Professional and Polite: Feedback in any form should maintain a respectful tone. Positive reinforcement can also be helpful, especially when team members are contributing creatively. A balance between constructive criticism and positive feedback helps build a collaborative environment.

4. Utilize Emojis and Formatting: Canva supports basic text formatting and emojis in comments, which can add an extra layer of communication. For example, a simple " " can indicate that a particular section is good to go, whereas " ? " can signify that something is unclear or needs further discussion.

5. Prioritize Feedback: As multiple comments accumulate, it's essential to prioritize feedback. Use labels like "urgent," "minor change," or "needs approval" to help team members quickly understand the priority level of each comment.

Managing Comments in Large Projects

For larger projects, managing a high volume of comments can become challenging. Canva provides several features to help teams stay organized:

1. Resolve Comments: Once feedback has been addressed, you can mark comments as "resolved." This not only keeps the workspace tidy but also ensures that team members know which feedback has been implemented. Resolved comments can still be reviewed later if needed.

2. Threaded Replies: Canva supports threaded comments, which allow team members to reply to individual comments and start a conversation around a specific piece of feedback. This feature is highly useful for back-and-forth discussions, ensuring that everyone's voice is heard and that feedback is thoroughly discussed before any changes are made.

3. Tagging Team Members: Canva allows you to tag specific team members in comments by using the "@" symbol followed by their name. This feature is great for directing feedback to the person responsible for making the necessary changes. For example, if the project needs a typography adjustment, you might tag the team member responsible for handling text elements by saying, "@John Can you adjust the font size on this header?"

4. Filtering Comments: Canva also includes a comment filtering feature. This is useful for projects with multiple ongoing threads of feedback. You can filter comments by those assigned to you, unread comments, or unresolved feedback, making it easier to stay on top of pending tasks.

Editing in Real Time: Tips for Seamless Collaboration

One of Canva's most powerful features for teams is real-time editing. This allows multiple users to work on the same design at the same time, a feature especially useful when deadlines are tight, and various elements of the design need to be completed simultaneously. To ensure a smooth editing process:

1. Communicate in Real-Time: While comments can be an excellent way to provide feedback asynchronously, real-time collaboration is most effective when team members communicate through chat tools like Slack, Microsoft Teams, or even Canva's built-in commenting system. This allows for immediate feedback and quicker decision-making.

2. Avoid Overwriting Changes: When working on the same design simultaneously, it's important to respect the work being done by others. Make sure you're editing the correct element and avoid overwriting changes made by team members unless agreed upon. Canva tracks changes in real time, but keeping communication open about what sections each team member is working on prevents confusion.

3. Version Control and History: Canva's "Version History" feature is a lifesaver for teams working on complex designs. If changes are made that need to be undone, or if a design was altered incorrectly, you can easily revert to a previous version. This adds a safety net for experimentation and reduces the risk of losing work.

4. Define Roles and Responsibilities: For smoother editing, assign roles and responsibilities within the team. For example, designate one person as the lead designer, responsible for finalizing the look and feel, while others handle content, images, or layout tweaks. This can help avoid conflicting changes and ensure a cohesive design.

Integrating Canva with Other Tools for Collaboration

To enhance collaboration even further, Canva can integrate with various third-party tools. Some of the most popular integrations for teams include:

1. Google Drive: You can easily link your Google Drive account to Canva, allowing seamless access to shared documents, presentations, and images. This integration is especially useful for teams working across multiple platforms.

2. Dropbox: Similar to Google Drive, Dropbox can be integrated with Canva to pull in assets directly from your cloud storage. Teams that already use Dropbox for file sharing will find this integration to be highly convenient.

3. Slack: Canva integrates with Slack for quick sharing of designs and feedback. Teams can set up a dedicated channel for design projects and use Slack to discuss changes, share links to Canva projects, and notify team members of updates.

4. Trello or Asana: If your team uses project management tools like Trello or Asana, you can link your Canva projects to tasks, allowing everyone to stay on top of deadlines and progress. This integration ensures that feedback, revisions, and approvals happen within the context of your overall project plan.

Best Practices for Collaborative Design in Canva

To ensure successful collaboration, here are a few best practices teams can follow when using Canva:

1. Set Clear Goals: Before starting any collaborative project, ensure that all team members are aligned on the objectives. This prevents unnecessary revisions and keeps the design process efficient.

2. Create a Style Guide: For teams that work on recurring design projects, such as social media posts or brand assets, having a Canva style guide is crucial. Canva's Pro version allows teams to create a Brand Kit, which includes your brand's fonts, colors, and logos. This ensures consistency across all designs.

3. Plan Regular Check-ins: Set up regular meetings or virtual check-ins to discuss the progress of the design. This keeps everyone on the same page and ensures that all feedback is considered.

4. Keep Designs Organized: Use Canva's folder system to keep your projects organized. Large teams can benefit from creating separate folders for different stages of the design process (e.g., drafts, final designs) or by categorizing designs by project type.

5. Leverage Templates: Canva's vast library of templates can significantly reduce design time. Teams can customize these templates to meet their needs, allowing them to focus more on content creation and less on design from scratch.

Conclusion

Canva's commenting and editing features allow teams to collaborate efficiently and creatively, helping them produce high-quality designs faster. By using comments to provide specific, actionable feedback and leveraging real-time editing features, teams can enhance communication, reduce revision cycles, and create cohesive, visually appealing designs. When combined with integrations like Google Drive and Slack, Canva becomes an even more powerful tool for teams to work together, no matter where they are.

CHAPTER V
Canva for Social Media

5.1 Creating Social Media Graphics

Social media platforms have become essential tools for businesses, influencers, and individuals to connect with their audience. Each platform has its own style and unique requirements, making it essential to design visuals tailored to each one. Canva simplifies this process by offering a wide variety of customizable templates and tools for creating engaging social media graphics. In this section, we will explore how to design for three of the most popular platforms: Instagram, Facebook, and Twitter.

5.1.1 Designing for Instagram, Facebook, and Twitter

When designing for social media platforms like Instagram, Facebook, and Twitter, it's important to keep in mind the visual preferences and technical specifications of each platform. While all three platforms allow users to share images, their unique audiences and content formats create different design challenges. Canva offers dedicated templates and tools to ensure your designs look great, no matter where they're posted.

Instagram Graphics Design

Instagram is a highly visual platform, with over a billion active users focusing on images and short videos. Whether you are sharing posts, stories, or reels, your design must be aesthetically appealing to grab attention and encourage engagement. Here's a breakdown of what to consider when designing Instagram graphics:

1. Image Size and Dimensions

Instagram supports different types of image formats, each with its own dimensions:

- Square Posts: 1080 x 1080 pixels (aspect ratio 1:1) – this is the most commonly used format, ideal for profile grids and maintaining consistency across your Instagram feed.

- Portrait Posts: 1080 x 1350 pixels (aspect ratio 4:5) – this takes up more vertical space on users' screens, making it more engaging for mobile users.

- Landscape Posts: 1080 x 566 pixels (aspect ratio 1.91:1) – though less common, landscape posts are perfect for wide images or panoramic shots.

- Instagram Stories: 1080 x 1920 pixels (aspect ratio 9:16) – these vertical images are designed to fill a user's screen, providing an immersive experience.

With Canva, selecting the right dimensions is easy. Canva's templates are preset with the correct sizes for posts, stories, and other Instagram formats, allowing you to focus on creativity rather than technical details.

2. Visual Style and Theme

Maintaining a consistent visual style on Instagram is crucial to building your brand identity. Canva helps you create and apply a cohesive theme across your posts by allowing you to:

- Use the same color palette and fonts across all designs.

- Add logos, watermarks, or brand symbols to keep your posts recognizable.

- Customize ready-made templates that align with your brand's voice (fun, professional, artistic, etc.).

For businesses, using Canva's Brand Kit feature helps ensure consistency in your visual assets. Upload your brand colors, fonts, and logos, so every new design adheres to your branding guidelines effortlessly.

3. Capturing Engagement with Instagram Posts

Instagram's algorithm prioritizes engaging content. Designing eye-catching visuals that encourage interaction (likes, comments, shares) is essential. Canva offers:

- Bold Typography: Use strong, legible fonts to convey your message clearly. Headings in bold or uppercase can draw attention.

- Call-to-Action (CTA) Designs: Include direct CTAs in your posts. For example, "Swipe up," "Link in bio," or "Tag a friend."

- Story Highlights: Design engaging cover images for Instagram Highlights to make your profile look polished and cohesive.

4. Instagram Carousels

Carousel posts, where you can swipe through multiple images, are becoming a favorite among Instagram users. They are great for storytelling, tutorials, or showcasing multiple products. With Canva, you can create a seamless flow across multiple images, ensuring each slide contributes to the narrative without feeling disjointed.

5. Image Editing and Filters

Instagram is known for its use of filters. Canva allows you to apply filters and adjustments (brightness, contrast, saturation, etc.) to make your images pop before uploading. Canva's filter options give you more control compared to Instagram's in-app filters, allowing for subtle or dramatic changes that fit your brand.

Facebook Graphics Design

Blue Gradient Simple Animated Global Warming Newsroom Facebook Post

Facebook Post (Landscape) • 940 • 788 px

By Studiotools Follow

Customize this template

More like this

Facebook remains a highly versatile platform for content sharing, from business pages to personal timelines. Visual content is crucial on Facebook, especially with image posts generating more engagement than text posts. Here's what you should focus on when designing for Facebook:

1. Image Size and Dimensions

Facebook supports various image sizes, and each serves a specific purpose:

- Profile Photos: 170 x 170 pixels – These images represent your brand across the platform and must be clear and recognizable, even at small sizes.

- Cover Photos: 820 x 312 pixels – Cover photos are prime real estate for showcasing your brand's message or personality. Canva's cover photo templates offer ideas ranging from product promotions to seasonal updates.

- Post Images: 1200 x 630 pixels – These dimensions are ideal for shared image posts on Facebook timelines, ensuring images appear clear without cropping.

- Event Images: 1200 x 628 pixels – If you're creating an event on Facebook, Canva's event image templates help create buzz and excitement.

2. Choosing Engaging Visuals for Facebook

Facebook users tend to engage more with visually appealing content. Canva's expansive template library includes options for various post types:

- Event Invitations: Use Canva's event templates to create custom invites for webinars, product launches, or special promotions.

- Polls and Surveys: Design interesting visuals for polls that encourage user participation.

- Promotions and Announcements: Canva's promotion templates allow you to highlight sales, deals, or upcoming announcements in an eye-catching way.

3. Facebook Ads

Facebook ads can be a powerful marketing tool. Canva offers templates specifically designed for ads, ensuring you meet Facebook's technical requirements while creating compelling visuals:

- Ad Images: 1200 x 628 pixels (recommended). Ensure the key message is in the center of the image, as Facebook may crop the edges when displaying the ad.

- Minimal Text Rule: Facebook limits the amount of text that can appear on ad images. Canva's built-in text overlay detection tool helps you meet these requirements.

4. Facebook Stories

Much like Instagram, Facebook stories use a vertical format with a 9:16 aspect ratio (1080 x 1920 pixels). Canva's story templates make it easy to create fun, engaging stories with features like animated elements, stickers, and interactive components like polls and questions.

5. Video Content for Facebook

With Facebook prioritizing video content, Canva's video templates let you create professional-looking video posts and stories. You can add text overlays, transitions, and music to make your videos stand out.

Twitter Graphics Design

Twitter is a fast-paced platform, and your visuals need to grab attention quickly in a feed filled with text-heavy content. Designing for Twitter involves a balance of clarity, simplicity, and eye-catching visuals:

1. Image Size and Dimensions

Twitter has a unique set of image size recommendations:

- Profile Photos: 400 x 400 pixels – Ensure your logo or brand symbol is clear and centered.

- Header Image: 1500 x 500 pixels – This long, horizontal format is ideal for panoramic images or banners that showcase your brand's message.

- In-Stream Images: 1200 x 675 pixels – Use these dimensions for standard tweet images, ensuring they display fully without cropping.

2. Designing Twitter Posts for Engagement

Twitter users are accustomed to concise, impactful content. Your visuals need to reflect this with:

- Minimalist Design: Since Twitter's character limit is low, your images should also follow a minimalistic approach. Canva offers templates that focus on bold visuals with minimal text, allowing your message to stand out.

- Clear CTAs: Use graphics that prompt engagement, such as "Retweet if you agree!" or "Reply with your thoughts."

- Infographics: Twitter is an excellent platform for sharing bite-sized information through infographics. Canva offers pre-made infographic templates that can be tailored to any message or data set you want to share.

3. Twitter Ads and Promoted Tweets

Twitter's advertising format is different from Facebook's, but Canva still provides templates for Twitter ad campaigns. Whether you're promoting a tweet or running a full-fledged ad, make sure your visual adheres to Twitter's 1200 x 675 pixel recommendation for best results.

4. GIFs and Animations

Twitter users love animated GIFs, and Canva lets you create custom GIFs to add some personality to your tweets. Simple animations, like moving text or objects, can draw attention and encourage more interaction.

Conclusion

Creating effective social media graphics requires a strong understanding of each platform's unique specifications and audience behavior. Whether you're designing for Instagram, Facebook, or Twitter, Canva provides all the necessary tools to produce high-quality visuals that align with your brand's goals. With its preset templates, easy-to-use interface, and customization features, Canva makes designing for social media simple and effective.

5.1.2 Optimizing Dimensions for Social Platforms

When it comes to designing for social media, getting the dimensions right is one of the most important factors. Every social platform has its own unique requirements for image sizes, and using the correct dimensions ensures that your designs are displayed correctly, without being cropped, distorted, or blurred. Optimizing dimensions not only enhances the visual appeal of your graphics but also maximizes engagement by ensuring your audience can easily view and interact with your content.

In this section, we'll explore the recommended dimensions for various social media platforms, including Instagram, Facebook, Twitter, LinkedIn, Pinterest, and YouTube, and how to optimize your designs for each.

Instagram

Instagram is a highly visual platform that prioritizes images and videos. It offers several formats for posts, including standard feed images, Stories, and Reels. Each of these formats has specific size requirements that need to be followed for the best results.

- *Instagram Feed Posts (Square, Portrait, and Landscape):*

Instagram allows three main formats for feed posts—square, portrait, and landscape. While square images are still the most common, portrait and landscape are gaining popularity.

- Square: 1080 x 1080 pixels

- Portrait: 1080 x 1350 pixels

- Landscape: 1080 x 566 pixels

Canva makes it easy to select the correct size when creating a new design by offering predefined templates. When optimizing for Instagram, it's important to remember that Instagram displays images at a width of 1080 pixels. To avoid pixelation, always ensure that your images are at least 1080 pixels wide. Anything smaller may result in blurry, low-quality images.

- Instagram Stories:

Instagram Stories occupy a full vertical screen, making them ideal for capturing attention. The dimensions are crucial for ensuring your images fill the screen without cropping important parts.

- Dimensions: 1080 x 1920 pixels

Since Stories only last for 24 hours (unless saved in Highlights), you want to make sure your graphics are as engaging as possible. Canva's Instagram Story templates allow you to create professional-looking stories with animations, images, and text overlays that perfectly fit the required dimensions.

- Instagram Reels:

Reels are Instagram's answer to TikTok—short, vertical videos designed for high engagement. For optimal results, your video should be formatted specifically for vertical viewing.

- Dimensions: 1080 x 1920 pixels

Always ensure that your most important content is centered, as Instagram crops the top and bottom of your video for previews on the feed.

Facebook

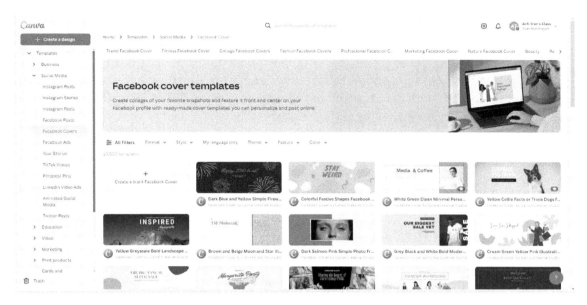

As the largest social media platform, Facebook offers a wide range of content types, including posts, stories, and cover photos. Each of these content formats has its own recommended dimensions to ensure that your designs are displayed crisply and attractively.

- Facebook Feed Posts:

Feed posts on Facebook can be in square or landscape formats, depending on the type of content you're sharing. The most common types of posts are image posts, link previews, and video content.

- Square: 1200 x 1200 pixels

- Landscape: 1200 x 630 pixels

To optimize your Facebook posts, make sure the images you design in Canva meet these resolution requirements. Higher resolution images help ensure that your graphics appear sharp and clear, even on large screens.

- Facebook Cover Photo:

The Facebook cover photo is one of the most prominent design elements on your page. It is displayed at the top of your profile or business page, so it's important that it is eye-catching and properly sized.

- Desktop Dimensions: 820 x 312 pixels

- Mobile Dimensions: 640 x 360 pixels

Since the cover photo is cropped differently depending on the device being used, it's crucial to design with both desktop and mobile views in mind. When using Canva, you can use guides to make sure that essential elements of your design are visible on both platforms.

- Facebook Stories:

Like Instagram, Facebook also has Stories, which are designed to take up the full vertical space of the screen.

- Dimensions: 1080 x 1920 pixels

Canva's Story templates allow you to quickly create engaging, full-screen content that is optimized for both mobile and desktop viewing on Facebook.

Twitter

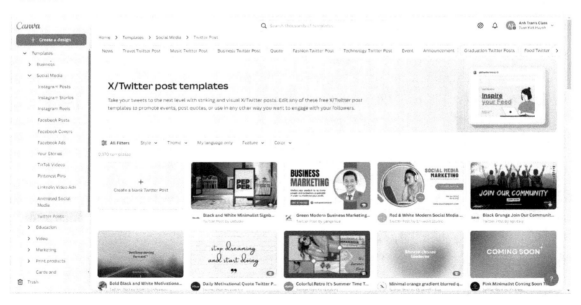

Twitter is a fast-paced platform where visuals can help your posts stand out in a crowded timeline. Whether you're sharing images, infographics, or videos, ensuring the right dimensions for each format will enhance the visibility of your content.

- Twitter Feed Images:

Twitter supports single-image, multi-image, and GIF posts, each with its own recommended size. For single-image tweets, using the correct aspect ratio is essential to avoid cropping.

- Recommended Dimensions: 1200 x 675 pixels

Designing your Twitter graphics at this resolution ensures that they display correctly across all devices. Canva provides easy-to-use templates for Twitter posts that maintain this aspect ratio, allowing you to create visually appealing designs with ease.

- Twitter Header Photo:

Your Twitter header photo is a large image displayed at the top of your profile. Like Facebook's cover photo, it's important to optimize this space to reflect your brand or personality.

- Recommended Dimensions: 1500 x 500 pixels

Canva offers a variety of header templates, allowing you to create a design that fits Twitter's size specifications while maintaining a professional appearance.

LinkedIn

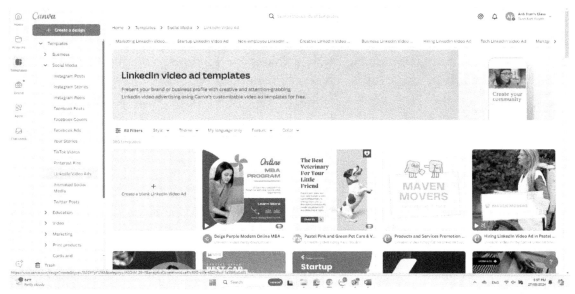

LinkedIn, being a professional networking platform, has specific requirements for profile and company page images, as well as content like posts and banners. Using the correct dimensions ensures your LinkedIn graphics look polished and professional.

- LinkedIn Posts:

LinkedIn post images can be either square or rectangular. The recommended size ensures that your visuals display clearly across both desktop and mobile views.

  - Recommended Dimensions: 1200 x 627 pixels

If you're sharing links or articles, make sure to optimize the image preview that accompanies the post, as this can significantly impact engagement. Canva's LinkedIn post templates are designed to meet these specifications.

- LinkedIn Cover Photo:

Both individual profiles and company pages have a header image, which serves as a banner at the top of the page.

  - Profile Header Dimensions: 1584 x 396 pixels

  - Company Page Header Dimensions: 1536 x 768 pixels

When creating cover photos, Canva's templates ensure that you can place important elements like logos or text in a way that they won't be cropped out by LinkedIn's layout.

Pinterest

Pinterest is a visual discovery platform where image quality and dimensions are crucial for getting more visibility. Optimizing your graphics for Pinterest ensures that your pins appear prominently in users' feeds and search results.

- Standard Pin Size:

The optimal pin size on Pinterest is a vertical image, as these perform better than square or landscape pins.

  - Recommended Dimensions: 1000 x 1500 pixels

Canva offers Pinterest-specific templates that allow you to create beautiful pins with text overlays, images, and icons. When designing, be mindful that Pinterest tends to favor high-quality, vertical images.

- Pinterest Infographics:

Infographics are highly popular on Pinterest because they offer a lot of information in a visually appealing format.

- Recommended Dimensions: 1000 x 3000 pixels

When creating infographics in Canva, focus on creating clean, readable designs with a logical flow. Keep important text and visuals within the center of your design to avoid any cropping.

YouTube

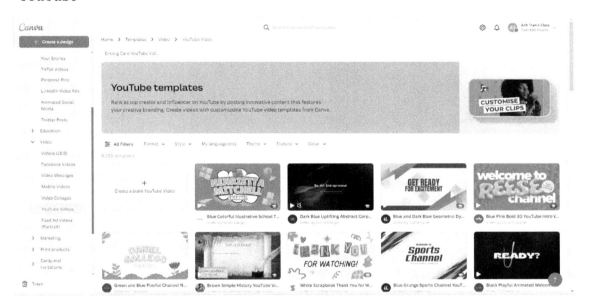

YouTube is a video platform, but it also relies heavily on visual graphics like channel art, video thumbnails, and social media posts to attract viewers.

- *YouTube Channel Art:*

Channel art is the banner image displayed at the top of your YouTube channel. It appears differently across devices, so optimizing the dimensions is critical.

- Recommended Dimensions: 2560 x 1440 pixels

Canva offers pre-sized templates for YouTube channel art, ensuring that you can design banners that look great on desktops, tablets, and mobile devices without worrying about cropping or low resolution.

- *YouTube Video Thumbnails:*

Thumbnails are the first thing viewers see when browsing videos, making them a critical part of your video's success.

- Recommended Dimensions: 1280 x 720 pixels

Canva provides templates for creating attention-grabbing thumbnails. Be sure to use bold colors, clear text, and engaging visuals to attract more clicks.

By using Canva's design tools and templates, you can ensure your designs are optimized for every social media platform, saving you time while enhancing your online presence. Always stay updated with platform changes to ensure your dimensions remain current, as social media platforms occasionally adjust their display sizes.

5.2 Using Canva for Videos

As the demand for video content continues to grow, Canva has become an essential tool for individuals and businesses alike to create engaging, professional-quality videos without the need for complex software. Whether you're designing a short social media clip, an informative video presentation, or a dynamic advertisement, Canva offers an array of easy-to-use tools to get the job done.

In this chapter, we will explore how you can harness Canva's video editing capabilities. We'll start with video templates and customization, which allow you to quickly create videos by modifying pre-designed layouts and elements, enabling you to produce high-quality videos in no time.

5.2.1 Video Templates and Customization

Canva provides a vast library of pre-made video templates tailored to various themes, social platforms, and purposes. From social media advertisements and promotional videos to tutorials and event announcements, these templates are designed to simplify the process of creating polished videos. By using these templates, you eliminate the guesswork involved in video design, making it easier for even a beginner to produce professional-looking content.

Finding the Right Video Template

The first step in creating your video is selecting an appropriate template. Canva's video template library is categorized based on the type of video you want to create, such as social media videos, YouTube intros, presentations, and more. Here's how you can find the perfect template:

1. Explore Canva's Video Template Library: Start by selecting the Videos section from Canva's homepage or the template search bar. Here, you can browse through templates by using specific keywords like "Instagram Story video," "YouTube intro," or "Facebook ad."

You can also filter templates based on categories such as "Business," "Education," or "Marketing."

2. Search by Platform: Canva templates are optimized for various platforms. You'll find options for Instagram, Facebook, TikTok, YouTube, and more. These templates are designed with the correct aspect ratios (e.g., vertical videos for Instagram Stories or square videos for Instagram posts) and dimensions to ensure that your video looks great across all devices.

3. Consider the Purpose of Your Video: Different templates serve different purposes. For example, if you're creating a product demo, you might want to choose a template with clean, simple designs that allow the product to be the focal point. If your goal is to create an announcement or event invitation, choose a template with bold text and visual effects to grab attention quickly.

Customizing Your Video Template

Once you've chosen a template, Canva makes it easy to customize it to fit your brand, message, or style. Here are the key customization features you can use:

1. Changing Text and Typography

Every video template comes with editable text placeholders. You can customize these placeholders to convey your message by clicking directly on the text boxes.

- Editing Text Content: Replace the placeholder text with your own copy. Make sure your text is concise and impactful, especially in short videos, where you have limited time to capture the viewer's attention.

- Font Selection: Canva offers a wide variety of fonts to match your brand's voice. Whether you need a modern, sleek font for a tech-related video or a bold, playful font for an event announcement, Canva has you covered. You can also upload your own fonts if you're using Canva Pro, ensuring your video remains consistent with your brand identity.

- Font Customization: Adjust the size, color, and style (bold, italic, underline) to make the text stand out or blend with the background. You can also apply text effects like shadows, outlines, and glow to add a visual pop.

- Text Animation: One of Canva's most powerful features for videos is the ability to animate text. You can choose from effects like fade-in, slide, typewriter, or bounce to create dynamic transitions that make your video more engaging.

2. Replacing or Adding Visual Elements

Video templates often come with placeholders for images, icons, and other visual elements. Customizing these elements is a crucial part of making the template your own.

- Images: You can replace any existing images in the template with your own visuals or search Canva's extensive stock photo library. Simply drag and drop the new image into the placeholder, and Canva will automatically crop or resize it to fit.

- Video Clips: Some templates feature built-in video clips. You can replace these with your own clips by uploading them from your device or selecting from Canva's stock videos. Canva's stock library includes thousands of free and premium video clips that cover a wide range of themes, from nature scenes to urban landscapes to business settings.

- Graphics and Icons: Enhance your video by adding custom icons, illustrations, or stickers from Canva's graphic library. Whether you're looking to add a logo, a call-to-action button, or decorative icons, Canva provides plenty of options.

3. Adjusting Colors and Themes

Color plays an essential role in video design, and Canva makes it simple to apply consistent color schemes to your entire video.

- Color Matching Your Brand: If you have brand colors, you can easily apply them to your video by changing the color of text, backgrounds, and other elements. Canva allows you to save brand colors using the Brand Kit feature (available in Canva Pro), so you can quickly access and apply them to future designs.

- Theme Consistency: Ensure that the colors used in your video align with your overall theme. For example, if you're creating a calming, nature-inspired video, soft greens and blues might work best. On the other hand, bold reds and yellows may be more suitable for a dynamic, high-energy promotion.

- Gradients and Patterns: In addition to solid colors, Canva lets you apply gradients and patterns to backgrounds and elements, adding depth and texture to your video.

4. Adding Music and Sound Effects

Audio is a vital component of any video. Canva allows you to add background music or sound effects to complement your visuals.

- Choosing the Right Music: Canva offers a library of free and premium music tracks that you can add to your video. Whether you need upbeat tunes for a product launch or soft background music for a tutorial, you'll find options to suit your needs.

- Uploading Custom Audio: If you already have specific music or voiceover files, you can upload them directly to your Canva project. Simply drag the audio file into your timeline and adjust its position and volume as needed.

- Syncing Audio with Visuals: It's essential to ensure that your audio syncs well with your video content. Canva provides basic timeline controls that allow you to trim, move, and adjust the timing of your audio files to match your video perfectly.

5. Working with Timelines and Transitions

Canva's timeline feature allows you to control the timing and sequence of elements in your video, making it easier to coordinate text, visuals, and effects.

- Adjusting Element Duration: Each element in your video (e.g., text, images, and animations) has its own duration on the timeline. You can extend or shorten the amount of time an element appears in the video by dragging its edges on the timeline.

- Adding Transitions Between Clips: Transitions create smooth visual flows between different video clips or scenes. Canva offers various transition effects, such as fades, slides, and wipes. Choose a transition that matches the mood and style of your video, ensuring the flow from one scene to the next feels natural and cohesive.

- Fine-Tuning with Preview: After customizing your template, you can preview the entire video to check for any issues. Ensure that transitions, animations, and audio align smoothly, and make adjustments where necessary.

6. Saving and Exporting Your Custom Video

Once you've finalized your video, Canva allows you to download it in multiple formats. For most platforms, downloading in MP4 format is the best option, as it ensures the highest quality. You can also adjust the resolution of your video depending on where you plan to publish it (e.g., social media, websites, or presentations).

- Resolution Options: Canva provides options to download videos in different resolutions (e.g., 720p, 1080p), allowing you to balance quality and file size.

- Saving Drafts: If your video is still a work in progress, Canva allows you to save drafts so you can return to them later without losing any changes.

With Canva's video templates and customization tools, creating high-quality, professional videos becomes an effortless process. Whether you're looking to produce engaging social media content, business promotions, or personal projects, Canva's intuitive interface empowers you to turn your creative ideas into visually stunning videos.

5.2.2 Adding Text, Music, and Transitions

Videos are an essential form of content, especially in today's digital age, where social media thrives on dynamic and engaging material. With Canva, creating and enhancing videos is straightforward, thanks to the intuitive interface and the ability to add elements like text, music, and transitions, which are crucial for engaging your audience.

Adding Text to Videos

Text is a powerful tool in video content. Whether you're creating an informative explainer video or an eye-catching promotional piece, adding text can help you convey your message more effectively.

1. The Role of Text in Videos

Text plays several roles in a video: it can provide clarity, emphasize key points, or simply add aesthetic value. For example:

- Titles: A title at the beginning of a video can give viewers a clear understanding of what the video is about. This is particularly useful in social media posts where videos autoplay without sound.

- Subtitles: Adding subtitles or captions is essential for accessibility and for viewers who might watch videos with the sound off. It can also help reinforce the message you're communicating.

- Annotations: You can use text to highlight key moments or explain complex information. This can be done subtly through small on-screen text that guides viewers through the video.

2. Steps to Add Text in Canva Videos

Canva's text feature is robust, allowing for customization while keeping the process simple:

- *Step 1: Select Your Video Template or Upload*

To begin, you'll either choose a video template or upload your video file. Once you're in the Canva video editor, you'll see the video timeline and the main canvas where the video will play.

- *Step 2: Click on the "Text" Option*

On the left sidebar, you'll find the "Text" option. Clicking this will open a range of preset text options, from simple headers to more stylized and animated text. You can also create your text box from scratch.

- *Step 3: Customize the Text*

Once you've added a text box, you can drag it to the desired position on the video. Canva allows full customization of text properties, including:

- Font style: Canva offers a wide variety of fonts, from professional to playful, allowing you to match your text style with your brand or video tone.

- Size and color: Adjust the size and color of the text to ensure it's easily visible against the video background.

- Alignment and Spacing: You can align your text horizontally and vertically, and adjust letter spacing and line height for a polished look.

- *Step 4: Timing the Text*

The ability to control when text appears and disappears is crucial in video editing. Canva allows you to adjust the timing of each text layer on the video timeline. Simply drag the edges of the text block in the timeline to extend or shorten its duration.

3. Best Practices for Adding Text

- Keep it Concise: While text can be incredibly useful, less is often more. Try to convey your message in as few words as possible so that it's easy for viewers to digest.

- Choose Readable Fonts: Avoid overly stylized fonts that may be hard to read, especially on small screens like mobile devices.

- Align with the Video's Tone: The text style should complement the tone of the video. A playful font works for an upbeat video, while a professional serif font might suit a corporate presentation.

- Use Animations Sparingly: Canva offers animated text options, but these should be used sparingly to avoid overwhelming your viewers.

Adding Music to Videos

Music can dramatically enhance the emotional appeal and engagement level of your videos. Whether you're adding background music to set the mood or using sound effects to emphasize certain moments, Canva makes it simple to integrate audio into your projects.

1. The Importance of Music in Video Content

Music is often the heartbeat of a video. It can:

- Set the Tone: A slow, ambient track can make a video feel calming and introspective, while a fast-paced beat can make it feel exciting and energetic.

- Create Emotional Connections: Music can invoke emotions that help viewers connect with your content on a deeper level, making them more likely to engage with and remember it.

- Improve Engagement: Videos with appropriate background music tend to hold the attention of viewers longer than those without.

2. Steps to Add Music in Canva Videos

Canva allows you to easily incorporate audio tracks into your video designs:

- Step 1: Choose a Video or Upload

Start by choosing a template that fits your video project or upload your own video file. Once your video is ready, move to the editing stage.

- Step 2: Click on "Audio" in the Sidebar

In Canva's editor, select the "Audio" tab from the left-side menu. This will open a library of music tracks that are available for use. You can filter these by genre, mood, or even by instruments to find the perfect track for your video.

- Step 3: Upload Your Own Music (Optional)

If you have a specific music track or sound effect that you want to use, Canva allows you to upload your own audio file by clicking the "Uploads" tab. Once uploaded, you can drag and drop the track into your timeline.

- Step 4: Sync Music with Your Video

Once the music is added, you can adjust its placement and duration on the timeline. If the track is longer than the video, you can trim it to fit. Canva also allows you to fade in and fade out the audio for smooth transitions between scenes.

- Step 5: Adjust the Volume

To ensure the music doesn't overpower any other elements, such as voiceover or important sound effects, adjust the volume of the track in Canva's audio settings. You can set different volume levels for different parts of the track if necessary.

3. Best Practices for Adding Music

- Match the Music to the Mood: Choose a track that complements the mood and message of your video. For example, a relaxing video might benefit from soft instrumental music, while an energetic promotion could use a fast-paced beat.

- Use Music as Background Support: The music should support the video's content rather than distract from it. Ensure it enhances the message, but doesn't compete with voiceovers or other key audio elements.

- Mind Copyright Issues: If you're uploading your video to social platforms, make sure to use royalty-free music or music you have the rights to. Canva provides a library of royalty-free tracks, so using one of their selections can help you avoid copyright issues.

Adding Transitions to Videos

Transitions are a subtle but effective way to keep your video flowing smoothly from one scene to the next. Canva offers a variety of transition options to help make your video more polished and professional.

1. The Purpose of Transitions

Transitions serve as the glue between different clips or elements in your video. They can:

- Create a Seamless Flow: Transitions can prevent your video from feeling disjointed by guiding viewers smoothly from one scene to the next.

- Emphasize Changes in Scenes: A dramatic transition can signal a shift in tone or highlight a significant moment in the video.

2. Steps to Add Transitions in Canva

Canva provides several easy-to-use transition options to help enhance your video:

- *Step 1: Break Your Video into Scenes*

In the Canva video editor, your video will be divided into individual clips or scenes. To add transitions between these scenes, first ensure the video is segmented appropriately.

- *Step 2: Select the Transition Option*

Between each scene, you'll notice a small icon representing a transition. Click on this icon to open Canva's transition menu, which offers several options such as fades, wipes, and slides.

- *Step 3: Customize Transition Settings*

After selecting a transition type, you can customize its speed and duration. A longer transition can create a more relaxed flow, while shorter ones keep the video feeling fast-paced and dynamic.

- Step 4: Preview and Adjust

Always preview your video after applying transitions to ensure they feel smooth and appropriate for the content. Adjust the timing or transition style as needed to achieve the desired effect.

3. Best Practices for Adding Transitions

- Keep It Simple: Overusing transitions can make your video feel chaotic. Stick to one or two types of transitions throughout the video for a cohesive feel.

- Match the Transition to the Content: Choose transitions that suit the tone and pacing of your video. For example, a gentle fade may work well in a calm, informative video, while a slide transition could add energy to a promotional video.

By effectively combining text, music, and transitions, Canva users can elevate their videos from simple clips to polished and engaging content. With these tools, your videos will not only capture the attention of viewers but also convey your message clearly and professionally.

5.3 Scheduling and Posting Directly from Canva

In the digital age, maintaining a consistent social media presence is crucial for businesses, influencers, and even individuals aiming to grow their online presence. One of the key challenges is posting consistently and at the right times to engage your audience. Canva offers a robust scheduling and posting feature that helps users plan and automate their social media content. This feature, combined with Canva's design capabilities, allows you to create, schedule, and post visually appealing content all from one platform. In this section, we'll explore how to connect your social media accounts to Canva and use its scheduling features to streamline your content distribution.

5.3.1 Connecting Social Media Accounts

To take full advantage of Canva's scheduling and posting features, you need to link your social media accounts directly to the platform. Canva supports popular social media platforms like Facebook, Instagram, Twitter, Pinterest, and LinkedIn, allowing users to post directly from Canva to these platforms.

Step-by-Step Guide to Connecting Social Media Accounts

1. Accessing the Content Planner

To begin the process, navigate to the Content Planner on the left side of Canva's dashboard. The Content Planner is your hub for scheduling posts. Once you've clicked on the Content Planner, you'll see a calendar interface where you can schedule and manage your upcoming posts.

2. Selecting the "Connect" Option

In the Content Planner, click on the "Create a Post" button or select a specific date on the calendar. You'll be prompted to connect your social media accounts if you haven't already. Canva will display a list of social platforms, such as Instagram, Facebook, Twitter, Pinterest, and LinkedIn, that you can connect to.

3. Authorizing Your Accounts

After selecting the platform you want to connect, Canva will guide you through the authorization process. This step is essential to grant Canva permission to post on your behalf. You'll be asked to log in to the selected social media account and approve the necessary permissions.

- For Instagram: You'll need to log in to your Instagram account and ensure that it's either a Business or Creator account, as personal accounts are not supported for direct posting. Additionally, you'll need to link your Instagram account to a Facebook page since Instagram's API requires this for automated posting.

- For Facebook: You'll log in to your Facebook account and select the pages or profiles you want to link. Canva allows direct posting to Facebook business pages.

- For Twitter, Pinterest, and LinkedIn: The process is similar. You log in, grant Canva access, and select the profiles or pages to connect.

4. Verifying the Connection

Once the account is authorized, Canva will display the connected profile. You'll see a checkmark or a confirmation message indicating that your social media account is now linked and ready for scheduling. You can connect multiple accounts across different platforms, making it easier to manage all your social media profiles from one place.

Benefits of Connecting Social Media Accounts to Canva

- Efficiency: By connecting your accounts directly to Canva, you eliminate the need to download designs and manually upload them to each platform. Canva handles the posting process for you, saving you time and reducing the risk of human error.

- Consistency: The ability to schedule posts ahead of time helps ensure that you maintain a consistent posting schedule, even if you're unavailable during peak times.

- Centralized Management: Canva acts as a central hub where you can manage multiple social media platforms. This is particularly useful for social media managers, content creators, or businesses with an active presence on more than one platform.

- Creative Flexibility: Canva's built-in design tools allow you to create a wide range of visual content (e.g., static images, carousels, videos) and post them directly from the platform, allowing for seamless creative control.

5.3.2 Using Canva's Content Planner

The Content Planner is one of Canva's most powerful features for anyone managing social media accounts. It allows users to schedule posts directly from Canva to their social media platforms, helping you stay organized and keep a consistent posting schedule. This section will guide you through understanding and effectively using Canva's Content Planner, from setting up a post schedule to managing multiple social media platforms simultaneously.

1. Introduction to Canva's Content Planner

Canva's Content Planner is a built-in tool that simplifies the process of scheduling social media posts. Instead of creating designs in Canva and then switching to another tool for scheduling, Canva integrates everything into one seamless workflow. This feature is especially beneficial for small business owners, social media managers, and influencers who need to plan and maintain a cohesive content strategy.

The Content Planner allows you to:

- Plan your social media content in advance.

- Schedule posts for Instagram, Facebook, Twitter, LinkedIn, Pinterest, and other supported platforms.

- View your scheduled posts in a calendar layout.

- Reschedule or edit posts as needed.

- Save time by scheduling posts directly from Canva's design interface.

The planner is available to both free and Canva Pro users, though Pro users enjoy additional features such as unlimited social media accounts, access to premium templates, and team collaboration tools.

2. Setting Up the Content Planner

Before you start using the Content Planner, you need to connect your social media accounts to Canva. This connection allows Canva to post on your behalf and manage your content calendar.

2.1 Connecting Social Media Accounts

To link your social media accounts:

1. Navigate to the Content Planner: On Canva's main dashboard, click on the "Content Planner" option in the left-hand menu.

2. Connect an Account: In the Content Planner interface, you'll see an option to "Connect Account." Click this and choose the platform you want to connect, such as Instagram, Facebook, or Twitter.

3. Authorize Canva: Once you select a platform, you'll be prompted to authorize Canva to post on your behalf. Follow the steps to log into your social media account and grant permission.

4. Repeat for Additional Accounts: If you manage multiple social media accounts, repeat the process to connect additional profiles. Canva allows you to connect several platforms for seamless content management.

After connecting your accounts, you'll be able to schedule posts to any of these platforms directly from the Content Planner. You can also manage multiple profiles, which is particularly useful for agencies or businesses with several brands.

2.2 Exploring the Content Planner Interface

Once your accounts are connected, you can start scheduling posts. The interface of the Content Planner is designed to be user-friendly, displaying your content in a calendar view. Here's what you can expect to see:

- Monthly Calendar: The Content Planner shows a monthly calendar view by default, allowing you to see your scheduled posts for the entire month. Each scheduled post appears as a thumbnail of your design, making it easy to review and adjust your content at a glance.

- Daily View: You can click on any specific day to get a more detailed view of the scheduled posts. This is helpful if you are managing multiple posts in a single day.

- Add a Post: There's an option to "Add a New Post" directly from the planner. This allows you to schedule new content without having to exit the Content Planner.

- Drag-and-Drop Scheduling: Canva's Content Planner features a drag-and-drop function, letting you easily move posts to different days if you need to adjust your schedule.

- Filter by Account: If you manage multiple social media accounts, you can filter your scheduled posts by the specific account. This ensures you stay organized and don't post the same content across different accounts unless intended.

3. Scheduling Posts with the Content Planner

Once your social media accounts are connected, you're ready to start scheduling posts. Canva makes this process straightforward by integrating the scheduling functionality directly into the design creation workflow.

3.1 Scheduling from the Design Editor

One of the most convenient aspects of Canva's Content Planner is the ability to schedule a post directly from the design editor. Here's how:

1. Create Your Design: Start by designing your post as you normally would. This could be anything from an Instagram story to a Facebook post or a Twitter image.

2. Click the Share Button: Once your design is complete, click the "Share" button in the top-right corner of the editor.

3. Choose Schedule: In the sharing options, select "Schedule" to open the Content Planner.

4. Select a Platform: Choose which social media platform you want to post to. If you're managing multiple accounts, make sure to select the correct one.

5. Choose a Date and Time: After selecting the platform, pick the date and time you want the post to go live. Canva uses your local time zone, so be mindful if you're targeting audiences in different regions.

6. Schedule the Post: Once everything is set, click "Schedule Post." Your design will now appear in the Content Planner, ready to be automatically published at the designated time.

3.2 Scheduling Multiple Posts

If you're working on a campaign or simply need to schedule multiple posts at once, Canva allows you to schedule several posts from the same design. This is particularly useful for creating consistent content across platforms. Here's how to schedule multiple posts:

1. Select Multiple Accounts: When scheduling a post, you have the option to select more than one social media account. This allows you to post the same content on different platforms (e.g., Instagram and Facebook) at the same time.

2. Customize for Each Platform: Canva lets you customize the post for each platform. For instance, you might want to use different hashtags on Instagram than you would on Twitter, or you might want to adjust the image dimensions to suit each platform.

3. Schedule in Bulk: Once you've made your adjustments, you can schedule the posts to all selected platforms in one go, saving time and ensuring consistency.

3.3 Editing and Rescheduling Posts

If you need to make changes to a scheduled post, Canva allows you to edit or reschedule it before it goes live. This is how you can modify a post:

1. Open the Content Planner: Go to the Content Planner and locate the post you want to edit.

2. Click on the Post: Click on the scheduled post to open its details. You can change the date, time, or even edit the design itself.

3. Reschedule or Edit Content: Make any necessary changes and either save the post or reschedule it for a different time.

This flexibility is key for staying agile with your content strategy, especially if you need to react to real-time events or trends.

4. Best Practices for Using Canva's Content Planner

While Canva's Content Planner makes scheduling posts easier, there are some best practices to keep in mind to ensure you're maximizing its potential and staying organized.

4.1 Plan Ahead for Consistency

Planning your social media content in advance is one of the most effective ways to maintain a consistent posting schedule. A regular posting cadence helps you stay top of mind with your audience and keeps your content flowing without scrambling at the last minute. Use the monthly view in the Content Planner to lay out your content strategy and ensure you're posting regularly.

4.2 Create a Balanced Content Mix

Make sure you're offering a variety of content to keep your audience engaged. Your posts should include a mix of promotional content, informative or educational material, and interactive content like polls or questions. Canva's templates and design tools make it easy to create different types of content, so use this to your advantage and avoid repetitive posts.

4.3 Monitor Analytics and Adjust

Although Canva's Content Planner helps with scheduling, you should still monitor the performance of your posts through your social media platform's analytics tools. Use these insights to adjust your strategy and fine-tune your content. For example, if you notice that certain types of posts perform better at specific times, adjust your schedule in Canva accordingly.

4.4 Collaborate with Your Team

If you're working with a team, Canva's collaboration tools allow multiple people to access and contribute to the Content Planner. Assign roles such as designer, editor, or social media manager, so everyone can play their part in the content creation process. This ensures that your team stays coordinated and that content is reviewed before it's posted.

5. Conclusion

Canva's Content Planner is a game-changer for social media management. By integrating the design and scheduling process into one platform, Canva simplifies the workflow for individuals and teams alike. Whether you're scheduling a single post or managing an entire month's worth of content, the Content Planner helps you stay organized, consistent, and efficient with your social media strategy.

With the ability to plan, schedule, and manage posts across multiple platforms, Canva's Content Planner offers a streamlined solution that saves time and effort, allowing you to focus on what matters most—creating engaging content that resonates with your audience.

CHAPTER VI
Printing and Exporting Your Designs

6.1 Downloading Your Designs

Once you've completed your design in Canva, the next critical step is downloading it for use in various contexts. Canva offers several download options, allowing you to export your design in the format that best suits your needs, whether it's for printing, web use, presentations, or videos. The flexibility in download options makes Canva an incredibly versatile tool, as different projects may require different file formats, quality settings, and even specific export features like transparent backgrounds or multiple pages.

Before diving into the various file formats available, it's essential to consider your end goal. The output format can significantly impact the quality of your design, its appearance on different platforms, and even the file size. For example, an image optimized for social media sharing may not have the same resolution requirements as one meant for large-scale printing. Likewise, downloading a video requires different settings than downloading a static image.

In this section, we'll explore the key considerations when downloading designs and how to choose the appropriate settings for different purposes

6.1.1 Choosing the Right File Format

Choosing the correct file format when downloading your Canva design is crucial for ensuring your design looks professional and functions as intended. Canva supports various file formats, each tailored for specific uses. Whether you are exporting a high-resolution image for print, a compressed file for the web, or a multi-page PDF for presentations, understanding the pros and cons of each format will help you achieve the best results.

Commonly Used File Formats

Let's take a look at the different file formats Canva offers and when you should choose each:

1. PNG (Portable Network Graphics)

The PNG format is one of the most popular choices for exporting images, particularly for web use. PNG is ideal when you want to preserve high quality and ensure that your design looks crisp and clean. It is a lossless format, meaning that no data is lost when the file is compressed. This makes PNG a great option when the highest possible image quality is a priority.

Key Features of PNG:

- High Quality: PNG files maintain their clarity even after being compressed, which is essential for designs that require sharp edges, such as logos, graphics with text, or detailed illustrations.

- Transparency: One of the major advantages of PNG is the ability to save images with transparent backgrounds. This feature is invaluable for logos, icons, or any design that needs to be placed over other backgrounds without a white box around it.

- Large File Size: The downside of PNG is that it tends to produce larger file sizes compared to other formats. This could be an issue if you need to upload the image to a website that has file size restrictions or if you're sharing the file with others via email or cloud storage.

When to Use PNG:

- For logos, icons, or illustrations that require transparency.

- When you need a high-quality image for digital use, such as on websites or in presentations.

- For social media graphics where clarity is crucial.

2. JPG (Joint Photographic Experts Group)

JPG is another widely used image format, particularly for web use. However, unlike PNG, JPG is a lossy format, meaning some quality is sacrificed when the file is compressed. This makes JPG files much smaller than PNG, but there is a trade-off in terms of image sharpness and detail.

Key Features of JPG:

- Compressed File Size: JPG is highly compressed, making it an excellent choice for situations where file size matters, such as uploading images to a website or sending via email.

- Good for Photographs: JPG is best suited for photographs or complex images with many colors. It handles gradients and soft transitions between colors better than PNG, making it ideal for designs that incorporate photos.

- No Transparency: Unlike PNG, JPG does not support transparent backgrounds. This limits its use for designs that need to be layered on top of other elements.

When to Use JPG:

- For designs that include photos or complex images with many colors.

- When you need a smaller file size for quicker load times on websites or for sharing via email.

- For social media posts where file size limits might apply, but transparency is not needed.

3. PDF (Portable Document Format)

PDF is one of the most versatile formats offered by Canva, especially for multi-page designs, such as brochures, presentations, and eBooks. A PDF file preserves the layout, fonts, and images of your design, ensuring that it looks the same no matter where or how it's viewed. Canva offers two types of PDF exports: PDF Standard and PDF Print.

- PDF Standard: This option is ideal for sharing online or via email, as it compresses the file size while still maintaining good quality. It is suitable for digital documents where recipients will view them on-screen.

- PDF Print: As the name suggests, this option is optimized for printing. It retains the highest resolution possible, ensuring that your design prints in the sharpest quality. Canva also allows you to include crop marks and bleed in your PDF, which is necessary for professional printing to avoid unintentional white borders.

Key Features of PDF:

- Preserves Design Layout: Your design will look exactly as intended, whether viewed digitally or in print.

- Supports Multiple Pages: PDFs are perfect for multi-page documents like presentations, portfolios, and brochures.

- Adjustable Quality: Choose between standard quality for digital sharing or high-quality resolution for printing.

When to Use PDF:

- For brochures, presentations, resumes, or eBooks that will be viewed online or printed.

- When you need a consistent, professional look across different devices or platforms.

- For multi-page documents that need to be shared or printed in high resolution.

4. MP4 (Video)

MP4 is the standard format for exporting video designs in Canva. This format is highly compressed, ensuring that your videos are small enough to be easily shared or uploaded to platforms like YouTube, Instagram, or Facebook without sacrificing too much quality.

Key Features of MP4:

- Small File Size: MP4 compresses video files, making them easy to share and upload.

- High Compatibility: MP4 is compatible with nearly every video player, web browser, and social media platform, making it a reliable choice for sharing video content.

- Quality: Although compressed, MP4 files maintain good video quality, which is especially important for social media videos or short presentations.

When to Use MP4:

- For social media videos, animations, or presentations that include motion.

- When you need a small file size for easy sharing or quick uploads.

- For video content that will be viewed on multiple platforms, ensuring compatibility.

5. GIF (Graphics Interchange Format)

GIF is a popular format for short, looping animations and is frequently used for memes, social media, or email marketing. Canva allows you to export simple animations as GIFs, which can be a fun way to create engaging content.

Key Features of GIF:

- Short Animations: GIFs are perfect for short, looping animations that catch the viewer's attention.

- Lower Quality: Because GIFs are optimized for fast loading, the image quality is lower than in formats like MP4.

- No Sound: Unlike MP4, GIFs do not support sound, making them suitable only for simple animations.

When to Use GIF:

- For social media posts, memes, or email campaigns where a short, engaging animation is required.

- When you want to create lightweight, fast-loading content.

- For short, looped animations without sound.

Conclusion: Making the Right Choice

The right file format depends on your project goals and the platform where your design will be used. PNG is ideal for high-quality images and transparency, while JPG works best for photos or when file size matters. PDF is essential for printing or sharing multi-page designs, while MP4 and GIF cover your video and animation needs. Understanding these formats and their applications will ensure that your Canva designs always look professional and perform as expected, no matter where they're displayed.

6.1.2 Quality and Resolution Settings

When it comes to downloading your designs, one of the most important factors to consider is the quality and resolution settings of your export. These settings can make or break the appearance of your design, whether it's viewed digitally or printed. Understanding how to adjust these settings appropriately ensures that your designs are crisp, clear, and meet the specific needs of your project.

Understanding Image Resolution

Resolution refers to the number of pixels displayed per inch (PPI) in an image. In simple terms, the higher the resolution, the more pixels there are in an inch of your design, which results in a sharper and clearer image. Conversely, a low-resolution image may appear pixelated or blurry, especially when enlarged. In Canva, ensuring that your design has the correct resolution is key to maintaining quality, whether your goal is to print or share it digitally.

Typically, there are two main resolution standards to consider:

- 72 PPI (Pixels Per Inch): This is the standard for most web-based designs and digital displays. While sufficient for online use, it is usually too low for print purposes, resulting in images that look fuzzy or grainy when printed.

- 300 PPI (Pixels Per Inch): This is the industry standard for high-quality prints. Any design that you intend to print should ideally be exported at 300 PPI to ensure that it looks professional and crisp on paper.

Canva allows you to control resolution indirectly by selecting appropriate file formats and ensuring you download in high quality, but understanding the basics of resolution is critical for knowing when and how to use it.

Choosing the Right Resolution for Different Use Cases

When exporting a design in Canva, the use case for that design should dictate the resolution you choose. Here are some common scenarios and recommendations for each:

1. Digital or Online Use:

For designs intended for websites, social media, presentations, or any other digital medium, a resolution of 72 PPI is typically sufficient. These designs do not need to be ultra-sharp since they will be displayed on screens, which have their own pixel density. Reducing the resolution here can also help minimize file size, making the design faster to load or share online.

2. Print Use:

If your design is destined for print — whether it's a flyer, poster, business card, or brochure — you'll need a resolution of at least 300 PPI. High-resolution exports ensure that your images, text, and graphics retain their sharpness and clarity when transferred to paper. Any design that's under 300 PPI might result in a subpar printout, with blurry text or grainy images.

3. Large-Format Print:

For larger prints such as banners, billboards, or posters, you'll still want a high-resolution export to avoid pixelation when the image is blown up. However, in some cases, printers can work with slightly lower resolutions like 150 PPI, as viewers will generally be standing farther away from these large-format prints, which means imperfections may not be as noticeable.

Exporting with Canva: File Formats and Resolution Impact

When you download a design in Canva, the file format you choose has a direct impact on the quality and resolution of your design. Canva offers several file formats to choose from, each with its own strengths and weaknesses in terms of quality, file size, and suitability for different types of projects. Let's break down each file format and its relation to resolution:

1. PNG (Portable Network Graphics)

- Best For: High-quality digital images, web graphics, and logos.

- Resolution: PNG files are lossless, meaning they retain their quality even after multiple edits or saves. When downloaded from Canva, PNGs can be exported in high resolution, making them suitable for both web and print use. Canva allows you to select the resolution manually before exporting, and this is the preferred format when you want sharpness and clarity in your designs.

- File Size: PNGs generally have larger file sizes than JPGs due to their high quality, but they also support transparent backgrounds, making them ideal for web elements like logos or icons.

2. JPG (Joint Photographic Experts Group)

- Best For: Web use, photography, social media images.

- Resolution: JPG files are lossy, meaning some quality is sacrificed in exchange for smaller file sizes. This format is perfect for digital designs that prioritize loading speed over pristine quality. While JPGs can be used for printing, they are generally not ideal for professional print projects due to their tendency to compress and lose details.

- File Size: JPGs are much smaller than PNGs, making them perfect for fast-loading web content. Canva's JPG export option allows you to adjust the quality and file size, which directly affects the resolution.

3. PDF (Portable Document Format)

- Best For: High-quality print designs, multi-page documents, brochures, and flyers.

- Resolution: PDFs are a vector format, which means they can scale up or down without losing quality. When exporting designs for print, PDFs ensure that the design maintains its sharpness and detail, no matter the size. Canva offers two types of PDF exports: "PDF Standard" for digital use, and "PDF Print" for professional printing. PDF Print will ensure the highest quality and resolution for all your print projects.

- File Size: PDF files, particularly PDF Print files, can be quite large due to their high resolution and embedded fonts. However, they are ideal for designs that will be printed professionally, as they ensure no quality is lost during printing.

4. SVG (Scalable Vector Graphics)

- Best For: Logos, icons, and illustrations that need to be resized without losing quality.

- Resolution: SVGs are vector-based, meaning they can scale indefinitely without losing clarity or resolution. This makes them perfect for logos and other designs that need to maintain their quality across various sizes. However, they are not ideal for photographs or complex designs that rely on pixel-based graphics.

- File Size: SVG files are generally small, which makes them an efficient choice for web use. Canva supports SVG export for elements like logos and icons, which require scalability.

5. MP4 (Video)

- Best For: Video designs, social media posts with animations.

- Resolution: MP4 is the most commonly used video format, and Canva supports exporting videos in high definition (HD). When exporting an MP4 video, you can choose between 720p (standard HD) and 1080p (full HD), depending on the platform you're posting on or the level of quality you need.

- File Size: Video file sizes depend on the length of the video and the resolution. Higher resolutions, like 1080p, will naturally produce larger files. If file size is a concern, you might choose a lower resolution or compress the file after exporting.

6. GIF (Graphics Interchange Format)

- Best For: Simple animations and looping designs for digital use.

- Resolution: GIFs are typically low-resolution formats due to their purpose for small, simple animations. Canva allows for GIF export, which works well for fun, short animations or moving elements, but it's not intended for high-resolution print work.

- File Size: GIFs are smaller in size compared to MP4s, making them ideal for quick web use or embedding in emails or websites. However, due to their resolution limitations, they should only be used for small-scale digital designs.

Adjusting Resolution Settings in Canva

Although Canva doesn't offer a direct PPI adjustment tool, you can still ensure high resolution by selecting appropriate file formats and paying attention to the size and quality options during the download process. Here's a simple guide to downloading high-resolution files from Canva:

1. Choose the Right File Format:

For most high-resolution needs, PNG or PDF (Print) should be your go-to choices. If your design involves photography or high levels of detail, opt for PNG. For larger designs or printed materials, PDF Print will ensure crisp quality.

2. Adjust the Size Slider:

Before exporting, Canva allows you to adjust the size of your design. Increasing the size percentage (e.g., from 100% to 200%) increases the overall resolution of your export. Keep in mind, however, that this can result in larger file sizes.

3. Enable Transparent Background (If Needed):

For designs like logos or web graphics, you might need to export with a transparent background. This option is only available for PNG files and will maintain the high quality and resolution of your design.

4. Select "High Quality" When Downloading:

If Canva prompts you to choose between standard or high quality, always opt for high quality for professional-looking results, especially if you're preparing for print.

Optimizing File Size Without Losing Quality

While maintaining high resolution is critical for quality, sometimes you'll also need to manage file sizes, especially for digital distribution. Canva's export options give you the flexibility to adjust both resolution and file size. Here are some tips for balancing file size and quality:

- Use Compression Tools: After exporting, you can use third-party compression tools (like TinyPNG or Adobe Acrobat for PDFs) to reduce file size without sacrificing much in terms of quality.

- Reduce File Dimensions: If the design doesn't need to be large, reduce the pixel dimensions (width and height) before exporting. This will naturally reduce the file size.

- Choose the Appropriate Format: If you need to strike a balance between quality and size, JPG may be a good compromise, especially for digital use.

With a good understanding of these quality and resolution settings, you can ensure that every design you download from Canva is optimized for its intended purpose. Whether it's a sharp, professional print or a quick, lightweight web graphic, Canva gives you the tools to fine-tune your exports to perfection.

6.2 Printing with Canva

Canva's versatility extends beyond digital designs; it offers robust options for printing physical products as well. Whether you're creating business cards, posters, flyers, or brochures, Canva provides tools to customize your design, ensuring high-quality prints. Canva's print service is particularly convenient because it offers integrated printing and shipping, meaning you can design, print, and have your items delivered to your doorstep without ever leaving the platform. In this section, we will explore how you can use Canva to print products, from selecting the right templates to customizing print sizes and configurations.

6.2.1 Print Products: Posters, Business Cards, etc.

Canva offers a range of products that can be designed and printed directly through the platform. Understanding the options available will help you decide how to tailor your designs based on the specific requirements of each product. Below, we'll go over the most popular print products Canva supports, along with tips for making the most of each item.

Posters

Posters are one of the most popular products in Canva's print lineup. Whether you're promoting an event, showcasing art, or creating educational material, posters are an eye-catching and versatile medium. Canva allows you to design posters in various sizes, with the ability to choose between vertical or horizontal layouts.

1. Selecting Poster Templates

Canva provides a wide range of customizable poster templates for different purposes, from movie posters to educational charts. When selecting a template, consider the purpose of your poster. For example, if you're creating a motivational poster for an office, you might want to choose a template that has strong typography and a clean background, allowing the message to stand out. On the other hand, if you're designing an event poster, you may prefer a vibrant, image-heavy design to grab attention.

Once you've selected your template, customize it by replacing the default text with your own, adding images, and adjusting the colors to match your desired theme. Canva's drag-and-drop editor makes it simple to add or remove elements.

2. Customizing for Print Quality

When creating posters, it's essential to ensure that your design is print-ready, especially when it comes to images and fonts. Canva automatically adjusts many of its templates to be suitable for printing, but it's a good practice to review the quality of each element in your design.

For images, make sure that any photos you use are high resolution to prevent blurriness when printed. Canva offers a wide range of stock images that are optimized for print, but if you're uploading your own, aim for at least 300 DPI (dots per inch) for the best print quality. Canva will notify you if the resolution of your image is too low for printing.

Additionally, check your fonts. Some fonts may look great on screen but become difficult to read when printed at smaller sizes. Use bold and readable fonts for the main message, and avoid overcrowding the design with too much text. Consider Canva's guidelines for margin safety zones to ensure that no important text or images get cut off during printing.

3. Poster Sizes and Paper Types

Canva offers several standard poster sizes, including:

- Small: 12 x 18 inches

- Medium: 18 x 24 inches

- Large: 24 x 36 inches

Each size serves different purposes. Small posters are great for indoor displays or smaller advertisements, while medium and large posters work well for public displays, such as on walls or bulletin boards.

Canva also offers different paper types for posters. You can choose between premium matte, which is great for indoor use and gives a non-reflective finish, or gloss paper, which adds a shiny finish and works well for more vibrant designs.

Once your design is finalized and you've selected your preferred size and paper type, you can place your print order through Canva's integrated service. Canva will then print your poster and ship it directly to your location.

Business Cards

Business cards are a professional necessity for many individuals and companies, and Canva's business card templates make it easy to design something that fits your brand's personality. With Canva, you can create standard or custom-sized business cards and print them on high-quality paper.

1. Designing Your Business Card

When designing a business card, simplicity and clarity are key. You want your card to be memorable, but also functional. Start by selecting one of Canva's business card templates, or create your own from scratch. Make sure your business card includes essential information, such as:

- Your name

- Job title

- Company name and logo

- Contact information (phone number, email, website)

Canva's design tools allow you to customize every aspect of your card, from fonts and colors to logos and images. Many templates feature placeholders for QR codes, which can link directly to your website or portfolio when scanned. This is especially useful if you're in a digital-heavy industry or want to stand out from traditional paper business cards.

2. Customizing for Print

Just like posters, business cards require attention to print quality. Since business cards are small, you need to make sure that all text is easily readable, even at smaller font sizes. Canva's text alignment and margin tools can help you ensure everything is perfectly placed on the card.

Canva offers standard 3.5 x 2 inch business cards, but you can also opt for square cards or other custom sizes. Consider the weight and feel of the paper, as this can influence the perception of your brand. Canva provides options such as matte, gloss, or eco-friendly recycled paper, which can further customize the texture and durability of your card.

3. Paper Types and Finishing

Canva offers several paper options for business cards, including:

- Standard Matte: A smooth, non-reflective finish that gives a professional look.

- Gloss: A shiny finish that adds a touch of elegance and is great for designs with images.

- Eco-Friendly: Made from recycled materials, ideal for environmentally-conscious brands.

In addition to paper types, you can choose to apply finishes such as foil accents or spot UV for a glossy highlight effect, giving your cards a premium feel.

Once your design is complete and ready for print, simply place your order through Canva. You'll receive your cards printed and delivered to your address, saving you the hassle of finding a separate print provider.

Flyers

Flyers are another popular product in Canva's print offering, widely used for events, marketing, or general promotions. Canva allows you to create single-page or double-sided flyers with ease.

1. Designing Your Flyer

Flyers need to communicate a lot of information quickly, so it's important to structure your design thoughtfully. Choose a flyer template that fits your purpose, whether it's a sale promotion, an event announcement, or a service offering. The key is to balance text with visuals. Canva's templates make it easy to replace placeholder text with your own, and you can adjust colors, fonts, and layout to fit your brand.

Ensure that your flyer has a clear hierarchy, with the most important information, such as the event name or promotion, standing out at the top. Consider adding bold headers, attractive images, and a call to action, such as "Visit Us Today" or "Join Our Event."

2. Customizing for Print

Like with posters and business cards, you want to ensure that your flyer design is print-ready. Use high-quality images and avoid overcrowding the layout. Canva's design tools will alert you to any potential issues, such as low-resolution images or text that's too small to read.

Canva offers standard flyer sizes, such as 8.5 x 11 inches (letter size) and smaller 5.5 x 8.5 inch options. You can also choose from different paper options, including gloss for a shiny finish or matte for a more understated look.

6.2.2 Customizing Print Sizes and Settings

When it comes to printing your designs with Canva, customizing the size and print settings is crucial to ensuring your final product meets your expectations. Canva offers flexible and intuitive tools that allow you to tailor the size of your designs to suit various print formats, such as posters, business cards, invitations, and brochures. Whether you're designing for personal use, marketing purposes, or professional projects, mastering Canva's print settings will guarantee your designs translate perfectly from screen to print.

Understanding Canva's Print Dimensions

Before delving into custom print settings, it's essential to understand Canva's default print dimensions. Canva provides a variety of pre-set dimensions for popular print products, including standard A4, letter size, and custom sizes for specific products like business cards, flyers, and brochures. If you're starting from a blank canvas, these dimensions are pre-configured to match standard industry sizes, so you don't have to worry about alignment or cropping during printing.

Standard Print Sizes in Canva:

  - A4 (210mm x 297mm): Common for letterheads, posters, and other documents.

  - Letter (8.5in x 11in): The standard size for documents in the United States.

- Business Cards (85mm x 55mm): Industry-standard dimensions for professional business cards.

- Postcards (6in x 4in): Ideal for greeting cards and promotional mailers.

- Flyers (210mm x 297mm or A5 size): A popular format for promotional content.

These sizes can be selected directly from the Canva interface when you start a new project. However, depending on your specific needs, you may want to customize these dimensions to create unique or non-standard prints.

Customizing Print Sizes

Customizing the size of your design in Canva is straightforward and allows you to tailor your output for specific requirements. Whether you're creating a banner for an event, a custom-sized poster, or a unique marketing brochure, you can easily adjust the dimensions by selecting the custom size option.

1. Setting Custom Dimensions:

- To set custom dimensions, open your project and click on the Resize button in the toolbar at the top of the screen. Canva's Resize feature allows you to enter specific dimensions for width and height.

- You can specify the units for your custom size by selecting from pixels (px), millimeters (mm), inches (in), or centimeters (cm). For print, it's best to use inches or millimeters to ensure accurate sizing during production.

2. Selecting the Right Units:

- Inches (in): Commonly used for larger prints such as posters, flyers, or banners, inches are preferred for North American printing standards.

- Millimeters (mm): Widely used internationally, millimeters provide precision and are ideal for smaller prints like business cards or brochures.

- Centimeters (cm): Used for a range of medium-sized prints, centimeters offer good flexibility for posters and custom document designs.

- Pixels (px): While pixels are great for digital designs, they should be avoided for print projects unless you are designing web-based documents that will also be printed.

When choosing your dimensions, it's essential to consider your project's print specifications. For example, if you're designing a poster for a large event, the dimensions might be much larger than a standard A4 sheet. Similarly, if you're printing custom invitations, you may want to set exact dimensions that suit your envelope size.

Custom Print Size Examples

Here are a few examples of custom print dimensions that you can create in Canva for specific projects:

- Banners: 3ft x 6ft or larger, depending on the space available at your event.

- Large Posters: 18in x 24in or 24in x 36in, perfect for visual impact at exhibitions.

- Custom Business Cards: Some professionals opt for square business cards, which can be set to dimensions like 2.5in x 2.5in.

- Event Invitations: 5in x 7in is a common size for invitations, but you could go larger or smaller depending on your preferences.

When working with custom sizes, it's essential to keep in mind how your design will look when scaled to fit different mediums. Canva's Resize tool provides a real-time preview, helping you see how your elements will adjust to fit the new dimensions. This can save you from potential cropping issues or text getting cut off when printing.

Bleed and Margins: Key Considerations for Print

One of the most critical aspects of preparing a design for print is ensuring that it has proper bleed and margin settings. These settings ensure that no important elements are cut off during the printing and trimming process. Canva offers a bleed setting option to help you extend your design slightly beyond the edge of the document, guaranteeing that when the final product is trimmed, there will be no unwanted white borders or cut-offs.

1. What is Bleed?

- Bleed refers to the extra space around your design that extends beyond the final dimensions. This ensures that your design reaches the edge of the paper when trimmed. Canva recommends a bleed of around 3mm (or 0.125in) for most print projects, though this may vary depending on your printer or print service.

- To add bleed to your Canva design, click on File in the upper left-hand corner and check the option labeled Show print bleed. This will display bleed margins on your canvas, allowing you to adjust your design elements accordingly.

2. Why Bleed is Important:

- Without bleed, there's a risk that important parts of your design will be cut off during trimming. For instance, if your design includes a background color or image that extends to the edges, failing to account for bleed might leave an undesirable white border around the edges after printing.

3. Margin Settings:

- Canva doesn't automatically add margin lines, but you can manually check your design's layout by ensuring all crucial text and graphics are kept away from the edge of the document. It's recommended to leave at least a 5-10mm margin between the edge and important design elements. This ensures nothing critical is cropped during the printing process.

Color Settings for Printing

When customizing print settings in Canva, it's essential to consider color accuracy. Designs intended for digital use often appear different when printed due to the difference between RGB (Red, Green, Blue) and CMYK (Cyan, Magenta, Yellow, Black) color formats. Canva designs are by default in RGB, which is optimized for screen viewing, but if you're preparing a file for professional printing, you should be aware of how color profiles affect the final product.

1. Understanding RGB vs. CMYK:

- RGB is best for designs that will be viewed on screens, such as digital posters, presentations, or social media posts.

- CMYK is the preferred color format for printed materials. Professional printers use this format to ensure accurate color reproduction.

2. Converting to CMYK:

- Currently, Canva does not allow you to directly convert your file to CMYK within the platform. However, many printers will accept your design in RGB format and adjust the colors accordingly. If you require a CMYK file, you may need to export your design from Canva and convert it using graphic design software like Adobe Illustrator or Photoshop.

3. Choosing Print-Friendly Colors:

- When designing for print, it's important to stick to colors that translate well in CMYK. Bright, neon colors, for example, may not appear as vivid on paper. Canva's color picker tool allows you to preview the colors you've selected, but always check with your printer for color accuracy or request a proof before final production.

Resolution Settings and Print Quality

Resolution plays a significant role in the clarity of your printed designs. Canva recommends using high-resolution images and elements to avoid pixelation or blurriness when printing large projects.

1. Recommended DPI for Print:

- DPI (dots per inch) is the standard measure for print resolution. For professional printing, a DPI of 300 or higher is recommended to ensure crisp, clear images and text. Canva's default settings export designs at 300 DPI, but always double-check this when exporting files intended for print.

2. Exporting for High-Quality Prints:

- When you're ready to print, download your design in PDF Print format. This option provides the best resolution for printing, ensuring that images and text appear sharp and colors are accurately represented.

- PDF Print also includes bleed settings if you have them enabled, allowing for precise trimming.

3. Avoiding Low-Quality Images:

- Canva includes a large library of high-quality images, but if you upload your own photos or graphics, ensure they are high-resolution (at least 300 DPI). Avoid using low-quality or pixelated images, as they will not appear sharp when printed.

By following these steps and understanding the nuances of print sizes and settings, you can ensure that your Canva designs translate beautifully into printed products, whether you're creating posters, business cards, or marketing materials. Properly adjusting your print settings guarantees that your final output looks polished, professional, and perfectly tailored to your specifications.

6.3 Sharing Online and Embedding Designs

In today's digital landscape, embedding designs from Canva into your website can significantly enhance the visual appeal and engagement of your content. Whether you're a business owner looking to showcase your products, a blogger wanting to add infographics, or an educator creating resources for your students, embedding your Canva designs can help you achieve your goals effectively. This section will guide you through the process of embedding your Canva designs, ensuring that they display beautifully and function seamlessly on your site.

6.3.1 Embedding Canva Designs into Websites

Understanding the Benefits of Embedding Canva Designs

Before diving into the how-to, let's briefly explore why embedding designs is beneficial:

1. Visual Appeal: A well-designed graphic can capture attention and convey information more effectively than text alone. Canva's templates allow you to create stunning visuals that elevate your content.

2. Interactive Elements: Canva offers interactive features that can make your designs more engaging for your audience. By embedding, you can utilize these features directly on your website.

3. Easy Updates: When you update a design in Canva, the changes reflect automatically on your website if you use the embed code. This ensures that your audience always sees the latest version of your content.

4. Accessibility: Embedding designs makes it easier for your audience to view your content without needing to download files or navigate away from your website.

How to Embed Canva Designs into Your Website

Embedding a Canva design into your website involves a few simple steps. Let's walk through them:

Step 1: Create Your Design in Canva

1. Open Canva: Log in to your Canva account and create a new design or select an existing design from your dashboard.

2. Design Your Visual: Utilize Canva's vast array of templates, graphics, and text options to create your desired design. Make sure it aligns with your brand's aesthetic and effectively communicates your message.

Step 2: Prepare for Embedding

1. Click on the Share Button: Once you're satisfied with your design, locate the "Share" button at the top right corner of the Canva interface.

2. Select Embed: In the share options, find and click on the "Embed" option. This will open a new dialog box with options for embedding your design.

Step 3: Customize Embed Options

1. Choose Embed Options: Canva offers different embed options, including:

   - Static Image: This option embeds your design as a static image.

   - Interactive: This option allows for interactive elements in your design (e.g., links or animated components).

   - Responsive: This makes your embedded design adjust to fit various screen sizes, which is essential for mobile-friendly websites.

2. Adjust Size Settings: You can set the width and height for your embedded design. Ensure that these dimensions fit well within the layout of your website.

Step 4: Copy the Embed Code

1. Copy the HTML Code: After customizing your embed options, Canva will provide you with an HTML code snippet. Click the "Copy" button to copy this code to your clipboard.

Step 5: Embed the Code into Your Website

1. Open Your Website Editor: Depending on the platform you're using (WordPress, Wix, Squarespace, etc.), navigate to the section of your website where you want to embed the design.

2. Add an HTML Block: Look for an option to add custom HTML or embed code. This may vary based on your website builder. For example, in WordPress, you can use the "Custom HTML" block.

3. Paste the Embed Code: Paste the copied HTML code into the designated area.

4. Save or Publish Your Changes: Once you've pasted the code, save or publish your changes to make the embedded design live on your site.

Tips for Effective Embedding

- Test the Embed: After embedding, always preview your website to ensure that the design displays correctly. Check for any issues with responsiveness and functionality.

- Consider Load Times: High-resolution images can slow down your website. Optimize your Canva designs for web use by ensuring they aren't overly large or complex.

- Monitor User Engagement: Use analytics tools to track how users interact with your embedded designs. This can provide insights into what types of content resonate best with your audience.

Common Challenges and Solutions

While embedding Canva designs is typically straightforward, you may encounter some challenges. Here are a few common issues and their solutions:

1. Design Not Displaying Properly: If your design doesn't appear as expected, double-check the embed code for any missing elements. Ensure that you've correctly copied the entire HTML code.

2. Responsive Design Issues: If your embedded design doesn't resize correctly on mobile devices, revisit the embed options in Canva and ensure you selected the responsive option.

3. Loss of Interactivity: If you notice that interactive elements (like links) are not functioning after embedding, ensure you used the interactive embed code and that your website supports interactive elements.

4. Slow Loading Times: If your website loads slowly due to the embedded design, consider optimizing the design by reducing the size of images or simplifying complex elements.

Conclusion

Embedding Canva designs into your website is an effective way to enhance your online presence and engage your audience. By following the steps outlined above, you can easily showcase your creativity and professional quality. Whether you're looking to display infographics, presentations, or marketing materials, Canva provides the tools necessary to make your website visually appealing and functional. With practice, embedding designs will become a seamless part of your content creation process, allowing you to focus on delivering valuable information to your audience.

As you continue to explore Canva's capabilities, you'll find even more ways to integrate your designs into various platforms, further enriching your digital content and enhancing user experience.

6.3.2 Sharing Direct Links to Your Designs

Once you have completed your design in Canva, sharing it with others can be as simple as providing a direct link. This feature is particularly useful when you want others to view or interact with your design without needing to download it. Canva makes it easy to share designs online, either for collaboration, feedback, or simply showcasing your work. In this section, we'll walk through how to share direct links to your Canva designs, explain the different types of access permissions available, and offer tips on managing your shared projects effectively.

1. Why Share Direct Links?

Sharing direct links to your Canva designs is an incredibly efficient way to distribute your work, whether it's for review, presentation, or collaboration. Here are some reasons why direct links can be useful:

- Real-time Collaboration: With Canva's direct link-sharing feature, multiple team members can access the same design, make changes, or leave comments simultaneously. This is perfect for teams working on a project remotely or for gathering feedback quickly.

- Accessibility: Recipients of your link don't need to have a Canva account or download any software to view your design. This makes sharing easy and hassle-free, especially for clients or collaborators who may not be familiar with Canva.

- Instant Updates: Any updates or edits you make to your design are instantly reflected for those with access to the link. This means you won't need to keep sending updated versions of your project every time you make changes.

- Customization Options: Depending on the purpose of sharing, you can control the level of access others have to your design, ensuring that only the intended people can edit, comment, or view the project.

2. How to Share a Direct Link

Let's go through the step-by-step process of sharing your design via a direct link in Canva.

Step 1: Completing Your Design

Before sharing a design, make sure it's in its final or review-ready form. Even if you're sending the design for feedback or edits, it's essential to ensure it's organized, free of placeholder text, and visually appealing.

Step 2: Accessing the Share Options

Once your design is ready:

- Click on the Share button located at the top-right corner of the Canva interface.

This will open a pop-up menu that contains various sharing options, including direct link sharing, social media posting, and email.

Step 3: Setting Permissions

Before generating a link, you'll need to decide the level of access you want to grant to the people receiving your design. Canva provides several options for permissions, including:

- Can View: This option allows recipients to view your design but not make any changes or leave comments. This is ideal for sharing completed designs with clients or showcasing work.

- Can Comment: If you're seeking feedback, you might opt for the "Can Comment" option. This allows recipients to view the design and leave comments without altering the content.

- Can Edit: For collaborative projects where multiple people need to make edits or adjustments, select the "Can Edit" option. This is useful for teams working together on the same design.

It's important to carefully consider the type of permission you grant, as giving editing rights can lead to unintended changes. If you're sharing with a client or someone unfamiliar with Canva, it's generally safer to stick to "Can View" or "Can Comment" unless otherwise agreed upon.

Step 4: Generating the Link

Once you've selected the appropriate permission level, click on Copy Link. Canva will generate a unique URL for your design that you can then share via email, messaging apps, or any other communication platform.

3. Advanced Link Sharing Options

Canva also provides a few advanced options when it comes to sharing direct links, especially for users on Canva Pro or Teams. Let's explore some of these features:

3.1 Expiration Dates for Links

If you're a Canva Pro user, you have the option to set expiration dates for your shared links. This feature ensures that your design won't be accessible indefinitely, which is particularly helpful when working on time-sensitive projects.

To set an expiration date:

- Click on the Settings button next to the generated link.

- Choose an expiration date from the calendar.

After the expiration date, the link will no longer be active, providing additional security for your designs.

3.2 Password Protection

For those concerned about security, Canva offers the ability to password-protect shared designs. This means that anyone trying to access the design via the direct link will be prompted to enter a password before gaining access.

To enable password protection:

- After generating the link, click on Settings next to the link.

- Toggle the Password Protection option and create a secure password.

Make sure to share the password only with intended recipients to avoid unauthorized access.

4. Best Practices for Sharing Links

4.1 Choosing the Right Access Level

It's critical to assess the nature of your design and the role of the person you're sharing it with before deciding on the access level. For instance, if you're sending a design to a client for review, granting "Can View" access ensures they can look at your work but won't accidentally make changes. On the other hand, if you're collaborating with a teammate who needs to make edits, "Can Edit" might be the right choice.

4.2 Monitoring Link Activity

Canva does not provide detailed analytics on how many times your link has been viewed or by whom. Therefore, it's good practice to regularly check back with the recipients of your link to ensure they've accessed the design and provided any necessary feedback.

4.3 Managing Multiple Versions of a Design

When sharing a link for collaboration, it's possible for others to make significant changes to your original design. To avoid confusion or loss of work, Canva allows you to create version history for your designs.

To view or restore a previous version:

- Click on File from the top menu bar.

- Select Version History to see the list of changes made to the design.

This is particularly useful if multiple team members are editing the same design and you need to revert to an earlier version.

5. Embedding Shared Links in External Platforms

Besides sharing a direct link via messaging or email, you can also embed your Canva design into websites or other platforms, making it accessible to a wider audience. This is especially useful for web designers, bloggers, or educators who want to integrate their Canva designs into their online content.

5.1 Embedding Designs into a Website

To embed a design:

- After clicking the Share button, select Embed from the menu.

- Canva will generate a line of HTML code that you can paste directly into your website's code.

Embedding a design allows it to be displayed directly on your website without requiring users to visit Canva. Any updates made to the design within Canva will automatically be reflected in the embedded version.

5.2 Embedding on Social Media and Online Portfolios

You can also embed your design into social media profiles or online portfolios to showcase your work. For example, if you're a graphic designer or social media manager, embedding your Canva designs can be an easy way to display your portfolio in real-time.

Many platforms like WordPress, Squarespace, and Behance allow embedding through custom HTML blocks, making Canva designs highly versatile for personal or professional websites.

In conclusion, sharing direct links to your Canva designs offers unparalleled convenience, flexibility, and collaboration potential. Whether you're sharing for feedback, collaboration, or simply showcasing your work, Canva's link-sharing options ensure that your designs are easily accessible to the right audience. Be sure to make use of the permissions, password protection, and embedding features to customize your sharing experience.

CHAPTER VII
Canva Tips and Tricks for Beginners

7.1 Time-Saving Shortcuts

7.1.1 Keyboard Shortcuts for Faster Designing

In the fast-paced world of digital design, efficiency is key, especially when working on multiple projects or creating content for clients with tight deadlines. Keyboard shortcuts are essential tools that can significantly reduce the time spent on repetitive tasks in Canva, helping you focus more on creativity and less on manual navigation. This section introduces you to the most useful keyboard shortcuts available in Canva, breaking down how each one can streamline your workflow and improve your overall design process.

1. The Basics: Navigational Shortcuts

Before diving into specific design actions, it's important to familiarize yourself with basic navigational shortcuts. These are shortcuts that allow you to move around the Canva interface quickly, reducing the need for excessive mouse clicks or manually scrolling through the menu.

- Ctrl + Z (Cmd + Z for Mac): Undo

Mistakes happen, and in the world of design, it's essential to have the ability to undo your actions quickly. This shortcut reverses your last move, whether it was adding an element, resizing an image, or moving an object.

- Ctrl + Y (Cmd + Y for Mac): Redo

If you accidentally undo an action and want to bring it back, this shortcut restores your last move. It's particularly useful when you're experimenting with designs and want to see which version looks best.

- Ctrl + A (Cmd + A for Mac): Select All

This is a powerful tool when you need to make changes across multiple elements on your canvas simultaneously. For instance, if you want to change the color or font of all the text boxes on your canvas, use this shortcut to highlight everything at once and then apply your desired edits.

- Esc: Deselect

If you have selected an element but decide you no longer want to make changes to it, pressing the escape key will quickly deselect it. This shortcut is handy when you need to reset your focus or start fresh on a specific task.

- Spacebar: Pan or Scroll Through Your Design

Holding the spacebar down while moving your mouse allows you to pan or scroll through your design without using the scroll bar. This is particularly useful for large, intricate projects where zooming in and out is necessary.

2. Text Formatting Shortcuts

When working with text in Canva, you'll often find yourself adjusting font styles, sizes, and alignments. Instead of manually selecting these options in the toolbar, you can use keyboard shortcuts to format your text more efficiently.

- Ctrl + B (Cmd + B for Mac): Bold

Apply bold styling to your selected text instantly. Bold text is great for emphasizing important points or headlines in your design, and this shortcut makes it easy to apply the style without navigating through the toolbar.

- Ctrl + I (Cmd + I for Mac): Italic

Italicizing text adds emphasis in a more subtle way than bold. Use this shortcut when you want to distinguish certain words or phrases from the rest of your content.

- Ctrl + U (Cmd + U for Mac): Underline

Underlining can be useful for headings or calls to action. This shortcut allows you to underline selected text without searching for the option in the formatting bar.

- Ctrl + Shift + L (Cmd + Shift + L for Mac): Left Align Text

If you want to align your text to the left, this shortcut will do the job. It's a common choice for blocks of text and works well with both paragraphs and single lines of copy.

- Ctrl + Shift + E (Cmd + Shift + E for Mac): Center Align Text

Centering text is perfect for titles, quotes, and other elements where symmetry is important. This shortcut instantly centers the selected text within its text box.

- Ctrl + Shift + R (Cmd + Shift + R for Mac): Right Align Text

Right alignment is often used for dates, quotes, or other design elements where a clean, minimal look is desired. Using this shortcut ensures quick access to right-aligned text.

- Ctrl + Shift + > (Cmd + Shift + > for Mac): Increase Font Size

Sometimes, you may need to increase the size of your font to create emphasis or improve legibility. This shortcut makes it easy to enlarge your text without manually selecting the size from the dropdown menu.

- Ctrl + Shift + < (Cmd + Shift + < for Mac): Decrease Font Size

Conversely, when you need to reduce the size of your text, this shortcut will decrease it incrementally. It's especially useful when fine-tuning the size of text elements to fit within a specific layout.

3. Object and Element Management Shortcuts

Designing in Canva involves managing multiple elements like images, shapes, text boxes, and icons. These shortcuts will help you manipulate objects quickly and effectively.

- Ctrl + D (Cmd + D for Mac): Duplicate Element

Duplicating an object is a common task when you're creating consistent layouts or patterns. With this shortcut, you can quickly make a copy of the selected element and place it elsewhere in your design.

- Ctrl + G (Cmd + G for Mac): Group Elements

When you have multiple objects that need to move or resize together, grouping them is the best solution. This shortcut groups selected elements into one, allowing you to manipulate them as a single unit.

- Ctrl + Shift + G (Cmd + Shift + G for Mac): Ungroup Elements

To break up a group and work with each element individually again, use this shortcut to ungroup them. This is particularly useful when you need to make detailed changes to a specific part of the design.

- Alt + Arrow Keys (Option + Arrow Keys for Mac): Nudge Elements

When fine-tuning the position of elements on your canvas, the arrow keys allow for precise movement in any direction. Adding the Alt (or Option) key lets you nudge the elements incrementally for even finer adjustments.

- Ctrl +] (Cmd +] for Mac): Bring Forward

In Canva, elements are layered on top of one another. If you want to bring an element forward so that it appears above others, this shortcut lets you move it up one layer at a time.

- Ctrl + [(Cmd + [for Mac): Send Backward

Similarly, if you need to send an object behind others, this shortcut moves it back one layer at a time, making it easy to control the stacking order of your elements.

- Shift + Click: Select Multiple Elements

This shortcut allows you to select more than one object at a time by holding the Shift key and clicking on each element. It's essential for grouping, aligning, or making changes to multiple objects simultaneously.

4. Layer and Alignment Shortcuts

Layering and aligning elements correctly are crucial parts of creating a professional and polished design. Canva provides several shortcuts to help you manage layers and ensure perfect alignment.

- Ctrl + ; (Cmd + ; for Mac): Show or Hide Gridlines

Gridlines are extremely useful when you need to align elements precisely. This shortcut toggles the gridlines on and off, giving you a clear reference point for spacing and alignment.

- Ctrl + Alt + L (Cmd + Option + L for Mac): Lock Element Position

Once you've positioned an element exactly where you want it, use this shortcut to lock it in place. This prevents accidental movements when working on other parts of your design.

- Ctrl + Alt + C (Cmd + Option + C for Mac): Copy Style

This powerful shortcut allows you to copy the style (such as color, font, or size) of one element and apply it to another. It's a great way to maintain consistency across your design without manually adjusting each object.

- Ctrl + Alt + V (Cmd + Option + V for Mac): Paste Style

After copying the style, this shortcut pastes it onto the selected element, ensuring that your design remains cohesive.

5. Miscellaneous Shortcuts

There are a few additional shortcuts in Canva that are useful for specific tasks or actions but might not fit neatly into the above categories. However, knowing these shortcuts can still significantly enhance your design experience.

- Ctrl + P (Cmd + P for Mac): Print Design

Once your design is complete, use this shortcut to quickly open the print dialogue and print your design directly from Canva.

- Ctrl + S (Cmd + S for Mac): Save Your Work

Although Canva automatically saves your design as you work, it's always a good idea to manually save at critical points, especially if you're working on a complex project. This shortcut saves your design instantly.

Conclusion: Mastering Efficiency with Keyboard Shortcuts

Using keyboard shortcuts in Canva is one of the most effective ways to speed up your workflow and enhance your productivity as a designer. As you incorporate these shortcuts into your design process, you'll notice a significant improvement in your speed and efficiency, freeing up more time for creativity and experimentation. Whether you're adjusting text formatting, aligning objects, or managing layers, mastering these shortcuts will enable you to work smarter and create stunning designs with ease.

7.1.2 Using Duplication and Alignment Tools

When working with design, speed and efficiency are essential to completing projects on time, especially when handling repetitive tasks. Canva's duplication and alignment tools can significantly accelerate your workflow while ensuring your designs remain polished and professional. This section will dive deep into how these tools function and their various applications in different design scenarios.

Understanding Duplication in Canva

The duplication feature in Canva allows you to quickly copy elements, such as text boxes, images, icons, or shapes, within your design. This tool is especially handy when you need to maintain consistency in your layout or replicate a specific element multiple times without having to recreate it from scratch.

Duplicating elements saves time and ensures uniformity, which is crucial for maintaining a cohesive look across your project. Whether you're working on social media posts, brochures, or business cards, duplicating design elements allows you to replicate styles and structures efficiently.

How to Duplicate Elements in Canva:

Duplicating elements in Canva is a straightforward process, designed to streamline your design experience. Here's how you can quickly duplicate any element:

1. Select the Element: Click on the element (text box, image, shape, etc.) you want to duplicate. This will activate the element with a bounding box around it.

2. Duplicate Command: With the element selected, you have two main options to duplicate:

   - Option 1: Use the keyboard shortcut `Ctrl + D` (or `Cmd + D` on a Mac). This instantly creates a duplicate of the selected element right next to the original.

   - Option 2: Right-click on the selected element and choose "Duplicate" from the context menu. This method also creates a duplicate directly on top of the original.

3. Move the Duplicate: After duplicating, simply click and drag the duplicated element to position it wherever you like on your design canvas.

Using this technique, you can quickly create identical copies of elements to maintain visual consistency, especially in multi-page documents, where repeated elements are often required.

Benefits of Duplicating Elements:

- Consistency: Duplication ensures that each copied element is identical in size, font, style, and color, reducing the risk of inconsistencies when manually recreating elements.

- Speed: Instead of manually creating new text boxes, images, or shapes that match previous elements, duplication saves you precious time during the design process.

- Efficiency: When creating layouts with multiple similar elements (such as icons or bullet points), duplicating them ensures spacing and sizing remain uniform, giving your design a professional touch.

For example, let's say you're designing a presentation slide and want to have five identical bullet points. Instead of manually creating each bullet point, you can simply create the first one, customize it, and then duplicate it four times. This ensures that all bullet points have the same size, spacing, and formatting.

Using Canva's Alignment Tools for Precision

Alignment is a fundamental aspect of good design. Ensuring that elements are properly aligned not only enhances visual appeal but also contributes to the professionalism and readability of your design. Canva provides various alignment tools that make it easy to arrange your elements in a structured and balanced manner, without the guesswork.

Alignment tools are invaluable when you're working with multiple elements on a canvas and want them to be evenly spaced or precisely aligned to a particular axis, whether vertically or horizontally. Proper alignment ensures your design feels cohesive, aesthetically pleasing, and easy to navigate visually.

Types of Alignment Tools in Canva:

Canva offers several alignment options, each designed to make positioning elements on the canvas a seamless process. These include:

1. Smart Guides:

 - Canva automatically displays alignment guides, known as smart guides, whenever you move an element around the canvas. These appear as pink lines and help you align your element to other objects on the canvas or to the center of the canvas itself.

 - For example, if you're moving a text box, a pink guide will appear when it's perfectly centered horizontally or vertically relative to the canvas or other objects. This feature helps you achieve balanced layouts effortlessly.

2. Align Buttons:

 - Canva has built-in alignment buttons located in the top toolbar when an element is selected. These buttons allow you to align objects relative to the entire canvas or to other selected objects.

 - The options include:

 - Align Left: Aligns the selected element(s) to the leftmost side of the canvas or group of elements.

 - Align Center: Centers the selected element(s) horizontally on the canvas or within the selected group.

 - Align Right: Aligns the selected element(s) to the rightmost side.

 - Align Top: Aligns the selected element(s) to the top edge.

- Align Middle: Centers the element(s) vertically.

- Align Bottom: Aligns the element(s) to the bottom edge.

3. Distribution Tools:

- In addition to aligning elements, Canva's distribution tools allow you to evenly space objects on the canvas. This is particularly useful when you have several elements and want to ensure they're equidistant from one another.

- The distribution options include:

- Horizontally Distributed: Ensures equal horizontal spacing between selected elements.

- Vertically Distributed: Ensures equal vertical spacing between selected elements.

- These tools ensure precision, eliminating the need to manually eyeball spacing.

How to Align Elements in Canva:

1. Select the Elements: Start by selecting the element(s) you want to align. If you're aligning multiple elements, hold down `Shift` while clicking each element.

2. Use the Align Buttons: With the element(s) selected, go to the top toolbar and choose one of the alignment buttons (Align Left, Align Center, etc.) based on your needs.

3. Check with Smart Guides: If you're manually moving an element around, pay attention to the pink smart guides, which will help you snap the element into place for perfect alignment.

Aligning Multiple Elements:

Aligning multiple elements at once can be particularly helpful when working with rows of images, text boxes, or shapes. Here's an example:

- Let's say you have three text boxes you want aligned along their left edges. You can select all three text boxes by holding down `Shift` and clicking each one. Then, click the "Align Left" button in the toolbar, and Canva will automatically align all the text boxes to the left side, creating a clean, structured look.

Using Distribution for Even Spacing:

If you have multiple elements and need them spaced evenly across the canvas, Canva's distribution tools are the perfect solution. For example, if you're placing four icons in a row, you can select all of them and use the "Distribute Horizontally" tool to ensure they're evenly spaced.

Best Practices for Using Duplication and Alignment Tools

- Maintain Consistent Spacing: When working on designs with multiple repeating elements (like business cards, social media posts, or presentations), ensure that spacing is consistent by using duplication and alignment tools. Evenly spaced elements create a harmonious and professional look.

- Avoid Overcrowding: While duplicating elements can be time-saving, avoid overcrowding your design with too many identical elements. Ensure that each duplicated element has a purpose and contributes to the overall balance of the design.

- Combine Tools for Maximum Efficiency: Use Canva's duplication and alignment tools together for maximum efficiency. For example, after duplicating an element several times, use the alignment and distribution tools to ensure they're perfectly spaced and aligned.

- Center Key Elements: For designs where balance and focus are essential, center-align your key elements, such as headlines, images, or call-to-action buttons, using Canva's smart guides and align buttons. This helps draw attention to the main message of your design.

Common Pitfalls to Avoid

While Canva's duplication and alignment tools are user-friendly and powerful, there are some common mistakes to avoid:

1. Overusing Duplicates: Duplicating elements is helpful, but overusing identical elements can make your design look repetitive and uninspired. Strive for balance between consistency and variety.

2. Ignoring Margins: Even with alignment tools, it's important to manually check margins to ensure that elements don't crowd the edges of your design. Proper padding around your elements gives your design breathing room.

3. Misusing Distribution Tools: Distribution tools can evenly space elements, but make sure the overall layout still looks aesthetically pleasing. Don't rely solely on automatic distribution—step back and visually assess the overall balance.

By mastering Canva's duplication and alignment tools, you can significantly enhance both the efficiency and precision of your design process. These tools ensure that your designs maintain consistency and professionalism, freeing you to focus on creativity rather than repetitive tasks. Whether you're designing a simple social media post or a multi-page brochure, these techniques will streamline your workflow and elevate your design game.

7.2 Best Practices for Consistent Designs

In the world of design, consistency is key to creating a professional, polished, and recognizable look. When designing in Canva, whether for personal projects or business purposes, maintaining consistency across all elements ensures that your designs resonate with your audience and reinforce the intended message. Inconsistent designs can confuse viewers and dilute the impact of your work. Let's explore how you can maintain consistency, starting with your branding.

7.2.1 Maintaining Consistent Branding

Branding is the process of creating a distinct identity for a product, service, or business. Consistent branding helps ensure that customers or audiences can easily identify your work, which can foster trust and loyalty over time. This is essential for businesses, organizations, and personal brands alike. Here are the key elements of maintaining consistent branding in Canva:

1. Establishing Brand Guidelines

Before diving into Canva, it's critical to develop a set of brand guidelines. These guidelines should cover all aspects of your visual identity, including:

- Logo: A consistent logo is often the centerpiece of branding. Make sure your logo is used the same way across all your designs, whether it's placed at the same location on marketing materials or scaled appropriately on different media types.

- Color Scheme: Select a set of colors (usually no more than five) that represent your brand. These colors should reflect your brand's identity, values, and emotions. Canva allows you to create and save color palettes, making it easy to apply the same colors across all your designs.

- Typography: Choose a primary font for headings and a secondary font for body text. Maintaining font consistency ensures that your designs look professional and well-structured. Avoid using too many fonts; two to three fonts across all platforms is ideal.

Canva has a vast library of fonts, and with Canva Pro, you can even upload custom fonts specific to your brand.

- Tone and Style: This is the overall feeling or attitude your brand wants to convey through visuals. Are you aiming for a modern, playful, or minimalistic tone? Ensuring consistency in the tone helps reinforce your message.

By following these guidelines, you'll make it easier to maintain consistency in every design you create.

2. Using Canva's Brand Kit Feature

One of Canva's most powerful features for branding is its Brand Kit. Available with Canva Pro, this tool allows you to save all of your branding elements in one place, making it easy to apply them to any new design. Here's how you can make the most of the Brand Kit:

- Add Your Logo: Upload your brand logo (or logos if you have variations for different platforms). This ensures your logo is easily accessible while designing. No more searching through folders for the right file.

- Create a Color Palette: Add your brand's primary and secondary colors to your Brand Kit. Canva will store these colors in a palette that's available every time you start a new design. The ability to have your colors readily available ensures that each design you create is consistent with your overall brand identity.

- Choose Your Brand Fonts: Canva allows you to set a primary font for headings, subheadings, and body text. This standardization is crucial for keeping typography uniform across various projects. By doing this, you prevent the accidental use of different fonts that could throw off the design's consistency.

With the Brand Kit, applying your brand's assets becomes second nature, freeing up more time to focus on creativity rather than repetitive tasks.

3. Applying Consistent Layouts

Consistency doesn't just apply to the brand's visual elements; it extends to the layout of your designs as well. Whether you are creating social media posts, presentations, or marketing materials, the layout plays a crucial role in maintaining a professional appearance.

- Template Usage: Canva provides thousands of templates that can be customized according to your brand. For consistent branding, pick one or two templates for each type of design (e.g., social media, flyers, business cards). Sticking with a few templates across your content creates uniformity. Additionally, you can create your own templates that follow your brand guidelines and use them across multiple designs.

- Grid Systems: Grids can be helpful for keeping your designs aligned and organized. They ensure that images, text, and other elements don't seem haphazardly placed. By using Canva's grid system or ruler guides, you can align objects in a way that keeps your designs neat and visually appealing.

- Hierarchy of Elements: Establish a clear hierarchy for the placement of text and visual elements in your designs. For instance, your logo might always go in the top-left corner, and the call-to-action could consistently be centered at the bottom. Maintaining this hierarchy helps audiences know where to look first and builds familiarity.

4. Reusing Elements Across Multiple Designs

When it comes to branding, repetition builds recognition. One way to ensure brand consistency is to reuse certain design elements in various projects. Canva makes this easy by allowing you to store and duplicate your designs. Here are some ways to reuse design elements:

- Logo Placement: Ensure that your logo appears in a consistent position in every design, whether it's in the header, footer, or watermarked across your design.

- Visual Elements and Icons: Choose specific visual elements that align with your brand. For example, if your brand uses a particular style of icon (minimalist, hand-drawn, geometric), make sure those icons are used consistently across your designs.

- Watermarks and Background Patterns: Watermarks or subtle background elements can be repeated across multiple designs to tie them together and maintain brand recognition.

5. Consistent Image Styles and Filters

Images play a huge role in defining your brand's visual identity. The types of images you choose (e.g., illustrations vs. photos) and how you present them (e.g., color vs. black-and-white, filters vs. no filters) should align with your brand's overall aesthetic.

- Use of Stock Photos: If you are using Canva's stock photos, select a style that fits your brand and stick to it. For example, if your brand is all about modernity, choose sleek, high-quality photos that exude a contemporary vibe.

- Filters and Image Effects: Canva offers a wide range of photo filters and effects. Applying a consistent filter to all your images can help create a uniform look. For instance, if you're aiming for a warm, nostalgic feel, applying the same sepia-toned filter across all your photos will give them a cohesive, branded look.

6. Cohesive Social Media Branding

Social media is one of the most critical places where consistent branding is essential. With Canva's social media templates, you can ensure your designs align with your brand's identity. However, consistency doesn't just mean sticking to the same colors and fonts — it's about ensuring that your entire online presence aligns.

- Profile Pictures and Banners: Make sure your profile picture (typically your logo) and banners are consistent across platforms like Facebook, Instagram, and Twitter. This reinforces your brand and makes it easily recognizable no matter where someone encounters your business.

- Post Templates: Create a set of branded templates for different kinds of posts, such as announcements, testimonials, product features, etc. This not only saves time but also ensures that each post maintains your brand's look and feel.

- Consistent Messaging: The way you present your brand visually should align with your messaging tone. For example, if your brand is playful, use bright colors, light-hearted images, and fun fonts. If it's professional and serious, stick with sleek, minimalistic designs.

7. Reviewing and Updating Branding

Finally, consistent branding doesn't mean being static. Brands evolve over time, and so should your visual identity. Periodically review your brand guidelines and assets to ensure they still reflect your business or personal brand's mission and values.

- Refreshing Elements: If certain aspects of your branding feel outdated (e.g., fonts, color schemes), don't hesitate to refresh them, but make sure to apply changes consistently across all platforms.

- Analyzing Feedback: Take feedback from your audience, clients, or team to see if your designs resonate the way you intend. Adjust your branding elements if needed to ensure it's making the right impact.

- Monitoring Trends: While it's important to stay true to your brand, staying aware of design trends can help keep your brand modern and relevant. Just make sure that any changes are cohesive with your existing identity.

In Summary, maintaining consistent branding across all of your designs in Canva ensures that your audience can easily recognize your work and associate it with your business or personal identity. By using tools like Canva's Brand Kit, reusing design elements, and applying consistent layouts, you can create professional designs that leave a lasting impression.

7.2.2 Using Canva's Brand Kit for Cohesive Designs

Consistency in design is essential, especially when you're creating content for a brand, business, or personal project that involves multiple pieces of visual communication. Maintaining the same fonts, colors, logos, and overall look across all your designs ensures that your audience can immediately recognize your work, whether it's on a website, social media platform, or physical materials like flyers or posters. Canva's Brand Kit is a powerful tool that helps you achieve this consistency effortlessly. In this section, we'll explore the importance of cohesive designs, how to set up and use Canva's Brand Kit effectively, and strategies for maintaining brand cohesion across all your creative outputs.

Understanding Brand Consistency

Before diving into the functionality of Canva's Brand Kit, it's important to understand why consistent branding matters. For businesses and even individuals building a personal brand, maintaining a recognizable and unified visual identity across platforms helps establish credibility, trust, and recognition.

When your designs follow a uniform pattern, they:

- Strengthen your brand's identity

- Create an immediate sense of familiarity with your audience

- Communicate professionalism

- Improve customer trust and loyalty

Inconsistent design, on the other hand, can confuse your audience and make your brand appear fragmented or unprofessional. Every piece of content you create should feel like it belongs to the same family, and Canva's Brand Kit makes this process incredibly simple, especially for those without formal design training.

What is Canva's Brand Kit?

Canva's Brand Kit is a feature designed to help users manage and store all the elements that make up their brand's identity, such as fonts, logos, and color palettes, in one centralized place. By setting up your Brand Kit, you ensure that these elements are always accessible and ready to be applied to any design project. This tool is especially useful for small businesses, entrepreneurs, and designers managing multiple brands.

Canva Pro users have the most access to Brand Kit features, allowing them to save multiple brand colors, fonts, and logos. Free users, however, can still set up basic brand elements like colors and logos but may need to manually select fonts each time.

The key components of the Brand Kit include:

1. Brand Colors – A palette of predefined colors that match your brand's identity.

2. Brand Fonts – Pre-selected fonts that are used consistently in all your designs.

3. Brand Logos – Easily accessible logos that can be inserted into any design quickly.

Let's break down each of these elements in more detail.

Setting Up Your Brand Colors

Color is one of the most immediate and powerful aspects of a brand's visual identity. It's often the first thing people notice about a design, and it plays a key role in evoking emotions and feelings. Think of iconic brands like Coca-Cola (red), Starbucks (green), or Facebook (blue) — their colors are so closely associated with the brand that they're recognizable even without the logo.

When setting up your Brand Kit, your first step should be to define your brand color palette. A good rule of thumb is to stick to three to five colors:

- Primary Color: This is the main color that represents your brand, often used in backgrounds, headlines, and key design elements.

- Secondary Colors: These are complementary colors that support the primary color, often used in smaller design details like buttons or icons.

- Accent Colors: These can be used sparingly to highlight or draw attention to specific parts of your design. Accent colors can be bold and contrasting, adding visual interest.

How to Add Brand Colors in Canva:

1. Navigate to the Brand Kit section under your Canva dashboard.

2. Click on "Add Brand Colors."

3. You can manually add colors using their HEX codes (if you have specific brand colors) or select colors from the color picker.

4. Save your palette.

Once saved, these colors will be available every time you design a project in Canva, ensuring that all your designs stay visually consistent with your brand identity. With Canva Pro, you can even create multiple color palettes for different brands if you're managing more than one.

Selecting Your Brand Fonts

Fonts are another critical aspect of maintaining cohesive branding. Consistent use of typography across all marketing materials reinforces brand recognition and helps to establish a clear voice or tone. Different fonts convey different emotions: serif fonts like Times New Roman can give a sense of tradition or formality, while sans-serif fonts like Arial are modern and clean.

In Canva's Brand Kit, you can save a combination of fonts for use across all designs. Generally, a brand should stick to no more than two to three fonts for clarity and visual balance:

- Primary Font: Used for headlines, titles, and other important text.

- Secondary Font: Used for body text and less prominent information.

- Optional Accent Font: Used for special text, such as quotes or call-to-action buttons, adding emphasis.

How to Add Fonts to Your Brand Kit:

1. In the Brand Kit section, find the "Brand Fonts" section.

2. You can select from Canva's wide array of preloaded fonts, or if you have custom fonts, you can upload them directly (available for Canva Pro users).

3. Choose a default font size, weight (bold, italic, etc.), and color to further customize your text.

With the Brand Kit, these fonts will automatically be suggested each time you add text to a design, helping to maintain visual consistency across different platforms and materials.

Uploading Your Brand Logos

The logo is the face of your brand and one of the most recognizable elements of your visual identity. It should be present in most, if not all, of your marketing materials, whether digital or print. By adding your logos to Canva's Brand Kit, you can quickly insert them into any project without having to search for files on your computer.

How to Add Logos to Your Brand Kit:

1. Under the Brand Kit, click on "Add Brand Logos."

2. Upload your logo files (PNG is recommended for a transparent background).

3. Canva Pro users can upload multiple versions of their logo, such as full-color, black-and-white, or icon-only logos.

Once uploaded, your logos will be easily accessible from the "Logos" tab in Canva's editor. You can drag and drop them into any design, and they will remain at a high resolution regardless of the design's size.

Using Your Brand Kit in Canva Designs

Once your Brand Kit is set up, you can begin using it to streamline the design process. Each time you start a new project, your brand colors, fonts, and logos will appear on the left-hand side of the Canva editor, making it easy to apply them with a single click.

Here are some practical tips for utilizing your Brand Kit effectively:

- Color Consistency: Stick to your brand palette when designing each element, from backgrounds to buttons. Avoid introducing new colors unless absolutely necessary.

- Typography: Ensure that you consistently use your primary and secondary fonts for headlines and body text, respectively. Limit the use of accent fonts to prevent visual clutter.

- Logos: Incorporate your logo tastefully, ensuring it appears on key materials such as flyers, social media posts, and presentations, without overwhelming the design.

Creating Templates for Consistent Designs

In addition to the Brand Kit, Canva allows users to create reusable templates, which is another powerful way to ensure that your designs are always consistent. By setting up templates for common materials like social media posts, business cards, or presentations, you can maintain uniformity across different platforms and campaigns.

How to Create Templates:

1. Design a sample layout using your brand's colors, fonts, and logos.

2. Save the design as a template by selecting "Save as Template."

3. The template can now be used repeatedly, ensuring that every new project stays consistent with your established visual identity.

This is particularly useful for teams or businesses with multiple designers working on the same brand. By providing them with a set of approved templates, you can ensure that all content produced remains aligned with your brand's visual guidelines.

Maintaining Brand Consistency Across Platforms

Canva's Brand Kit helps you maintain consistency within Canva, but how do you ensure that consistency extends across all platforms? Whether you're posting on social media, designing print materials, or creating presentations, it's important to adhere to your brand guidelines beyond just Canva's workspace.

Here are a few tips for ensuring brand cohesion across all platforms:

- Social Media: Use the same color schemes, fonts, and logos for every post, story, or ad. Canva even allows you to schedule social media posts directly through its platform, further simplifying the process.

- Printed Materials: Make sure your print designs, such as business cards, flyers, or brochures, adhere to your Brand Kit. Export designs in high resolution and ensure that your printer is using the correct color profile (CMYK vs RGB).

- Website: Use the same fonts, colors, and logos on your website for a seamless transition between digital marketing and online presence.

By using Canva's Brand Kit and implementing these strategies, you can create a cohesive, recognizable, and professional brand identity across all your designs, strengthening your brand and creating lasting impressions with your audience.

7.3 Troubleshooting Common Issues

Canva is a powerful design tool, but like any platform, users may face some challenges, especially when it comes to alignment and formatting. Whether you're creating a simple social media post or a detailed marketing brochure, proper alignment and formatting are crucial for a professional and polished look. In this section, we'll explore some of the most common alignment and formatting issues that users encounter in Canva, and provide step-by-step solutions to address these problems efficiently.

7.3.1 Solving Alignment and Formatting Problems

One of the most frequent challenges Canva users experience is getting their design elements perfectly aligned. Misaligned text, images, or icons can give the design a cluttered and unprofessional appearance, which can detract from the overall message you are trying to convey. Canva provides several tools that make alignment easy, but understanding how to use these tools correctly is essential. This section will walk you through common alignment and formatting issues, and how to resolve them step by step.

1. Understanding Canva's Alignment Tools

Before diving into specific issues, it's important to familiarize yourself with the alignment tools Canva offers. These tools include guides, grids, rulers, and alignment buttons.

- Grids and Rulers: Canva provides grids and rulers to help you align elements with precision. To enable these, click on the "File" menu and select "Show Rulers" and "Show Guides." Grids give you a visual framework, while rulers help you place elements accurately along the x and y axes.

- Snap to Grid: This feature ensures that elements align automatically as you move them. When dragging text boxes, images, or shapes, they will "snap" into place based on Canva's underlying grid system. While this feature is useful, it may sometimes misalign elements slightly due to spacing or formatting. You can toggle this feature on and off based on your needs.

- Alignment Buttons: Located in the top toolbar, these buttons help you align objects to the left, right, center, or top/bottom of the canvas. For example, to align multiple elements horizontally, select them all, and click the "Align Horizontally" button. These tools are essential when working with several elements that need to be evenly spaced or aligned.

2. Common Alignment Issues and Solutions

Let's now explore some common alignment problems you may encounter in Canva and how to address them.

2.1 Text Boxes Not Aligned with Images or Other Elements

Problem: One of the most common issues is misalignment between text boxes and images or other graphic elements. Often, when resizing or moving text boxes, they may not perfectly align with other design components, leading to a disjointed appearance.

Solution:

1. Use Canva's Alignment Guides: As you move the text box around, Canva's built-in alignment guides will appear in the form of solid lines. These guides will indicate whether your text box is centered or aligned with other objects. Always look for these visual cues as they will help you place the text correctly.

2. Manual Alignment with Position Tool: If the guides don't appear, or if the alignment still seems off, select the text box, go to the top toolbar, and click "Position." This tool allows you to adjust the placement of the text box either manually or by snapping it to a specific part of the design (left, center, right).

3. Using Grouping for Precise Alignment: When dealing with multiple text boxes and elements, grouping them is often the best way to ensure alignment. Select all the elements you want to group, right-click, and select "Group." This ensures that the elements move as one, maintaining their alignment and relative positioning.

2.2 Misalignment of Multiple Elements

Problem: When working with multiple elements—such as icons, shapes, and text—keeping everything aligned can be challenging. Slight misalignments can result in a messy look.

Solution:

1. Use the Distribute Tool: To evenly space multiple elements horizontally or vertically, select all the elements, click on the "Position" button in the toolbar, and choose "Tidy up." Canva will automatically adjust the spacing between the elements, ensuring they are evenly distributed.

2. Turn on the Gridlines and Guides: Grids and guides offer a more manual approach to alignment. By turning on the gridlines (through the "File" menu), you can manually place each element within the grid for perfect alignment. This method works well for designs that require precise, pixel-perfect placement.

3. Align and Tidy Up: Another useful option when dealing with multiple elements is Canva's "Align" and "Tidy up" tools. Once you've selected the items, you can align them to the left, right, top, or bottom edges of the canvas or tidy them up by equalizing the spacing between each item. This works especially well for social media posts or presentations where symmetry is important.

2.3 Issues with Text Wrapping and Spacing

Problem: Sometimes, the text within a box doesn't wrap correctly or appears too close to other elements, creating a cramped design. Improper text spacing and wrapping can disrupt the flow of a layout.

Solution:

1. Adjust Line Spacing and Letter Spacing: Canva provides controls for both line spacing (the space between lines of text) and letter spacing (the space between individual characters). Select the text box, and in the toolbar, adjust these settings to improve the spacing between lines or letters. Proper spacing creates a cleaner, more readable design.

2. Use Padding for Better Readability: If text appears too close to the edge of a text box or other elements, increase the padding by adding a blank margin around the text. You can do

this by resizing the text box or adjusting the text area boundaries. This provides breathing room for the text and improves its alignment with other design elements.

3. Text Box Boundaries: Ensure the text box boundaries are wide enough to contain the full text, especially when working with long paragraphs. By adjusting the width and height of the text box, you can improve how the text wraps and aligns with nearby elements.

2.4 Elements Overlapping or Misaligned After Resizing

Problem: Sometimes, after resizing elements or the entire design, elements overlap or become misaligned.

Solution:

1. Locking Elements in Place: To prevent accidental misalignment when resizing, lock elements that are in their correct position. Select the element, right-click, and choose "Lock." Locked elements cannot be moved or altered unless they are unlocked, which ensures that your design maintains its structure during resizing.

2. Resizing with Precision: When resizing images or text boxes, hold down the Shift key to maintain the aspect ratio. This prevents distortion or uneven resizing, which often leads to misalignment. After resizing, use the alignment guides or Position tool to reposition the element.

3. Using the Snap Feature: Canva's snap-to-grid feature can help realign overlapping elements by snapping them back to their correct position. Simply drag the element near its original position, and it will automatically align with nearby objects.

3. Best Practices for Preventing Alignment Issues

While Canva's alignment tools are powerful, the best way to avoid misalignment issues is through careful planning and implementation of best practices. Below are some tips to help you prevent alignment problems before they occur.

1. Start with a Grid: Before adding any elements, activate the grid or ruler features. This will give you a visual framework to work within, ensuring that all elements are aligned from the start.

2. Work in Layers: Canva allows you to move elements forward or backward in the design using layers. By organizing your elements in layers (text on top, images in the middle, and background at the bottom), you can maintain alignment even as you add new elements.

3. Keep Consistent Margins and Padding: Be mindful of the margins and padding in your design. Consistent margins between elements help create balance and improve the overall alignment.

4. Use Canva Templates: If you're unsure about alignment, starting with a Canva template can help. These templates are pre-designed with alignment and spacing already optimized. You can customize the template while maintaining the structure of the design.

By following these steps and using Canva's alignment tools effectively, you can solve common alignment and formatting problems that may arise during the design process. With practice, you'll find that proper alignment becomes second nature, and your designs will have a more polished, professional look.

7.3.2 Avoiding Blurry Images and Text

When working with Canva or any design software, maintaining the clarity and quality of your visuals is crucial to producing professional-looking content. Blurry images and text can detract from the impact of your design, reduce its readability, and convey a lack of polish. In this section, we'll explore the common reasons for blurry images and text in Canva and provide detailed solutions to ensure your designs are always sharp and clear.

Understanding the Causes of Blurry Images

Blurry images are one of the most frequent issues encountered by designers, especially beginners. Several factors contribute to image blur in Canva, and knowing the root cause is the first step to avoiding it. Below are the common causes of blurry images:

1. Low-Resolution Images:

The resolution of an image is a measure of how many pixels it contains. When you upload or use a low-resolution image, the software can't generate more pixels to fill the gaps, resulting in a blurry or pixelated appearance, especially when resized. Canva's default image settings are optimized for web use, meaning that if you're using an image for print, you need to ensure it has a high enough resolution.

2. Resizing Images:

Enlarging a small image beyond its original dimensions will often cause it to become blurry. This is because the software attempts to stretch the existing pixels, leading to a loss of clarity. While Canva provides tools to resize images, it's essential to use images that are the correct size for your design from the outset.

3. Exporting at the Wrong Resolution:

When downloading designs, selecting the appropriate resolution is crucial. Canva allows you to export in different formats and resolutions, and if you opt for a low-resolution option (such as a small JPG), your images might appear blurry, especially when viewed at larger sizes or printed.

4. File Format and Compression:

Different file formats handle compression differently, which can affect image clarity. For instance, a highly compressed JPEG might lose detail, making images appear blurry. On the other hand, formats like PNG retain more image quality but result in larger file sizes.

How to Prevent Blurry Images

Now that we've covered the common causes, let's look at how you can prevent blurry images in your Canva designs.

1. Use High-Resolution Images from the Start:

Always start with high-resolution images, particularly if you plan to resize them or use them in print designs. A good rule of thumb is to use images that are at least 300 DPI (dots per inch) for print, and around 72 DPI for web use. You can find high-resolution images in Canva's image library or upload your own from a trusted source. If your image is too small, consider finding an alternative image rather than resizing it.

2. Resizing Images Properly:

Avoid enlarging small images beyond their original resolution. If you need to resize an image, try to reduce its size rather than enlarging it. When resizing, always check the image's clarity by zooming in to 100% to see if the quality remains sharp. Canva provides resizing tools, but it's essential to preview your design after resizing to make sure there's no loss of quality.

3. Export at the Right Resolution:

When you're finished designing and ready to download your file, choose the appropriate resolution based on how the design will be used. For web use, 72 DPI is usually sufficient, but for print materials, 300 DPI or higher is necessary. Canva's "Download" options allow you to choose the size and quality of the image. Always select "High Quality" or "Print Quality" when clarity is essential, especially for larger prints like posters or banners.

4. Choose the Right File Format:

The file format you export in will also affect image clarity. For high-quality images, PNG is often the best option because it retains detail without compressing the image too much. JPEG can be used for web images, but keep in mind that it uses compression, which can lead to a reduction in quality. If you're exporting for print, consider using PDF print format to ensure the best image quality, especially for text and logos.

5. Use Canva's Built-in Tools:

Canva offers several tools that can help you maintain image clarity. For instance, you can use the "Adjust" tool to fine-tune the sharpness, contrast, and brightness of your images. Increasing sharpness slightly can often improve the clarity of images, but be careful not to overdo it, as it can introduce artifacts or distortions.

6. Avoid Over-Editing Images:

Applying multiple filters or making significant adjustments to an image can sometimes lead to a loss of detail and clarity. If you find that an image looks blurry after several edits, consider starting over with the original image and applying only the necessary adjustments.

Preventing Blurry Text in Canva

Blurry text is another common issue, especially when working with smaller font sizes or exporting designs for different platforms. Clear, sharp text is essential for readability and professionalism. Here's why text can appear blurry and how to fix it.

1. Font Size Too Small:

One of the most common reasons text appears blurry is that the font size is too small for the medium you're using. If you're creating designs for print, a font size that looks fine on the screen might not print as clearly. Conversely, if you're designing for web, using a font that's too small can make it hard to read when viewed on different devices.

2. Incorrect File Resolution:

As with images, the resolution at which you export your design can impact text clarity. Text in a low-resolution image will appear pixelated or blurry, especially when zoomed in or printed. Exporting your design at a higher resolution can make a significant difference in text sharpness.

3. Improper Alignment or Layering:

When text is not properly aligned or is layered over complex backgrounds, it can become difficult to read or appear fuzzy. Canva's alignment tools can help ensure that your text is positioned correctly, while using contrast and background elements can help improve its visibility.

4. Compression Issues with JPEG Files:

As mentioned earlier, JPEG files use compression, which can negatively impact the sharpness of text. If you notice your text is becoming blurry after exporting, try using the PNG or PDF format instead. These formats retain the clarity of text better than JPEG, which can introduce noise or blur through compression.

How to Ensure Crisp, Clear Text

1. Choose the Right Font Size:

For web designs, aim for a minimum font size of 14-16px to ensure readability. For print designs, adjust your font size according to the medium. For example, a business card might use 8-12pt fonts, while a poster might require 24pt or larger fonts for clear visibility. Always test your design by zooming in to ensure the text remains clear at the intended size.

2. Export in High Resolution:

As with images, text needs to be exported in high resolution to maintain clarity. Canva offers different export options such as PDF Print, PNG, and high-quality JPEGs. For best results, choose PDF Print for any print designs, as it maintains the highest level of detail for both text and images. For web designs, use PNG to keep text sharp without compressing the design.

3. Avoid Overlapping Text with Complex Backgrounds:

Text that is layered over busy or complex backgrounds can appear blurry or hard to read. To prevent this, make sure your text has enough contrast with the background. You can add a semi-transparent overlay behind the text to help it stand out, or use bold, simple fonts that are easier to read at smaller sizes.

4. Use Canva's Alignment Tools:

Proper alignment and spacing can also affect the clarity of your text. Use Canva's built-in grid and alignment tools to ensure your text is evenly spaced and positioned correctly. This helps to avoid distortions or blurriness caused by improper layout.

5. Avoid Excessive Formatting:

While text effects such as shadows, outlines, and highlights can enhance your design, too many effects can reduce the clarity of your text, especially at smaller sizes. Use these effects sparingly to ensure your text remains sharp and easy to read.

6. Preview Before Downloading:

Always preview your design at 100% size before downloading to make sure the text and images appear clear. Canva allows you to zoom in and out of your design so you can check for any issues with text or image clarity. This step can save you time and frustration later, especially if you're printing the design.

Conclusion

Avoiding blurry images and text is essential for producing professional-looking designs in Canva. By understanding the causes of blurriness, using the appropriate image resolution and file formats, and leveraging Canva's tools for alignment and exporting, you can ensure your designs always look sharp and clear. Whether you're designing for print or web, keeping these best practices in mind will help you avoid common pitfalls and create polished, high-quality visuals that stand out.

CHAPTER VIII
Expanding Your Skills with Canva Pro

8.1 The Benefits of Canva Pro

Canva Pro offers a comprehensive suite of advanced features designed to enhance the user's experience and efficiency. While the free version of Canva is incredibly powerful and versatile, Canva Pro elevates the user's capabilities with access to premium content, additional tools, and functionalities aimed at professional-level design. Whether you are a freelancer, small business owner, or part of a large team, Canva Pro can significantly impact your workflow, making it easier to create stunning visuals in a fraction of the time. One of the standout advantages of Canva Pro is access to premium templates and images, which are crucial in maintaining high-quality output, especially for professional or business purposes.

8.1.1 Access to Premium Templates and Images

One of the most enticing benefits of Canva Pro is the enormous library of premium templates and images. While Canva's free version offers a wide variety of design resources, the Pro version unlocks an additional array of exclusive elements that significantly elevate the quality and flexibility of your designs. This extensive collection gives users the tools they need to make their designs truly stand out, whether for social media, business presentations, marketing materials, or personal projects.

Access to High-Quality Premium Templates

In Canva Pro, users gain access to over 610,000 premium templates, spanning a wide range of industries, design styles, and purposes. These templates are not only visually superior but also highly customizable, allowing users to personalize designs while maintaining professional aesthetics. Whether you're designing an Instagram post, an email newsletter, a business card, or a presentation, these premium templates provide a solid foundation to start from, saving users time and effort compared to creating from scratch.

The ability to access premium templates is especially advantageous for users who are not professional designers but want their work to have a professional look. With these templates, you don't need to spend time worrying about design principles like layout, typography, or color schemes. Canva's design experts have already done that work for you, ensuring that the templates are optimized for impact and readability. This is ideal for small business owners, marketers, or freelancers who need to produce polished designs quickly and consistently.

Moreover, the premium templates are updated frequently, which means you'll always have access to the latest design trends. This helps keep your brand's visual identity modern and fresh, especially if you're using Canva for social media marketing or promotional materials. Each template is also pre-formatted for various platforms, so you won't have to worry about resizing or reformatting your designs for different types of media like print, digital, or social.

Unlimited Access to Premium Stock Photos and Videos

Another significant advantage of Canva Pro is the ability to access over 100 million stock photos, videos, and graphics, all included as part of the Pro package. This is a game-changer, especially for businesses and content creators who need high-quality visuals to enhance their projects.

Stock photography can be expensive if purchased separately from traditional stock libraries, but Canva Pro eliminates this additional cost. Having access to a vast collection of premium images means you can find the perfect visuals for any project without spending extra time searching across different platforms. This is particularly useful for industries where branding and imagery play a significant role, such as marketing, real estate, education, and more.

The premium stock photos available on Canva Pro are diverse, covering a wide range of subjects, ethnicities, environments, and situations. This inclusivity makes it easy to find images that resonate with your audience, allowing you to create content that feels relatable and authentic. Additionally, these photos are of high resolution, ensuring that your designs look sharp whether viewed on a screen or printed out.

Beyond static images, Canva Pro also includes access to premium videos, a critical feature for businesses or creators who want to engage their audience with multimedia content. Video content is becoming increasingly essential for marketing and branding purposes, and Canva's Pro video collection allows you to seamlessly integrate high-quality video clips into your designs. Whether you're creating video ads, social media posts, or presentations, the ability to pull from this vast library can save time and money while improving the overall professionalism of your content.

Elevating Your Brand with Customizable Content

The premium templates and stock photos are designed with flexibility in mind, allowing users to customize each element to align with their brand's identity. Canva Pro gives you the freedom to modify colors, fonts, and other elements of these templates, ensuring that the final product matches your brand's tone and aesthetic. This is particularly useful for businesses that need to maintain a consistent look across all their marketing materials, from social media graphics to printed brochures.

Furthermore, the premium templates are built for functionality. For instance, many premium presentation templates are designed to communicate information clearly and concisely, making them ideal for business pitches, webinars, or client meetings. You can also adjust the layout to fit the specific content of your presentation, while the premium visuals ensure that the overall look remains professional and cohesive.

Saving Time and Boosting Productivity

One of the greatest benefits of having access to premium templates and images is the time saved. As a Canva Pro user, you no longer need to spend hours searching for high-quality visuals or experimenting with design layouts. With premium resources at your fingertips, you can streamline your workflow and focus on other important aspects of your projects.

For example, if you're working on a social media campaign, you can simply select a premium template, customize it with your branding, add high-quality stock images, and have your design ready to publish in minutes. The intuitive drag-and-drop interface combined with Canva's extensive library of premium content makes the design process much faster and more efficient.

Moreover, Canva Pro allows you to save your customized templates for future use. If you're running multiple campaigns or producing recurring content, this feature can save you even more time, as you'll be able to quickly modify and reuse templates without starting from scratch. This is particularly valuable for businesses and social media managers who need to produce a large volume of content on a regular basis.

Unlocking Creative Freedom

The premium templates and images available in Canva Pro offer users greater creative freedom, allowing them to push the boundaries of their designs without worrying about limited resources. For content creators, marketers, and designers, the vast selection of premium content can serve as a source of inspiration, helping you come up with new ideas and approaches to your projects.

In addition, Canva Pro's premium resources are ideal for those who want to experiment with different design styles. Whether you want to create minimalist designs or more elaborate layouts, Canva's Pro templates and images provide the flexibility needed to execute your creative vision. The abundance of choices means that you can try out various design approaches and find what works best for your specific audience or project.

Building Professionalism and Trust

For businesses, the quality of your designs directly impacts how your brand is perceived. Canva Pro's premium templates and stock images help you maintain a high level of professionalism, ensuring that your designs look polished and cohesive across all platforms. This can help build trust with your audience, clients, or customers, as high-quality visuals often lead to higher engagement and a stronger brand presence.

Whether you're creating a marketing campaign, a business proposal, or a social media post, using premium resources elevates your design, making it clear that your brand values quality and attention to detail. For small businesses or startups, this can be especially important, as well-designed materials can make a big difference in how your company is perceived in a competitive market.

Staying Ahead of the Competition

In today's fast-paced digital world, staying ahead of the competition is crucial. Canva Pro's access to premium templates and images allows you to create designs that not only meet but exceed industry standards. With access to top-tier resources, your designs will stand out in crowded markets, whether you're competing for attention on social media, showcasing your products, or pitching ideas to potential clients.

By using Canva Pro's premium tools, you can ensure that your designs are always at the cutting edge of design trends, giving you a competitive advantage. Whether you're running a marketing campaign, launching a new product, or creating content for your audience, Canva Pro enables you to produce high-quality designs that capture attention and leave a lasting impression.

In conclusion, Canva Pro's access to premium templates and images is a valuable feature for anyone looking to improve the quality and efficiency of their designs. Whether you're a beginner or a seasoned designer, having access to these premium resources will save you time, boost your productivity, and elevate the overall professionalism of your work. With Canva Pro, the design possibilities are virtually limitless, empowering you to create stunning visuals that resonate with your audience and help you achieve your goals.

8.1.2 Advanced Photo and Video Editing Features

One of the most compelling advantages of Canva Pro is its advanced photo and video editing capabilities. These features go far beyond the basic functionalities available in Canva's free version, allowing users to create more professional and polished visual content. Whether you're editing images for a website, designing marketing materials, or producing engaging social media videos, Canva Pro provides a comprehensive set of tools to enhance your designs and streamline your creative process.

1. Enhanced Photo Editing Tools

In the free version of Canva, you can apply simple edits such as adjusting brightness, contrast, and saturation, or adding basic filters to photos. However, with Canva Pro, you gain access to more sophisticated photo editing tools that allow for greater customization and control over your images. These advanced features give you the flexibility to manipulate photos more precisely, helping you to achieve the exact look and feel you want for your designs.

1.1. Advanced Filters and Effects

One of the standout features of Canva Pro is its expanded library of filters and effects. While the free version offers a limited range of filters, Canva Pro unlocks access to a broader variety of both subtle and dramatic effects, helping you to create more visually striking images. These effects can dramatically alter the mood and tone of a photo, from vintage and sepia effects to modern, high-contrast looks that make your images pop.

In addition to the pre-set filters, Canva Pro also allows you to create your own custom filters. By adjusting various settings, such as tint, vignette, and warmth, you can develop a personalized filter that reflects your brand's style or personal preferences. Once you've created the perfect filter, you can save it and apply it across multiple designs to maintain visual consistency.

1.2. Background Remover

The Background Remover is one of Canva Pro's most powerful tools, enabling you to isolate the subject of an image by effortlessly removing the background. This feature is particularly useful for product photos, portraits, and other images where you want to place the subject on a new background or make it stand out in the design. With just one click, Canva Pro analyzes the image and removes the background, leaving you with a transparent cutout of the subject.

This tool eliminates the need for third-party photo editing software, like Photoshop, which can be complex and time-consuming to use. Canva Pro's Background Remover streamlines the editing process, making it easy for even novice designers to create professional-quality images. Furthermore, if the automatic background removal isn't perfect, you can manually refine the edges using Canva's precision eraser tool.

1.3. Image Cropping and Resizing

While image cropping is available in Canva's free version, Canva Pro offers more advanced options for resizing and positioning images within your design. You can crop images to custom dimensions or use Canva's built-in aspect ratio templates, ensuring your images are perfectly sized for various platforms like social media posts, websites, or print materials.

Additionally, Canva Pro's Magic Resize tool allows you to resize your entire design with just one click. This feature is especially valuable for businesses and marketers who need to create multiple versions of the same design for different platforms. Instead of manually adjusting each element for different sizes, Magic Resize automatically adjusts the layout, saving you significant time and effort.

1.4. Image Adjustments and Corrections

Canva Pro offers a more robust set of image adjustment tools compared to the free version. You can fine-tune various aspects of an image, including:

- Sharpness: Improve the clarity of your image by adjusting sharpness, making details more defined and enhancing overall quality.

- Blur: Add a blur effect to create a soft, dreamy look, or blur the background to make the subject of your image stand out more prominently.

- Clarity: Boost the clarity of an image to enhance its contrast and make textures and details more vivid.

- Color Adjustments: Control the temperature, hue, and tint of your images to create warmer or cooler tones, or to achieve specific color schemes that match your branding or design goals.

- Curves Tool: The Curves tool allows you to make advanced color and brightness adjustments. You can manipulate the shadows, midtones, and highlights separately, giving you more control over the lighting and tonal balance of the image.

These tools make it easy to correct imperfections in photos, such as poor lighting or imbalanced colors, ensuring that every image you use in your design is polished and professional.

2. Advanced Video Editing Tools

As video content continues to dominate the digital landscape, Canva Pro's advanced video editing tools are increasingly essential for businesses, content creators, and marketers. Canva makes it easy to create eye-catching videos without needing expensive software or extensive editing experience. The advanced video editing features in Canva Pro allow users to produce professional-quality videos for a wide range of purposes, from social media to presentations and advertisements.

2.1. Access to Premium Video Templates and Assets

Canva Pro offers a vast library of premium video templates, which are tailored to various platforms and purposes. Whether you're creating a YouTube intro, an Instagram story, or a Facebook ad, you'll find professionally designed templates that are fully customizable to meet your needs. Additionally, Canva Pro includes access to millions of premium stock videos and animations, allowing you to incorporate high-quality footage into your designs.

This access to premium assets means you can create engaging, dynamic videos without needing to shoot your own footage or pay for third-party stock video subscriptions.

2.2. Customizable Animations

Animations are a great way to make your designs more engaging, and Canva Pro offers a wider selection of animation effects than the free version. You can apply various animations to text, images, and other elements within your design, choosing from effects like "Rise," "Pop," "Slide," and "Bounce." These animations help draw attention to key elements in your video and create a more dynamic viewing experience.

Canva Pro also allows you to customize the speed and duration of animations, giving you greater control over the pacing and flow of your videos. For instance, you can create smooth transitions between scenes or add subtle motion to static elements, ensuring that your video feels polished and professional.

2.3. Video Trimming and Splitting

Canva Pro provides more advanced video editing tools, such as the ability to trim and split video clips. You can easily cut unnecessary portions from the beginning or end of a clip, or split a video into multiple sections to rearrange or edit them individually. These features make it easy to create concise, impactful videos that maintain the viewer's attention.

The ability to trim and split videos also allows you to repurpose content for different platforms. For example, you can take a longer YouTube video and create shorter clips for Instagram or TikTok, ensuring your content reaches a wider audience across multiple channels.

2.4. Audio Editing and Integration

In Canva Pro, you can enhance your videos with audio tracks, adding music, sound effects, or voiceovers to complement your visuals. Canva's library includes a range of free and premium audio tracks, or you can upload your own custom audio files to use in your designs.

Canva Pro also allows you to adjust the volume levels of your audio tracks, ensuring that background music doesn't overpower dialogue or other important sounds. You can also trim audio clips to fit specific sections of your video or apply fade-in and fade-out effects to create smooth transitions.

2.5. Exporting High-Quality Video

When it comes time to export your video, Canva Pro gives you the option to download it in full HD (1080p) resolution. This higher-quality export ensures that your videos look sharp and professional, whether they're viewed on social media, websites, or larger screens.

In addition to downloading, Canva Pro offers seamless sharing options. You can publish your video directly to social media platforms, embed it on a website, or share it via a direct link. This flexibility makes it easy to distribute your content to the right audience, without needing to navigate multiple platforms or file formats.

In summary, Canva Pro's advanced photo and video editing features provide users with a powerful toolkit for creating high-quality visual content. From sophisticated photo adjustments and background removal to customizable animations and premium video templates, these tools enable you to produce professional-level designs with ease. Whether you're enhancing images for print materials or crafting engaging videos for digital platforms, Canva Pro simplifies the process, making it accessible for beginners and experienced designers alike.

8.2 Pro Features for Business Branding

In this chapter, we'll delve into one of the most powerful uses of Canva Pro: branding. Canva's Pro features enable businesses to maintain consistency in their visual identity and brand presence across all digital and printed materials. Whether you're running a small startup or managing the marketing department of a large company, Canva Pro can significantly simplify and enhance your branding efforts.

8.2.1 Setting Up Your Brand Kit

One of the standout features of Canva Pro is the Brand Kit, a comprehensive tool designed to help businesses create a consistent look and feel for their brand across various marketing materials. Whether you're designing business cards, social media posts, or company presentations, the Brand Kit makes it easy to stay on brand by providing quick access to your brand's assets. In this section, we'll guide you through setting up and using the Brand Kit effectively.

What is a Brand Kit?

A Brand Kit is a collection of your brand's core visual elements, such as logos, color schemes, fonts, and images. These are the building blocks of your visual identity and play a vital role in making your brand instantly recognizable. Canva's Brand Kit feature allows you to organize all of these assets in one convenient location, ensuring that you and your team always have access to them when designing.

Here's why a Brand Kit is important:

- Consistency: A Brand Kit ensures that your team maintains a consistent look and feel across all marketing channels, from social media to print.

- Efficiency: Having a centralized location for your brand assets saves time, as you no longer need to search for logos or fonts each time you start a new design.

- Professionalism: A well-structured Brand Kit enables you to produce polished, professional designs that reflect your brand's identity in a cohesive manner.

Setting Up Your Brand Kit

Setting up a Brand Kit in Canva is straightforward and can be done in a few easy steps. Once it's set up, you'll have all the essential assets at your fingertips, ready to use in any design. Here's how to set up your Brand Kit:

Step 1: Access the Brand Kit Feature

To begin, log in to your Canva Pro account and navigate to the Brand Kit section. You can find it on the left-hand menu of the Canva homepage. If this is your first time using the Brand Kit, you'll be prompted to create one from scratch.

Step 2: Upload Your Brand Logos

The first element of your Brand Kit is your logo. Logos are a crucial part of any brand's identity, and Canva Pro allows you to upload multiple versions of your logo to ensure flexibility in your designs. For example, you may have different versions of your logo in various color schemes or file formats (such as PNG or SVG for transparent backgrounds). Canva supports these file types, making it easy to ensure your logo looks sharp and professional in any design.

Simply click the "Upload" button under the Logos section and select your logo files from your computer. You can upload multiple versions if needed, such as a colored version, a black-and-white version, and a transparent version.

Once your logos are uploaded, you can access them directly from the Brand Kit in the design editor. This saves time and ensures your branding is consistent, no matter who's working on the design.

Step 3: Define Your Brand Colors

Next, it's time to define your brand colors. Colors are one of the most important elements of visual branding as they evoke emotions, convey messages, and contribute to brand recognition. Canva's Brand Kit allows you to set up a custom color palette, making it easy to apply your brand colors across all designs.

To set up your brand colors:

- Click the Add New button under the Colors section of the Brand Kit.

- You'll see a color picker where you can input specific hex codes for your brand colors. If you don't know your brand's exact color codes, you can use Canva's color picker tool to match them.

- Once you've added your primary and secondary colors, Canva will save the palette for easy access. You can set up multiple color palettes if your brand requires different sets of colors for various marketing campaigns or product lines.

By establishing a brand color palette, you ensure that your brand maintains a consistent look, whether you're designing a social media post, website banner, or business card.

Step 4: Set Your Brand Fonts

The next step in setting up your Brand Kit is defining your brand fonts. Typography is a key component of your visual identity, and using consistent fonts helps create a cohesive brand image. Canva Pro allows you to upload custom fonts or choose from its extensive library of typefaces.

To set up your brand fonts:

- Under the Fonts section, click on the Add New Font option. Here, you can either upload your own brand-specific fonts or select from Canva's built-in font library.

- When choosing fonts, it's essential to pick one or two that represent your brand well. For example, a modern, sans-serif font might convey innovation and simplicity, while a classic serif font might give a more formal and traditional feel.

- After uploading or selecting your fonts, you'll need to specify their usage. Most brands have at least two fonts: a primary font for headers and titles and a secondary font for body text. Canva allows you to assign specific fonts for headings, subheadings, and body text in your Brand Kit, ensuring that your designs remain visually consistent.

Having your fonts easily accessible in the Brand Kit eliminates the guesswork from designing text-heavy materials. It ensures that everyone on your team is using the same typefaces, sizes, and styles, contributing to a polished and professional look.

Step 5: Add Other Brand Assets

In addition to logos, colors, and fonts, Canva's Brand Kit also allows you to add other brand assets. These can include:

- Images: If your brand uses specific imagery or stock photos repeatedly, you can upload them to your Brand Kit for easy access. This is particularly useful for brands that rely heavily on visual content, such as fashion or lifestyle businesses.

- Icons and Illustrations: Some brands use specific icons or illustrations in their marketing materials. These assets can also be added to your Brand Kit so that they're available whenever you need them.

These additional assets help keep your designs on-brand and ensure that everyone on your team has access to the same resources.

Best Practices for Using Your Brand Kit

Now that your Brand Kit is set up, it's important to understand how to make the most of it. Below are some best practices for using Canva's Brand Kit to ensure brand consistency and efficiency in your design process:

1. Regularly Update Your Brand Kit

Your brand may evolve over time, and so should your Brand Kit. If you update your logo, introduce a new color palette, or change your fonts, make sure to update your Brand Kit to reflect these changes. This keeps your designs up-to-date and ensures that your team is always using the correct assets.

2. Set Clear Brand Guidelines

While Canva's Brand Kit helps automate consistency, it's still important to have clear brand guidelines. These guidelines should explain how to use your logos, fonts, and colors appropriately. For example, you may want to specify that your logo should only appear on a white background or that a specific color should only be used for call-to-action buttons. Canva's Brand Kit can store these guidelines as part of your design process.

3. Train Your Team on Using the Brand Kit

To get the most out of Canva's Brand Kit, ensure that your entire team knows how to use it effectively. Take the time to train new team members on accessing and applying your brand assets within Canva. This will minimize mistakes and help everyone work more efficiently.

4. Leverage Templates for Consistency

Once your Brand Kit is set up, Canva allows you to create custom brand templates for different types of marketing materials. These templates come pre-loaded with your brand fonts, colors, and logos, ensuring that every design you or your team produces is consistent with your brand guidelines. Whether it's social media posts, business cards, or presentations, using templates can save time while maintaining a unified brand identity.

Setting up a Brand Kit in Canva Pro is one of the most effective ways to streamline your business branding efforts. It ensures that all design materials remain consistent with your visual identity, enabling your business to maintain a professional and recognizable presence across all platforms. The next section will dive into how to utilize these branding elements to create and use templates for brand consistency.

8.2.2 Using Templates for Brand Consistency

Consistency in branding is one of the most critical factors in establishing and maintaining a professional image across all platforms and communication channels. Whether you're a small business, a start-up, or a large enterprise, creating a consistent brand experience can significantly influence how customers perceive your business. Canva Pro provides powerful features that help users maintain this consistency, especially through its use of customizable templates.

In this section, we will explore the importance of brand consistency and how Canva's templates can streamline this process for your business. By the end, you'll have a clear understanding of how to use Canva templates to create cohesive, on-brand materials for all your design needs, from social media posts to presentations and printed materials.

Why Brand Consistency Matters

Brand consistency refers to the way your business presents itself across all marketing channels and customer touchpoints. Whether it's your website, social media, emails, or printed materials, maintaining a cohesive look and feel is crucial for building trust and brand recognition.

There are several reasons why brand consistency is important:

- Recognition: The more consistent your visual branding is, the easier it is for people to recognize your brand instantly. This helps in building a stronger brand identity over time.

- Professionalism: Inconsistent designs can make your business appear disorganized or unprofessional. A consistent brand, on the other hand, conveys reliability and credibility.

- Emotional Connection: Consistent branding ensures that your brand evokes the same feelings and emotions across all platforms. Customers should associate your brand with a specific tone, aesthetic, and message no matter where they encounter it.

- Efficiency: Maintaining brand consistency can streamline design processes. When you already have a predefined set of templates, you don't have to reinvent the wheel each time you need to create new content.

Templates in Canva Pro are designed with these factors in mind, allowing businesses to create content that is not only beautiful but also consistent with their brand's image.

Understanding Canva Templates for Brand Consistency

Templates are one of the most powerful tools Canva offers. Whether you are creating a simple Instagram post, an email banner, or a more complex brochure, templates allow you to start with a pre-designed layout that can be customized to fit your brand's identity. Canva Pro takes this a step further by offering premium templates and customization options designed specifically to keep your brand on point.

Key Elements of Templates That Support Brand Consistency:

1. Color Schemes: Using consistent colors across all designs is essential for brand recognition. Canva Pro allows you to save your brand's color palette in its Brand Kit feature, which you can easily apply to any template. This ensures that your colors remain uniform across all designs.

2. Fonts and Typography: Fonts play a key role in the perception of your brand. For example, a modern, clean font may signal innovation, while a more traditional serif font may evoke a sense of trust and heritage. Canva Pro lets you upload your brand's fonts into the platform, so you can apply them consistently across all your templates.

3. Logos and Imagery: Your logo is the face of your business, and it should appear in all your designs. Canva Pro allows you to store and easily insert your logos into any template. Additionally, having a consistent style for imagery (such as photography, icons, or illustrations) can further strengthen your brand's visual identity.

4. Layout Structure: Templates in Canva Pro come with a set layout, but they are highly customizable. However, the key to maintaining consistency is ensuring that the structure of your designs doesn't vary wildly. For instance, if your business card template uses a central logo and left-aligned text, you should maintain this general layout across all business cards. Similarly, if you use a specific placement for your call-to-action in social media posts, it should remain uniform across all posts.

5. Tone and Style: While this is less about the physical attributes of a template and more about the overall aesthetic, your brand's tone should be reflected in every template you use. For example, a luxury brand might opt for minimalistic and elegant designs, while a vibrant tech company might choose bold colors and modern fonts.

How to Use Canva Templates for Brand Consistency

Now that we've covered the importance of brand consistency and how Canva templates can support it, let's dive into the practical aspects of using these templates effectively for your business.

1. Choosing the Right Template for Your Brand

Before customizing, it's important to select a template that aligns with your brand's overall tone and style. Canva Pro offers thousands of templates in various categories—social media, email marketing, posters, presentations, and more.

When selecting a template, keep the following in mind:

- Purpose: What is the template being used for? The design requirements for a social media post will differ from a PowerPoint presentation. Choose a template that aligns with the specific platform or medium.

- Aesthetic: Does the template match your brand's visual identity? Look for templates that reflect your brand's values and personality. For example, if you are a wellness brand, you might look for calm, soothing designs with ample white space.

- Flexibility: Ensure the template is flexible enough to be customized with your brand elements without losing its core structure. A template that requires too many changes may end up looking inconsistent with your overall branding.

2. Customizing the Template with Your Brand Elements

Once you've selected a template that fits your brand's purpose and tone, the next step is to customize it with your brand elements. Canva Pro allows you to quickly and easily swap out default elements for your brand assets.

Steps for Customizing a Canva Template:

1. Apply Your Brand Colors: In Canva Pro, you can access your saved Brand Kit, which contains your company's specific color palette. When editing a template, replace the default colors with your brand colors to ensure consistency. Canva even highlights your brand colors in the editor, making it easier to stay on-brand.

2. Add Your Logo: Every template in Canva Pro can be customized with your logo. You can upload your logo directly to Canva or use the logos stored in your Brand Kit. Place the logo in a consistent spot across all templates—for example, in the header or footer—so it becomes easily recognizable to your audience.

3. Customize Fonts: If you've uploaded your brand's specific fonts to Canva, you can easily apply them to any template. Make sure to keep the font hierarchy consistent, using the same fonts for headings, subheadings, and body text across all designs.

4. Adjust Imagery: Replace the default images or icons in the template with visuals that align with your brand. Canva Pro gives you access to millions of premium stock photos, but you can also upload your own. Just be sure the style of imagery remains consistent with your brand guidelines.

5. Edit Layouts for Consistency: While it can be tempting to heavily customize a template's layout, it's best to stick with the core structure that aligns with your brand's visual style. Small tweaks, such as adjusting margins or adding extra elements, are fine, but avoid making changes that drastically alter the template's flow.

3. Saving and Reusing Templates

One of the major benefits of Canva Pro is the ability to save templates for future use. Once you've customized a template to fit your brand's specifications, you can save it to your account. This allows you or your team to reuse the template for future designs, ensuring consistency across multiple projects.

Here's how to save and manage templates for your team:

- Save Customized Templates: Once your design is complete, save it as a template so that it can be reused for similar projects in the future. This can save time and effort while also maintaining brand consistency.

- Create Template Folders: Organize your templates by project or category to make them easier to find and access. For example, you might have folders for social media templates, email templates, and print materials.

- Share with Team Members: If you're working with a team, you can easily share your saved templates with other members through Canva Pro's collaboration tools. This ensures that everyone is working from the same set of templates, which helps maintain consistency across all projects.

4. Using Templates for Cross-Platform Consistency

Brand consistency is not just about using the same design across different touchpoints; it's also about adapting your brand assets to suit different platforms. Canva Pro's templates make it easy to create platform-specific designs while maintaining a cohesive brand identity.

For example, you can create a template for Instagram posts that mirrors the design of your Facebook banners or email headers. Even though these are different platforms with different design requirements, using Canva templates ensures that the visual branding remains consistent.

Best Practices for Using Templates Effectively

To ensure that your use of Canva templates contributes to a strong, consistent brand image, follow these best practices:

1. Develop a Clear Brand Style Guide: Before you start using templates, create a brand style guide that outlines your brand's colors, fonts, logos, and overall design principles. Canva Pro's Brand Kit feature can store these elements for easy access when customizing templates.

2. Stick to Predefined Layouts: While Canva templates are highly customizable, avoid making too many drastic changes to the core layout. Keeping the structure consistent will help reinforce your brand's identity.

3. Regularly Update Templates: As your brand evolves, make sure to update your templates to reflect any changes in your branding. For example, if you update your logo or color palette, ensure that your saved templates are updated as well.

4. Train Your Team: If you have multiple team members working on designs, ensure they are all trained on how to use Canva templates effectively. This will help ensure consistency across all designs, no matter who is creating them.

By using Canva Pro's templates effectively, businesses can create a consistent, professional brand presence across all platforms and materials. Templates not only save time but also ensure that every piece of content aligns with the company's overall visual identity, making it easier for customers to recognize and trust the brand.

8.3 Creating and Managing Teams

Canva Pro offers advanced team collaboration features that allow multiple users to work together on designs. Whether you're working with colleagues in a corporate setting, collaborating with clients on a project, or engaging in group work for a school assignment, Canva's team functionality can significantly improve the design process. In this section, we'll explore how to create and manage teams effectively in Canva Pro, and how these features can streamline collaborative efforts, ensuring smooth workflows and well-coordinated projects.

8.3.1 Collaborating on Projects with a Team

Collaboration is a fundamental aspect of Canva Pro's offerings, and it allows teams to work simultaneously on designs in real time. This feature is particularly useful for businesses, educational settings, or any scenario that involves group design projects. By integrating team functionality, Canva ensures that design workflows remain consistent, organized, and accessible to all team members.

Setting Up Your Team for Success

To begin collaborating with a team in Canva, the first step is to set up a team within the platform. As a Canva Pro user, you have the ability to invite people to your team, assign specific roles, and define their permissions within the workspace.

1. Creating a Team in Canva Pro

To create a team, navigate to the "Account Settings" section of Canva, and under "Teams," you will find the option to start a new team. You can customize the name of your team based on your project or organization's needs. Once the team is created, you can begin adding members by sending them an invitation via email.

One advantage of Canva Pro is that it allows you to invite people who may or may not already have a Canva account. If the recipient is new to Canva, they can easily create an account and join your team. Additionally, you can organize team members into groups within your main team, which is particularly useful for larger organizations where multiple departments or teams are working on different projects simultaneously.

2. Assigning Roles and Permissions

Once your team is set up, it's essential to define roles for each member. Canva Pro provides three main roles: Administrator, Template Designer, and Member. These roles come with different levels of access and functionality.

- Administrator: This role has full access to the team settings, including the ability to invite new members, assign roles, and manage team permissions. They can also create, edit, and delete designs across the team's folders.

- Template Designer: Users with this role can create and edit design templates for the team. This is particularly useful for businesses or organizations that want to ensure brand consistency across multiple users.

- Member: Members have access to the team's designs and can contribute by creating or editing their own designs. However, they don't have the administrative capabilities to manage team settings or invite new members.

By assigning roles thoughtfully, you can ensure that everyone has access to the tools and features they need without overwhelming them with unnecessary functions. Defining roles also prevents accidental changes to critical design elements, ensuring smooth workflows.

Real-Time Collaboration and Editing

Canva Pro allows team members to collaborate on designs in real time, meaning multiple users can be working on the same project simultaneously. This is particularly beneficial for teams working under tight deadlines, as changes can be made, reviewed, and approved without needing to email files back and forth.

1. Live Collaboration Features

When multiple team members are working on a design at the same time, Canva's live collaboration feature shows exactly who is editing the project. Each team member's cursor will be highlighted with their name, allowing for smooth coordination and communication. For example, if one person is adjusting the text, others can focus on image placement or graphic elements without interfering with each other's work.

Canva also allows for commenting within the design, which is invaluable for team discussions and feedback. By simply selecting an element within the design, users can leave comments or suggestions. This feature is particularly useful for clients or managers who want to provide feedback without directly editing the design. For example, a manager might leave a note saying, "Change this font to something more professional," or "The logo should be bigger." Team members can respond to comments, resolve issues, and keep the conversation organized within the design itself.

2. Version Control and File History

Real-time collaboration can sometimes lead to accidental changes or overwritten designs. To address this, Canva Pro provides version history that allows users to revert back to earlier versions of a design. This feature is especially useful in larger teams where multiple people are working on the same project, as it helps prevent mistakes or unwanted changes from becoming permanent.

Canva Pro stores a comprehensive revision history that enables team members to track the development of a design. You can go back to previous versions, compare changes, or even restore an older version if the current one no longer meets your requirements. This history helps maintain the integrity of your design and ensures that nothing gets lost during the collaboration process.

Leveraging Shared Folders for Organization

An important part of effective team collaboration is keeping designs, templates, and assets organized. Canva Pro offers shared folders, which make it easy to categorize and store designs in an accessible way for all team members.

1. Creating and Managing Shared Folders

Shared folders are a great way to keep design assets in one place. For example, if your team is working on a marketing campaign, you can create a folder for that campaign and store all relevant designs, logos, images, and templates in it. Everyone on the team will have access to these assets, making it easy to locate and use them in new projects. Additionally, by setting folder permissions, you can control who can view, edit, or organize the contents.

2. Organizing Templates and Brand Assets

For businesses that need to maintain consistent branding, shared folders can also house templates and brand assets. This allows all team members to access pre-approved design templates that adhere to your brand guidelines, such as the correct fonts, colors, and logo placements. Instead of starting each design from scratch, team members can simply pull from these templates and customize them as needed.

Canva Pro's Brand Kit feature integrates seamlessly with shared folders, allowing you to store your brand's fonts, color palettes, and logos in one easily accessible location. By having these assets on hand, your team can quickly and efficiently create designs that align with your brand identity.

Efficient Feedback and Approval Processes

Team collaboration often requires multiple rounds of feedback and approvals. Canva Pro simplifies this process by offering tools that streamline communication and ensure everyone is on the same page.

1. Commenting and Suggesting Changes

As mentioned earlier, Canva's comment feature allows team members to leave feedback directly on the design. This eliminates the need for external email chains or messaging platforms, keeping all communication in one place. Feedback can be provided in real time, and once a comment has been addressed, it can be marked as resolved, helping to keep the workflow organized.

2. Approval Workflows

For teams that need formal approval processes, Canva Pro allows you to set up an approval system. For example, junior designers can submit their work for approval, and team leaders or managers can review and either approve the design or request changes. This feature helps maintain quality control and ensures that the final design meets all necessary standards before it's published or shared.

Integrating External Tools for Seamless Workflow

In addition to Canva's built-in features, teams often use other tools to manage projects, communicate, or share files. Canva Pro integrates with several third-party platforms, such as Slack, Google Drive, Dropbox, and Trello. These integrations allow you to streamline your workflow by linking Canva with your existing project management or communication tools.

For example, if your team uses Slack for internal communication, you can easily share Canva designs directly within Slack channels, making it easy for the whole team to review and discuss the design. Similarly, integrating Canva with Google Drive or Dropbox allows you to save designs in your cloud storage, ensuring that all your assets are backed up and easily accessible.

Ensuring Smooth Team Collaboration

To sum up, Canva Pro's team collaboration features are designed to facilitate seamless communication, organization, and design workflows. By setting up teams, defining roles, and utilizing tools like shared folders and real-time editing, you can ensure that your team works efficiently and effectively, no matter where they are located. Collaboration becomes smoother, feedback processes are faster, and the overall design quality improves when everyone is aligned on the same platform.

8.3.2 Assigning Roles and Managing Permissions

When managing a team in Canva Pro, one of the critical aspects is defining roles and permissions. Not every team member may require the same level of access or control over projects, and Canva Pro offers a flexible system that allows for tailored access depending on the role of each individual within the team.

This section explores how to assign roles within a Canva team, manage permissions, and ensure that the right people have the right level of control over design assets and projects. Understanding how to allocate permissions effectively will help streamline workflows, avoid unnecessary edits, and maintain consistency in your designs.

Understanding Canva Team Roles

Canva Pro offers predefined roles that make it easier to organize and manage team members. These roles include Administrators, Template Designers, Members, and Guests, each with varying levels of access and capabilities. By assigning these roles based on the team members' responsibilities, you can maintain control over your designs while allowing others to contribute efficiently.

1. Administrator:

The Administrator role has the most control in Canva. This role is typically assigned to a team leader or someone responsible for overseeing the entire project. Administrators have the authority to invite or remove members, assign roles, manage the team's settings, and control billing information. In addition to these administrative tasks, they also have full access to all design projects, allowing them to edit, review, or approve designs before they are published.

2. Template Designer:

Template Designers are crucial for businesses or organizations that rely on maintaining brand consistency across multiple projects. These team members are responsible for creating templates that others in the team can use. Template Designers ensure that colors, fonts, and brand elements are used consistently, saving time for team members who need to create new designs quickly. While they may not have the same level of administrative privileges as the Administrator, their role in ensuring brand compliance is vital.

3. Member:

Members are the core users in a Canva team. They have access to shared projects and can create, edit, and collaborate on designs. However, unlike Administrators, Members cannot manage team settings or billing information. This role is ideal for individuals who need to contribute to design tasks but do not require administrative privileges. Members can comment on designs, suggest changes, and implement edits based on feedback, making them essential contributors to any design project.

4. Guest:

Guests are users who may need temporary access to a specific project or design. They can view and sometimes comment on designs, but their permissions are more limited compared to other roles. This role is ideal for clients or external collaborators who only need to provide feedback or approve a design. Guests cannot make changes to the designs themselves, ensuring that the integrity of the work remains intact while still allowing for input.

Managing Permissions Effectively

Now that we've explored the different roles within Canva, it's important to understand how to manage permissions effectively. Permission management is key to controlling who can access, edit, or delete design projects. Mismanagement of permissions can lead to accidental changes, loss of important files, or inconsistent branding across designs.

1. Design Permissions: Viewing vs. Editing

Canva allows administrators to control whether team members can view or edit designs. When sharing a project, you can decide whether other members can make changes or simply view the design without the ability to edit. This is particularly useful for maintaining control over sensitive projects, where only a few individuals should have editing capabilities, while others can review the design before it's finalized.

For instance, in a large marketing campaign, the design team may have editing permissions, allowing them to make adjustments to the layout, images, and text. Meanwhile, the content team may only require view permissions to ensure that the copy fits well within the design without altering any visual elements. This division of access reduces the risk of accidental edits while ensuring that the appropriate teams can collaborate smoothly.

2. Template Permissions: Ensuring Brand Consistency

One of the most valuable aspects of Canva Pro is the ability to create and share templates across a team. Templates are especially useful for businesses that need to maintain brand consistency across all designs, such as social media graphics, presentations, or marketing materials.

Administrators or Template Designers can lock certain elements within a template, such as the logo, color scheme, or font style, ensuring that other team members cannot alter these key brand components. This feature prevents deviations from brand guidelines and ensures that even team members with less design experience can create professional, on-brand designs quickly and easily. Team members with fewer permissions can still use the template to create new designs, but they won't be able to modify the locked elements, thus preserving the brand's visual identity.

3. Sharing Permissions: Internal vs. External Collaboration

In some cases, you may need to collaborate with individuals or teams outside of your organization. Canva Pro allows you to share designs with external collaborators by sending them a link. When sharing designs externally, it's important to manage permissions carefully to ensure that sensitive information is protected.

You can choose whether external collaborators can view, comment, or edit the design. If you only need feedback from an external client, providing view or comment access is ideal. This ensures that they cannot make changes directly but can still provide input on the design. Alternatively, if you are working closely with an external team, you may grant them editing access, allowing for more hands-on collaboration. Canva's permission settings make it easy to toggle between these options, giving you control over how much access external users have.

4. Organizing and Managing Team Folders

Another powerful feature in Canva Pro is the ability to organize designs into team folders. Team folders make it easier to manage projects and ensure that all team members have access to the resources they need. Folders can be organized by project, client, or design type, allowing for efficient navigation and collaboration.

Administrators can control who has access to specific folders, ensuring that only relevant team members can view or edit the designs within. For example, a folder dedicated to social media graphics may only be accessible to the marketing team, while a folder containing internal documents could be restricted to the HR department. By using team folders, you can streamline collaboration and prevent confusion over where designs are stored.

Collaborative Workflow with Canva Pro

The collaborative capabilities of Canva Pro go beyond simple design sharing. Canva includes several features that make real-time collaboration intuitive and seamless, allowing multiple team members to work on the same design simultaneously.

1. Real-Time Design Collaboration

Canva Pro allows team members to collaborate on designs in real time. Multiple users can work on the same project simultaneously, making it possible to see edits and updates as they happen. This feature is particularly useful for teams that need to work quickly or when time zones differ, as it allows everyone to contribute without waiting for a file to be passed around.

2. Commenting and Feedback

Collaboration in Canva is made easier with its built-in commenting system. Team members can leave comments directly on the design, making it easy to provide feedback or ask questions. Comments can be tagged to specific design elements, ensuring that feedback is clear and actionable. Administrators or team members can also reply to comments, creating a dialogue around design changes. This eliminates the need for external communication tools and keeps all feedback centralized within the Canva platform.

Best Practices for Team Management in Canva Pro

Managing teams in Canva Pro is straightforward, but to ensure smooth collaboration and consistent results, it's important to follow some best practices.

1. Define Clear Roles from the Start:

Before inviting team members, define their roles and responsibilities. This prevents confusion and ensures that everyone knows what they are accountable for. Assigning roles upfront also reduces the risk of unauthorized changes and keeps the project organized.

2. Lock Key Elements in Templates:

For teams working with strict brand guidelines, it's a good idea to lock essential design elements such as logos, fonts, or colors. This ensures that even as different team members contribute to a design, the core branding remains consistent.

3. Use Team Folders for Organization:

Create team folders to store designs and resources for specific projects. This helps avoid confusion about where files are saved and ensures that team members can quickly access the materials they need.

4. Regularly Review Permissions:

As projects evolve, team dynamics may change. Regularly review permissions to ensure that the right people have the correct level of access. For example, if a team member no longer needs to edit a design, downgrade their permissions to view-only.

5. Encourage Collaboration Through Comments:

Use the commenting feature to promote collaboration and discussion. This not only helps provide clear feedback but also keeps the design process transparent and inclusive. Encourage team members to ask questions or suggest improvements through comments rather than making changes directly to the design.

With Canva Pro's robust team management tools, businesses and organizations can significantly streamline their design workflows. Whether you're managing a small team or collaborating across departments, understanding roles, permissions, and best practices will ensure that your team works efficiently and produces high-quality designs consistently.

Conclusion

Final Tips for Mastering Canva

As you've journeyed through this guide, you've likely realized how versatile and user-friendly Canva is, regardless of your design experience. Whether you're creating social media graphics, presentations, or printed materials, mastering Canva can transform how you approach visual communication. To wrap up, let's go over some final tips that will ensure you maximize Canva's potential and solidify your design skills. These tips are designed to help you elevate your design process, enhance creativity, and streamline your workflow.

1. Plan Your Designs Before You Begin

One of the most common pitfalls of design is diving in without a plan. Canva makes it easy to jump right into a project with its vast array of templates and intuitive tools, but it's still important to take a moment to plan your design before starting.

- Understand the Purpose: Ask yourself what the primary goal of your design is. Are you trying to inform, inspire, promote, or entertain? The purpose of the design will influence everything from the layout to the color scheme and font choices.

- Audience Awareness: Understanding your target audience is crucial. Who are you designing for? What appeals to them visually? Designing for a professional audience may require a more conservative approach, while a younger, creative audience may appreciate bold colors and playful fonts.

- Sketch or Outline: Even though Canva offers easy drag-and-drop functionality, sketching out a rough layout on paper or digitally before starting can save you time in the long run. By outlining where key elements like text, images, and graphics will go, you'll have a clear direction when you sit down to design.

2. Organize Your Canva Workspace for Efficiency

When working with multiple designs or collaborating with others, organization is key to maintaining an efficient workflow. Canva offers several tools to help keep your projects, assets, and templates organized.

- Use Folders: Canva allows you to create folders to categorize your designs. Organize by project, client, or design type. This makes it easy to locate past designs, templates, or assets quickly, saving you from the frustration of endlessly scrolling through your past work.

- Label Your Files Clearly: Give your designs and folders descriptive names so you can easily identify them later. A naming convention like "Client_Project_Date" or "SocialMedia_InstagramPosts_September" will ensure you can always find what you're looking for, especially if you manage multiple projects at once.

- Utilize the Brand Kit: If you're working with a team or for a business, the Brand Kit is a lifesaver. It allows you to store and access brand-specific fonts, colors, and logos to maintain consistency across all your designs. If you're using Canva Pro, you can even create multiple brand kits for different projects or clients.

3. Use Templates as a Starting Point, Not a Limitation

Canva's library of templates is one of its strongest features. However, while templates are a great way to jumpstart your design, it's important not to rely on them too heavily or limit your creativity.

- Customize Templates Fully: While Canva's templates are beautifully designed, it's important to personalize them to fit your project's needs. Change colors, swap out fonts, and replace placeholder images with your own. Customizing templates ensures that your design stands out and aligns with your brand's voice or your creative vision.

- Create Your Own Templates: Once you've mastered the basics, consider creating custom templates for recurring projects. Whether it's for Instagram stories, email headers, or presentations, having your own templates can save you time and ensure consistency across different designs.

4. Be Intentional with Color Choices

Color is one of the most powerful elements of design. It influences the mood of your audience and impacts how your message is perceived. Canva provides a robust color tool that allows you to create custom palettes or use pre-existing ones, but it's essential to be intentional with your color choices.

- Understand Color Psychology: Colors evoke emotions. For example, blue can evoke feelings of trust and calm, while red can create a sense of urgency or excitement. Familiarize yourself with basic color psychology to ensure your design aligns with your message.

- Use Canva's Color Wheel: If you're unsure which colors work well together, Canva's color wheel is an invaluable tool. It allows you to experiment with different combinations and see how they interact in real time. Use complementary, analogous, or triadic color schemes to create visually appealing designs.

- Maintain Consistency with Your Brand: If you're designing for a brand, stick to your brand's colors. Canva Pro's Brand Kit makes it easy to store and access your brand's specific hues, ensuring consistency across all of your projects.

5. Pay Attention to Typography

Typography, or the art of arranging type, plays a critical role in the overall impact of your design. Canva offers hundreds of fonts, but knowing how to combine and utilize them effectively can make or break your design.

- Limit Font Combinations: A common mistake is using too many fonts. Limit yourself to two or three fonts in a single design to maintain readability and a cohesive look. One font can be used for headings, another for body text, and a third for accents.

- Hierarchy Matters: Establish a clear visual hierarchy by differentiating the size, weight, and color of your fonts. This helps guide the viewer's eye to the most important elements of the design first.

- Readability Is Key: No matter how beautiful a font may be, if it's hard to read, it's ineffective. Choose fonts that are legible at all sizes, especially for body text. Canva allows you to adjust line spacing and letter spacing, so take advantage of these tools to improve readability.

6. Leverage Canva's Design Grids and Guidelines

Canva offers built-in grids and guidelines that can significantly enhance your design's structure and alignment, creating a professional, polished look.

- Use Grids to Organize Content: Canva's grid feature helps you arrange elements symmetrically and balance your layout. This is especially useful for image-heavy designs like photo collages or product catalog pages.

- Align and Distribute Elements: Make use of Canva's alignment tools to ensure elements like text boxes, images, and shapes are properly aligned. Proper alignment leads to a cleaner, more professional design. Canva also has an auto-align feature that snaps elements into place as you move them.

7. Keep File Sizes in Mind for Exporting

As you prepare to export your design, it's important to understand the appropriate file formats and sizes for your project. Canva offers several options for exporting designs, from PNGs for high-quality images to PDFs for print.

- Use the Right Format for the Job: For digital graphics, PNG and JPG are the most common formats. PNG is best for designs that need a transparent background, while JPGs are useful for smaller file sizes. For print, opt for PDF or high-quality PNG to ensure clarity.

- Adjust File Size for Web: If you're creating content for the web, you may need to reduce file sizes to ensure quick loading times. Canva's export settings allow you to adjust the resolution or quality of your download to balance quality with file size.

8. Stay Updated on Canva Features

Canva is constantly evolving, with new features being rolled out regularly. To stay ahead of the curve, it's essential to familiarize yourself with Canva's updates and new functionalities.

- Explore Canva's Blog and Tutorials: Canva frequently posts new tutorials, design tips, and case studies that can help you discover new ways to use the platform. Subscribing to their newsletter or regularly visiting their blog will keep you informed about the latest features and trends.

- Experiment with New Tools: Don't hesitate to experiment with new tools or features as they are released. For example, Canva's introduction of video editing tools or animated elements opens up new possibilities for multimedia design. Staying curious and experimenting with new functionalities will allow you to expand your skill set and find fresh ways to approach design projects.

9. Keep Designs Simple and Focused

In design, less is often more. While Canva offers a wide range of design elements, it's crucial not to overcrowd your design with too many images, fonts, or colors. Simple, clean designs are often the most effective.

- Focus on the Message: Your design should serve to amplify your message, not distract from it. Keep only the essential elements and remove anything that doesn't add value to your project.

- White Space is Your Friend: Don't be afraid of white space (also known as negative space). It helps break up the design, increases readability, and guides the viewer's eye to key elements. White space creates balance and keeps your design from feeling cluttered.

10. Consistency is Key in Design

Whether you're designing a one-off project or a full suite of branding materials, consistency is key to creating professional, cohesive designs.

- Create a Visual Identity: If you're creating designs for a brand or business, it's important to establish a consistent visual identity. This includes using the same fonts, colors, and logo placement across all designs. Canva's Brand Kit feature helps ensure this consistency.

- Use Canva's Templates for Consistency: Canva's ability to save templates makes it easy to maintain consistency across recurring projects. Create templates for social media posts, email headers, and presentations that follow the same design rules, and reuse them for future designs.

In conclusion, mastering Canva is about more than just learning how to use its tools—it's about applying design principles, staying organized, and always striving to improve your skills. By planning ahead, organizing your workspace, customizing templates, and paying attention to color, typography, and consistency, you'll be well on your way to becoming a Canva expert. Keep experimenting, stay curious, and remember that design is a journey, not a destination. Whether you're designing for fun or for business, Canva provides the perfect platform for bringing your creative ideas to life.

Acknowledgments

First and foremost, I would like to extend my deepest gratitude to you, the reader, for purchasing this book. **Canva Basics: A Beginner's Guide to Designing with Ease** *was created with the goal of helping you unlock your full creative potential, and the fact that you've chosen to invest your time and resources into this guide means the world to me.*

In today's fast-paced world, where information is abundant and time is precious, your decision to turn to this book is something I deeply appreciate. Whether you are a complete beginner or someone looking to sharpen your design skills, it is my hope that the content of this book not only equips you with practical knowledge but also inspires you to explore new creative horizons. Canva is a powerful tool, but it is your imagination and dedication that will turn your ideas into reality.

I want to take a moment to acknowledge your commitment to growth. Learning any new skill, including graphic design, requires patience and perseverance, and it is your willingness to learn and improve that will ultimately lead to success. This book is not just a collection of tutorials and instructions—it is a guide designed to empower you to confidently use Canva to bring your visions to life.

I would also like to thank you for placing your trust in this resource. There are countless guides and tools available, and I am truly honored that you have chosen this one to accompany you on your creative journey. My goal has always been to create a book that is as accessible as it is informative, and your support serves as a reminder of why I love sharing knowledge with others.

To all the dreamers, the creators, the problem-solvers, and the innovators who pick up this book—thank you. Your support fuels my passion for writing and education. I hope that as you turn these pages, you'll discover new ways to express yourself, solve design challenges, and share your unique perspective with the world.

Finally, I want to encourage you to continue pushing the boundaries of what you can achieve with Canva and beyond. The world of design is vast and full of possibilities, and I am confident that this book is only the beginning of what you will accomplish. I look forward to seeing the incredible work you will create, and I am honored to be a small part of your journey.

From the bottom of my heart, thank you for making this book a part of your design toolkit. I wish you all the best in your creative endeavors, and I hope this guide serves as a lasting resource for years to come.

With deep appreciation,

www.ingramcontent.com/pod-product-compliance
Lightning Source LLC
LaVergne TN
LVHW081334050326
832903LV00024B/1156